Dear Mary &

I am very grateful for your contribution to my success.

Love,
Marlene XO

ROADMAP to Success

AMERICA'S TOP INTELLECTUAL MINDS MAP OUT SUCCESSFUL BUSINESS STRATEGIES

Copyright © 2012

Published in the United States by
Insight Publishing Company
707 West Main Street, Suite 5 • Sevierville, Tennessee • 37862

All rights reserved. No part of this book may be reproduced in any form or by any means without prior written permission from the publisher except for brief quotations embodied in critical essay, article, or review. These articles and/or reviews must state the correct title and contributing authors of this book by name.

Disclaimer: This book is a compilation of ideas from numerous experts who have each contributed a chapter. As such, the views expressed in each chapter are of those who were interviewed and not necessarily of the interviewer or Insight Publishing.

ISBN   978-1-60013-921-5

10 9 8 7 6 5 4 3 2 1

Message From The Publisher

The interviews in this book were conducted by David E. Wright, the President and founder of Insight Publishing and ISN Works

I'VE DONE A LOT OF DRIVING IN MY LIFE and one thing I have been smart enough to have is a dependable road map. If you don't have a good plan to get from where you are to where you want to go, you will get lost.

I've known many people who have started out in business and thought they had a good plan, but did not achieve the success they wanted. A major problem for many of these people was that they had not sought good advice from people who had achieved success. If you don't learn from the experience of others, you might achieve success but you will probably get there the hard way. You might get lost down many side roads before you find the right one.

ROADMAP to Success, is a mini-seminar on how to plan for your success. The successful people in this book have the experience that will help you find what you need to create your ROADMAP to Success. These perceptive businesspeople were fascinating as they unfolded their own personal road maps and told me about their various success journeys.

I invite you to set aside some quiet time and learn from these exceptional authors. I assure you that your time won't be wasted. It's not often that you can access such a large quantity of quality information that will either get you started or help you get further along on your road to success. This book is an investment in your future—your successful future!

—*David E. Wright*

Table of Contents

Leadership in the Family-Owned Business
  Dr. George Kastner and Brenda Erickson 1

Fundamental Success Principles and Strategies
  Catharine Wright 29

The Powers of Success
  Rebecca Bales 47

The Careers You LOVE Model for Success
  Marlene Haley 59

Discover Your Inner Resource
  Dr. Deepak Chopra 79

A Journey to a Place Called There
  Cheryl Washington 91

Be Legendary
  James Carter 105

Journey to Achievement
  Melanie White 123

Living a Vibrant Life - The Power of Dreams
  Marc Drizin 135

The Successful Life You Deserve
  Dr. Elise Stevenson 151

An Interview With
  Dr. Kenneth Blanchard 165

As You Think You Are: Your Thoughts Create Success
  Kandy Graves 181

Wellness Within
  Marlene George 199

Creative Visualization:
Disciplined Thinking for Leadership Success
  Liz Dallas 217

Self-Activate and Create Transformation
  Jennifer Kern Collins 229

Let Your True Self Shine!
  Caterina Alberti 251

Chapter One

LEADERSHIP IN THE FAMILY-OWNED BUSINESS

DR. GEORGE KASTNER
AND
BRENDA ERICKSON

DAVID WRIGHT (WRIGHT)

Today I'm talking with Dr. George Kastner and Brenda Erickson. Dr. Kastner is CEO and Founding President of First GTK, international management consulting firms focused on strategic support to entrepreneurial and family business firms. As an executive coach in the United States and Latin America, Dr. Kastner mentors executives, deans, teachers, fellows, and entrepreneurs through difficult and developmental experiences. From his dedication to advancing the level and quality of business practices, he is known for bringing new perspectives and innovative approaches to business issues. His consulting and coaching engagements take him throughout the world where he has a chance to see firsthand the challenges of international businesses. Most recently he has concentrated on business issues, growth and entrepreneurial businesses, and family-owned businesses in Latin America while continuing his passion for teaching management practices, operations management, and entrepreneurial growth and leadership. He has taught students and business leaders in Venezuela, Colombia, Saudi Arabia, China, the Czech Republic, and the United States.

Brenda Erickson is a business development consultant and frequent speaker in the Washington, D.C., area. As Founder of Erickson Consulting, she works with a consortium of sales and marketing professionals throughout the United States to mentor small companies in their early stages of growth and development. Her background in psychology, technology, and management, and experience as a business professional in both large corporations and small growing businesses provide a unique perspective for her clients who want to grow and develop high integrity businesses. A popular and motivating speaker, she speaks on technology vision, communications, and management. Focusing now on her work with a growing company, ITpreneurs, she is known in the industry as a business leader, executive coach, and consultant.

Dr. Kastner and Brenda Erickson, welcome to *ROADMAP to Success*.

DR. KASTNER (KASTNER)
Thank you.

BRENDA ERICKSON (ERICKSON)
It's good to be here with you, David.

WRIGHT
Why is the family-owned business discussed as a separate topic from other privately held businesses?

KASTNER
When we talk about businesses, we tend to separate two groups: businesses that are public and are traded on the stock exchange, and businesses that are privately held. Privately held businesses are business entities that are funded by a family, or small group of unrelated investors. This ownership group may participate in the running of the business, or may choose to hire a professional management team and remain as "silent partners" in the background, but certainly interested (financially or

otherwise). Most new entrepreneurial ventures start out as privately held and are funded by family and friends' investments. Many of these ventures successfully attract the market success that spurs growth and eventually may make the decision to sell shares and become public.

Figure 1 Business interactions

Roles:
1. Only Management / Employees
2. Only the Owner
3. Only Members of the Board of Directors
4. Management – Board of Directors
5. Management – Owners
6. Owners – Board of Directors
7. Management – Owners – Board of Directors

Family businesses are a special category of privately held businesses that are owned by one person, or majority owned by one or two families, and where the family members work in the business. Generally, when we study organizations from an outsider's high-level view, we expect to find multiple types of interactions between owners, managers, and board members. Sometimes you'll find complex interaction and activity matrices such as owners who also participate as managers, owners who also participate as board members, and board members who participate as managers. With that level of potential complexity, there are seven types of interaction (see Figure 1).

Figure 2 Family Business interactions

Roles:
1. Only Management / Employees
2. Only Owner
3. Only Board of Directors
4. Only Family
5. Family – Owner
6. Family – Management/Employee
7. Family – Board of Director
8. Family – Management – Board of Directors
9. Family – Board of Directors – Owner
10. Family – Owner – Management
11. Owner – Management/Employee
12. Owner – Board of Directors
13. Owner – Board of Directors – Management
14. Management – Board of Directors
15. Family – Owner – Management – Board of Directors

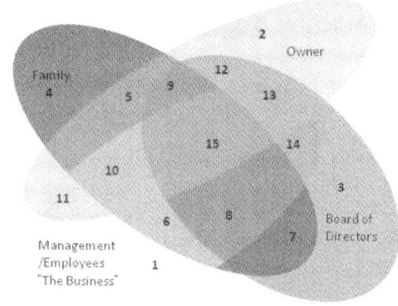

When you superimpose the set of interactions onto the business structure and within company daily activities, the seven basic types jump to fifteen as shown in Figure 2. If you can imagine sitting in a meeting room and talking about issues related to the business with these owners and relatives, you can see how you may suddenly become unclear about "who" is participating in the conversation. "Who" may be your brother, father, in-laws, a fellow manager, owner, board member, or someone you hired in as an objective professional. Each communication transaction may require a different style and approach to achieve acceptance and to realize value from the discussion.

The complexity and difficultness of clarifying the different roles require dealing with family businesses in a different fashion. There is an additional variable that complicates things. In most countries you have regulation that stems from structured government characterizations and requirements for doing business. Some countries will call it commerce, other countries will refer to it as business registration. All of those refer to general businesses, none refers specifically to family-owned businesses, and they are not taking into account the additional complexity. These additional complexities require that we assess the additional daily challenges that the family relationship component adds in a separate way with a different lens.

WRIGHT

Are the leadership requirements in the family-owned business different from what is required in other businesses, or are there special considerations that the leadership in a family-owned business must understand to be successful?

ERICKSON

Leading a business is challenging and exhilarating for any professional. With the added dimension of the family members who share a common history, value systems, and language, the management in such an organization can complicate communication and management. The reality of dealing day-to-day with family members on business issues can be too much for many leaders. Clear structure and responsibilities and communication provide a formal channel for keeping the business as objective and professional as possible. As the business evolves, change is inevitable. It is important to prepare the managers (family members and longtime employees who are treated like family and professionals with no relationship other than employment) with equal challenges and with professional development opportunities so that all levels in the company can reach their potential as leaders in the business.

Governance and rules of engagement must be clear, clearly communicated, and honored by all participants. Sometimes, in contentious situations, it may help to bring in an objective third party such as a consultant experienced in family businesses to coach and guide the leadership during the process of business growth and change. In family businesses and in life, emotionally charged situations can have far-reaching effects, not always positive.

Maturity, self-awareness, and alignment of individual skills with company goals are leadership traits that support success in the family business.

KASTNER

Leadership in corporations stems from several things, but first, we look at the structure and hierarchy of the organization. We see the CEO as the leader of the company, and the officers at higher organizational positions in the company as the leaders of certain areas. Secondly, leadership stems from specific knowledge or specialty areas such as the project manager who leads a special critical project or activity within the company. When we look at situations that bring into the company specific types of risks, sometimes, due to the company culture, such leaders become situational leaders and assume responsibilities as the demands of circumstances change. Only a few companies have an open structure where this fluid leadership shift can occur, but those organizations do exist.

If we look at these points through the prism of family ownership, we ask, "Who has the hierarchical leadership strength?" There we see that when the person who assumes the higher-level positions in the organizational structure is a blood relative (father, brother, sister, or senior cousin), then that family relationship introduces additional complexities. In most families, the older child from a young age is motivated and guided by the parents to assume the role of being an example to younger siblings. Oldest children anywhere will confirm this responsibility that parents universally introduce during childhood. It is called "setting the example" for the others. As such, there is a message and a role that is bestowed without regard to competence or skill level.

As an adult, with this message firmly enforced, the adult child may feel motivated or obligated to take a leadership position in the family-owned business. Or it may be that the father wants to maintain the position of the patriarch of the family and does not have the objectivity to realize the business strengths and weaknesses of the individual. So the added elements of family affiliation, birth order, age, role, and historical events, may unduly influence the leadership and could hinder the ability to recognize the right individual strengths and competencies so that the organization builds the structure from objective strength. As you can see, it is not as simple as one may think in terms of commonly accepted corporate structure.

WRIGHT

I have always thought of family ownership differently from other corporations. Even though it is a corporation, most corporations, I would think, would hire a CEO, almost like owners would hire a baseball coach or a football coach. But then generally most of the stock, if it is corporation, is owned by the father, the mother and father, and that person assumes the role of leadership. But you're adding a lot more complex elements that are very interesting. How would you define leadership in the family-owned business?

KASTNER

Leadership needs vary, depending on where the business sits in the business growth and development cycle, and whether or not the founder (or leader who inherits the leadership role) is prepared educationally and experientially to lead. More and more we see family-owned business leaders willingly step aside to assume an active shareholder role in order to recruit professional leadership in the top management position.

There are many examples. Look at what may be the largest of the large family-owned businesses in the United States, where the daughter of the founder assumed the role of CEO after her father. In the next cycle of succession, as she stepped aside, she openly declared that her only son was not qualified to assume the CEO position because of his demonstrated attitude and personal characteristics. Instead, she appointed one of her senior executives as CEO (and first nonfamily leader) of the company.

It is important to note that the appointment of a new CEO does not change the structure of ownership. Many key decisions and guidance regarding issues continue to be directed from the boardroom. When the patriarch of this company, the family-owned company, feels that by letting go he will lose control, it's mostly related to the fear of losing relevance. For an aging leader, it's one thing to age and continue to demonstrate leadership and use the power of the office, and quite another thing to recognize the time has come to gracefully release the power, move away from the CEO post, and to reinvent himself or herself as an advisor, community leader, or contributor in another capacity. That move takes courage, confidence, and vision.

Leadership, regardless of the ownership structure, focuses on one primary goal—to drive the company to generate value on an ongoing sustainable long-term. That is why the individual's integrity, competence, and vision are fundamental to business leadership. The way they deal with their constituents, internally and externally, means that clients, suppliers, and employees will define the style of leadership. They assume, "Is it hierarchical? Is it power-driven? Is it motivational?

Recently, Brenda and I looked at specific experiences. Two years ago I was working on a consulting engagement with a Mexico-based steel company. The company provides steel pipes to the oil industry. At a young eighty-plus years old, the founder and original CEO of the company who still maintains a 98 percent ownership but not official position in the company, feels within his rights to lecture the current CEO (his only son out of five who survived the tyrannical rule and stayed with the company). He ends his talks with, "You'd better do what I say." Well-meaning? Perhaps, but this is not an example of good leadership, supportive mentorship, or graceful retirement. Some people just cannot let go; but unlike other businesses, family members do not just go away. That can cause problems.

WRIGHT

What about the outward leadership? Is outward leadership much different from the inward leadership?

KASTNER

Yes, it is very different. Generally speaking, the outward (or external) environment knows the company by company reputation and performance in terms of providing the right responses, whether products or services, to its constituents outside of the company rather than recognizing organization structure and hierarchy.

For example, in dealings with banks, suppliers, or associations, these external entities do not care about the company ownership. Family-owned and operated, closely held, or public company, the CEO is the CEO of the company—indisputable. If the company maintains the desired terms of performance and has documentable assets and the capability to do its work, then they get the approach and the support and service they require, the same way as any other company, whereas the ownership structure is only important in new projects. I'll come back to that in a minute.

In terms of the internal nature of leadership, we have already mentioned the complexities that stem from the family relationships and the history of the family. Also, there are some additional elements. The non-family employees and managers who support the company, and thus the family at least economically, often have a very complicated situation. They may have been in the company with the founding CEO from early days, even before his or her other family members joined the company as professionals or as people who hold influential positions. They often understand what the younger generation wants to do in the company to move it forward; however, the original loyalty is with the older generation who gave them the opportunity to be part of this family and they become, as said earlier, an extended family member. Internally, they tend to side with the older generation or with the founding generation who gave them the opportunity to move forward and they become like an extension to support exercising the internal leadership. You may hear the reminder your father said this or that, and obviously that may lead to problems. While this is the internal reality in any company, it is more obvious and there is often more opportunity for skipping the formal channels in the family-owned business because of previous loyalties. The smaller the company, the more evident this reality is. In larger companies, there are bigger distances between the professional managers and the original founders or founding families so this is less likely. That said, in the sometimes-murky informal organizational structure and the mesh of relationships throughout, this reality is always lurking.

I can share with you an anecdotal situation about such leadership. I know a founder of a business who today is still CEO of this family-owned business. Today, after some thirty years in business, he can call the bank that his company does business with, ask for a line of credit and, without question, the bank will approve his request on a virtual handshake. Later they will send the paperwork to formalize the transaction, he will sign it, and it is done. On the other hand, his son who is an executive in the same company and has his father's name and years of work in the company, will call the bank and request the same service, but his request will not be honored. The bank does not care what his familial relationship is with the father (the CEO). Since he is not a known entity to the bank, he cannot qualify for the same business treatment.

That is the difference in the external characteristic. Internal to the company the son may command the same leverage as the father because of his relationship and his name. External to the organization he must professionally build his reputation if he wants to command the same respect as his father. Different realities.

ERICKSON

When you're working within any business, leadership is both art and science. Leaders are challenged to balance power, which is important to effectively seize and maintain control with trust and permission, enabling creative and innovative actions within the bounds of what is good for the organization.

In the family business, due to the established reputation of the leadership, talent is attracted to the key positions because of the opportunity to work with and learn from an established leader. This established reputation also makes it easier to attract established suppliers, financiers, and others who can be instrumental in boosting the business success. There is often an unconscious competence in the management of people that bodes well for the early stages of getting the group aligned and moving forward. Inward leadership starts with hierarchical recognition, but consistent performance and truthfulness generates the business environment and builds the culture.

In an inward situation, when you are leading internally, you have that captive audience because of your hierarchical position in the company. Employees respect and trust when they feel they are respected and receiving communications that are sincere. Leaders would do well to remember that.

In the external world, you are your business card until you prove your credibility and veracity. Because the external leadership is more intermittent and distant, it is worthwhile to work with the internal communication team to determine how to consistently communicate and show the world what the company stands for. Harmony between the internal leadership mode and the external leadership mode is necessary; however, the actions may be somewhat different.

In the external world, the CEO is the face and the voice of the company. Actions taken by the company are attributed to the CEO, even if the CEO claims to have no knowledge of the action. And they should be held responsible—just ask the leadership of Enron.

WRIGHT

So what are the main skills required to ensure leadership success in such companies?

ERICKSON

Relative to a company, whether it's a family business or a public business, if you look at the relative similarity in nature, size, and complexity of that business, in that respect the leadership skills in each segment would be the same—energy, capacity to listen, speaking the truth, and courage. Sometimes, in a family business, speaking the truth to a family power may be a little more difficult than speaking truth to an objective power. It can complicate things, it can make things better, and you have to have spontaneity and a sensitivity to work as we do everywhere, both with and through people.

KASTNER

I think there are many points worth mentioning that require a very special focused directive and the coordination of characteristics and behaviors to maintain that leadership.

Let me just set the ground by suggesting the following; first, family members tend to have a family language of their own. So when they speak, they may be less likely to fully explain the context of their remark and non-family members in the management team miss some of the nuances. Second, family members talk about the business at all times—at family dinners, weddings, funerals, sports events. Basically, any family gathering presents the opportunity for a business discussion. Undoubtedly, the business is a common and important interest; however, common does not mean that they are all in agreement or even in alignment. Discussions are valuable and the end result can be to strengthen the business, but at times the disagreements may weaken the family bonds and even destroy the unity of purpose in the family business model. As in any organization, leadership with open dialogue is essential to clear decision-making and communication.

Having said that, the elements of leadership internally require a very high level of flexibility and objectivity. Why? If you look at the situation of succession for example: what will be the criteria of succession other than the person best suited to the job? The person best suited to take over the CEO reins of a company does not mean the oldest child or the son or nephew. Family members may have a different idea of "who" in their personal immediate family is best suited. The decision must be discussed early and before it is an issue and all must understand that the best person for the job is the person who best understands the business and its strategy and has the skills to learn and lead. Without such objectivity, the leadership breaks down because the nature of the decision-making breaks down and destroys value.

Here is an example in a textile corporation that was founded by what today would be the grandfather generation. The founder falls ill. The founder had four sons working in the business. One of his grandsons was groomed with education at an Ivy League school, graduating first in his class with two majors, and then attended a top MBA school.

When the grandfather fell ill, he called in his four sons who still worked in the business and his recently graduated grandson to discuss succession. The founder announced to them that he had chosen his grandson to take over the leadership in the company based on an assessment of the professional skills that he had acquired and his understanding on the business. He told his sons that while their service was appreciated, none of them possesses the capabilities and education that the grandson had acquired. The founder transferred leadership and expressed his decision in an objective argument. The grandson accepted the challenge and from the onset demonstrated leadership, compassion, and finesse. In both internal and external leadership, the grandson enabled his uncles and his father to gracefully accept the business decision of the founder. The new CEO converted the business into a very profitable growth business during the next thirty years.

WRIGHT

So how does the ownership structure in a family-owned business affect succession?

KASTNER

There are two aspects of succession: the art of succession transition and the science of succession. The science of the succession of ownership deals with the process, paperwork, and timing of the ownership succession with respect to the business and its ownership. The family hires lawyers, investment bankers, and accountants who draw up the legal document for transfer of ownership to the next generation in a very well-defined structure designed to minimize the financial effect on the individual and on the corporation. This is a well-documented and predictable process.

Then, there is the art of succession transition. How do you emotionally and organizationally transfer the leadership from the outgoing generation to the incoming generation? This transfer of leadership is a complex and often overlooked process.

After twenty-five to thirty years with a founder at the helm, how do you prepare the company to accept another person at the head? How does that person prepare? When do you make the decision public? The company suppliers, major clients, and management staff have all dealt with an individual they learned to trust, accept, respect, and understand. They trust the actions and have observed behavior long enough to know how to respond to the leader. When that individual steps down and the new leader is introduced, it should not be a surprise to the individual or to the organization (internal and external). Preparation in all directions is necessary to ensure a smooth transition.

Internally, leadership is simply not an easily transferable relationship. In other words, the vision of the incoming Founder CEO and the qualifications and vision of the incoming CEO must be planned, nurtured, and communicated. Respect is earned, over time, but there are ways to make the transition easier and more successful.

You can, of course, dictate change, but we all know that that does not guarantee that the change will take place. In fact, individuals who are most resistant are often some of your most loyal employees. Unless you are an insular dictatorship, mandate just simply does not work in the modern world. So if the element of success is to sustain the business ongoing, even through the change of leadership at the top, then the new leadership should move into the positions with some credibility and understanding established upfront. This means that succession must be a planned process, emotionally as well as legally.

A few years ago, I worked with a company where succession was an event. When the founding CEO died suddenly and unexpectedly, with no plans of succession and transition, it was a relatively simple process to transfer the assets of the company to his two adult children. However, when the fight for leadership started between the brother and the sister, although the sister was better qualified and prepared to assume the leadership role internally, she deferred to her male sibling because of the cultural bias in this Latin American. Eight years after he assumed leadership, the corporation was in shambles and the whole conglomerate disappeared.

In a similar situation, a second-generation founder of the corporation chose his younger son as his successor. Why? Because the CEO considered the strategy of the company and evaluated the characteristics of the candidates, then made his selection objectively. The son chosen as the future leader of the company went to school, after graduation his path was employment in a manufacturing company in a field position, then MBA school, then he spent some time as an investment banker—all before he returned to the company. He was scheduled to work in the company for a period of seven years. He was scheduled to work in each one of the eleven areas of the company for at least six months. His father's death ended his last task early (he had two more areas to work in), but because of the early decision and his dedicated preparation, he readily and competently assumed the reigns of the company. Due to the experience he accumulated through work and the rotations, he understood workers, suppliers, and clients. Having performed in the field over the previous seven years, he ably assumed control of the company, was accepted internally and externally, and served as CEO for the next ten years successfully doubling the size of the company.

ERICKSON

It's a good example of how he built his integrity, trust, and credibility base within the company. He had all those skills already but his credibility skills and integrity continued to keep the company together. Planning proved successful because of the dedication of the individual and the objection analysis and planning of the founder.

WRIGHT

So what drives continuity during the growth of the family-owned business and helps ensure the survival rate?

KASTNER

Well, the survival rate in family-owned businesses is actually very tricky. If you study family-owned businesses, it is difficult to assess their full importance to the economy. Generally speaking, the sheer number of family-owned businesses is very large in every economy. Look at some statistics of a few years back. Holland reports about 54 percent of businesses are family-owned, 82 percent in Germany, 95 percent in the United States, and just under 99 percent in Italy. Why is that? Because we don't think of the owner of the service station or the corner restaurant as family-owned businesses but according to the definition that we have provided they qualify.

The sheer number of such businesses in this society is significant; however, it is not clear what percentage of the heirs want to continue with the family business and not all businesses are successful, thus the mortality rate is very high. Some fail or struggle due to changes in the economy, others expire when the heirs sell or decide not to continue the business, or sometime because the internal fight over succession kill the company.

The mortality rates from relatively recent statistics show that when companies transition to second generation ownership 24 percent of companies in this group worldwide die. With transition to the third generation ownership, the death rate for such companies is 10 to 14 percent. Only a small percentage of family-owned companies survive beyond the fourth and fifth generations. However, there are actions that companies can take to ensure longevity of existence from the time they are founded.

WRIGHT

What drives the continuity during the growth of a family-owned business and helps to ensure the survival rate of a privately-owned business?

ERICKSON

Families own their businesses for an average of seventy-eight years. One activity that drives continuity during growth in the family business is active planning for long-term success. Once the family agrees on a plan to move forward, a true solid succession plan ensures fewer issues when it comes to transition.

Necessary is agreement among all family members participating in the business. They must agree that the success, growth, and continued survival of the business are critical to the key goal and they support longevity. An element that drives continuity in a family-owned business is culture and shared values of the family community.

Very ugly territorial fights can occur in business. Respecting the culture, the CEO and leadership team must earn respect, manage competing priorities, preserve the business strategy, and communicate a direction consistent with the culture leading the changes that must occur to make progress. In family-owned businesses, the CEO often stays in the leadership position much longer than you see in most public firms where they're governed by shareholders and by quarterly reports. Another statistic worth noting is that in family-owned business, CEOs are typically paid about 15 percent less than their non-family business counterparts in public corporations.

KASTNER

The issue is one of sustaining the family dynasty. The issue is also one of overcoming the complexity of multi-generations and differences in the same business and the growing family who owns the investment in the business.

Here are some scenarios that may occur: Two brothers in the business, children (if the children come into the business) who are married, and they have additional children. If you look at the third generation of the family members, the pyramid has opened up so much that now you could be looking at about more than twenty-five people who feel a right to some kind of ownership in the business. In addition, there are deaths, divorces, separations. Suddenly you have another business partner who is not related by blood. So here are the things that families start doing to guarantee continuity and support and the possibility of continuity and success for sustainability of the business.

Prenuptial agreements may be unromantic but they are practical and essential in family businesses to protect the shares, define the participation in business, and clearly define the rules that structure a plan for continuity and resolution.

One of the oldest family-owned businesses was founded in the Far East in the late 1600s and is now in its seventeenth or eighteenth generation of family ownership. At the time this business was founded, the founding families in the 1600s were more autocratic and traditional. The patriarch managing the family business grew impatient with all of the relatives during the second and third generation transitions because they wanted to benefit from the business without working in it. He introduced the concept that today is referred to as either the family protocol or the family constitution.

The constitution defines most of the aspects of the rights to the family business, it defines who can be employed, who cannot be employed, who has the right to benefit from the company, what happens in the case of death or divorce, who has the right to inherit, and so on. By defining that, it also defines how those rules can be changed. Setting this protocol made the structure and rules clear and transparent to everybody and created rules of engagement to support continuity.

To highlight what the family business constitution is and is not:

- It is a managerial document that is accepted by all family members at the time it is created.
- It is not a long, tedious, complicated legally structured document, it's a document of understanding that the family members agree to and self-impose.
- It is not an accounting document because it sets rules of behavior.
- It generally separates the business from the general family interests by creating the "family office."

It takes a concentrated effort of exchange back and forth between the family and an experienced, prepared, and sophisticated managerial consultant to help a family create the business protocols appropriate to their specific business. An important element that adds to the continuity is that the document specifies separately the family office, or the family treasury, from the business treasury.

By having such an agreement, protocol, or constitution, a family office is created. This so-called office has a set of rules and lays the foundation for family activities that are not related to this specific business to be carried out under certain given rules.

WRIGHT

How are professional managers—non-family members who are connected to the ownership structures—affected by succession and growth and change?

ERICKSON

When a non-family member professional is hired by the family to come into a leadership role in the organization, the family members must consciously and deliberately include these recruits as partners in the running of the business. Joining forces will make the transition easier for the professional managers to learn the business and it is important to the family and the family business that professional, outside managers integrate into the culture quickly so they can provide critical insights in the early stages and add value to the business.

KASTNER

In family businesses, more so than in other businesses, managers may bring family prejudices into the office and may be inclined to make decisions regarding ownership and stock distribution with their hearts. So it's uncommon to see important portions of the stock or stock options handed out to family. They will be much more willing to allow external professional managers to participate in profit sharing rather than handing over even a small portion of ownership.

The outside professional hired into the CEO position may not be willing to deal with the family complexities in the course of leading the business unless some explicit rules are in place. Such rules may include, for example, the definition of the scope of authority and territory of action, and the scale and form of compensation for the CEO. As a general rule, the CEO will seek a broad scope of influence and the opportunity to build a strong capital base. CEO stock participation ensures a strong sense of authority for themselves, not only for the family.

To begin the process of radical change that may accompany the appointment of a non-family member to the CEO position, external directors may be included to catalyst the change. External directors must understand the nature of business sustainability, the politics of family participation, and possess a commanding and flexible ability to think strategically. Since they are not family members, they do not have to abide by the unwritten rules of family hierarchy and they can abide by the rules of driving business value and strategic positioning. When an external CEO comes in at the same time that you have external independent board members, this alliance between the two may drive a positive situation that is more conducive to the changes that need to be made organizationally.

WRIGHT

So let's talk about the strengths of family-owned companies. Are they different from other privately-held companies?

KASTNER

Family-owned businesses have similar strengths as other businesses, but there are several elements where family-owned businesses excel over public organizations. For example, family-owned businesses tend to be more family-oriented, or family-aware, than other places of work.

A good example of this is a very successful software company in North Carolina where Brenda worked for many years. The CEO, one of the original founders of the company, has led the company from start-up to a very large enterprise of more than ten thousand employees worldwide and he is still very active in all areas. In support of employees and their families, the company provides onsite health clinics, sports facilities, educational facilities, and even some concierge services, so employees understand that their life is part of this family-owned life cycle. Until recently, they also actively promoted from within and selectively hired outside professionals as needed. Things change as the organization gets larger, but in family-owned businesses the leadership certainly has more control of how much they invest in their employees to get the best performance.

Family-owned businesses, because of their ownership, have more freedom regarding how they spend resources and structure human talent benefits. For example, in some companies, when you get married you are allowed five days of holiday outside of vacation time; or if there is a death in the family, you are allowed three days of bereavement leave. In a family-owned business the leaders may have more latitude with respect to these issues.

Also, family values become an important benefit. In family-owned businesses, investors tend to be more patient than in a non-family-owned business because most of the capital comes from family members. Such companies may be willing to provide a "long runway" to innovative projects and be more patient with results at times. That's not necessarily good, but it's different and it stimulates and encourages creative approaches to problem-solving, which can help the business. It's different in terms of the pyramid of hierarchy, which tends to be longer and steeper than in non-family-owned businesses. Also they have a longer capacity to endure. The sense of belonging and proprietorship encourages and supports high levels of commitment. There is a willingness to further build the company and there is a willingness to protect and advance the values that it embodies.

About two years ago in a business magazine interview, Bill Marriott said that people like to go to Marriott because they know there is a Marriott behind the business. When the family name is attached to the business, the endurance capability is much bigger and much longer and they also know that the board members are related somehow to that value of endurance of the business.

An element that is important in the family-owned business and differs from other structured businesses is a willingness to protect the employees and their relationships with the external agencies that provide support. That element is much bigger than the willingness in others to do the same in other companies, why? Because they understand that those suppliers and the people who work in the company have family who need to be protected, need to be fed, need to be developed. While in the other companies it's narrowly an issue of balance sheets and cash flow. Not to say that any one of those elements—the balance, sheet, cash flow, and the financial performance—of family-owned businesses is not important, or it is not number one on the list, the point is that it is number one on the list, and number two, three, four, and five on the list are very close to number one, not like the nonfamily-owned businesses.

ERICKSON

One of the strengths of a family business is shared values. As mentioned earlier, because there are family members who own the business and working in the business and have come up through the same culture, there is shared history, a shared value system, and the there are internal discussions that go on within the business. So that can contribute to a strong culture, which can be a strength for attracting strong candidates to the organization. Knowing who you are as a business and a culture builds strength and in many ways helps family-owned businesses get a jump-start on identity and focus. This is true even without any explicit effort to define it. It is like an unspoken family DNA.

As a business, the primary function is to increase shareholder value for the long-term and to build a viable business that will be sustainable through generations. There is the vision and pride along with the hope that other generations will be interested in perpetuating this family business. That's a huge strength and builds resilience. Individuals work for many reasons—economic viability, being a part of a larger vision, contributing to success of a larger entity, and fulfilling dreams. In a family-owned business, it is often easier to see the results of the efforts and to feel appreciation because of the culture and size of the company. Inclusion is often felt more strongly in the family business.

WRIGHT

Can we look at some success stories?

ERICKSON

The Marriott Corporation is a great place to start. It is a successful business that started as a family-owned motel system for travelers in the Mid-Atlantic. Even in tough economic times, the company has lived by its values and supported employees whenever possible. For example, when hurricanes in 2005 destroyed most of Cancun, including the J.B. Marriott Hotel there, Marriott was the only hotel that continued to keep their employees on payroll. This effort paid off in satisfied and loyal employees who remain dedicated to customer satisfaction with the Marriott experience.

Another example is SAS Institute. One of the largest family-owned businesses is a privately held software company in North Carolina. Incorporated in 1976 by the remnants of a research project from a local university, it is today the largest privately held software company in the world with revenues of more than a billion dollars and more than ten thousand employees worldwide. Another strength there is that it is a company that still continues to remain very true to its values and continues to grow in market share.

KASTNER

The success of family-owned business depends on the achievement and balance of several very important things: entitlement, responsibility, and accountability. When these elements are clearly defined, the longevity and continued growth of the business will be nearly guaranteed. Secondly, the business is the business. Every other activity, even if it was a business activity but not related to the current business entity, should be handled, decided upon, and defined by the family office. Separating these elements protects the business from external pressures of family members who may want to gain control or start a new business that is not related to the current entity.

This refers to the founder, an individual who ran the business, with an autocratic, old-fashioned strong-arm demeanor. He divorced wife number one after having seven children (six daughters and one son). He then married wife number two and they had one son.

When the founder died, about twenty-five years later, two very important things happened. First, there was no will. Second, there was no separation of property with wife number one at the time of divorce. These facts led to a vicious ownership battle. In order to try to bring some order to the business after the founder's death, the son from marriage number one, who was working in the business, took the position that they would consider the two groups a single family with eight children. So personal property was settled and then they had to deal with the original business (a media business).

The children then hired a prominent management consultant to develop a family constitution. After review, all children signed off on the family constitution and the business carried on. Today, the business is still very profitable; four other businesses were incorporated through family decisions governed by the constitution. They are prosperous and amicable because of the foresight, courage, and insistence of that young man and his focus on the continuity of the business.

I will close with just one other success story from a family business in Argentina. Some Spanish immigrants started a business in the energy industry. Their success stems from the fact that, instead of blindly falling in love with the original business, they fell in love with the business area, and they decided to protect the family values rather than protect the original business.

Their business started with a focus on the business of electrical energy, but they decided that electricity was too highly regulated by government and they could no longer sustain a profitable practice. They were not willing to sacrifice family values to deal with the government and remain in the business. They made a clear choice to honor their values. At that time, the petroleum industry was being privatized and they continued the family business in a more viable industry sector. As of yet, two generations later, they talk not only about corporate values, but also about family values and why those are important to them. They will uphold those values under any circumstances rather than just protect the business.

WRIGHT

Lastly I'd like to pose this question that might help our readers: if you were having your first meeting with a new CEO of a family-owned business, what are the top concerns that need to be understood and addressed to position the company for long-term success?

KASTNER

The new CEO upon accepting the leadership role must be absolutely and totally familiar with the history of the family business. He or she cannot afford to be challenged by any element about the history of the business and the involvement of the family in it. Total transparency and familiarity is imperative. The new CEO will need to invest time reading history and press, and interviewing in multiple scenarios the key players in leadership and production throughout the organization.

An entering CEO cannot simply come in with the attitude that we are going to change everything now that we are "professionals." Unless this is an extreme and critical turnaround situation, such an approach will lose the hearts and minds of many long-time employees and will risk damaging the credibility of the new leadership. On the other hand, at this critical time, the new CEO has the opportunity to communicate unity and vision, building on the strong foundation built by the founders and supported by the loyal employees throughout the years.

The new CEO must demonstrate respect and future direction to create the team that will be stronger as a company going forward. This new era must be a joint effort with family members who are still able to lead many aspects of the business, with the professional managers who have contributed to the success, and with the leadership team who craft the new initiatives, and ultimately with the CEO who, like a maestro, directs the orchestra—not trying to play any instrument or outshine any team members. So this sets the vision, tone, and pace while inviting the participation of the organization moving forward.

With this approach, the CEO invites followership. If you are the CEO, this continued approach becomes a best practice, not just lip service, and your followers will support direction, contribute in all aspects appropriately, and you will stay steadfastly and successfully on your road to success for the organization.

WRIGHT

Well, this has been a great conversation, especially for me. I fit in the category of family-owned business with four businesses, all family-owned. You really have given me a lot of information here today that I can use. I'm sure that our readers will also benefit from the same good information. I really do appreciate both of you taking all this time this afternoon to answer these questions. I appreciate your participation in this book.

KASTNER

Thank you very much, David, and thanks for inviting us to this exciting project. We hope to hear from you soon.

WRIGHT

Today I have been talking with Dr. George Kastner and Brenda Erickson. As a management consultant, executive coach, and international speaker, Dr. Kastner has dedicated his professional life to excellence in academia and business. He has ideas that grow from entrepreneurial roots to successful enterprises and is an expert in family business issues, succession planning, and governance models.

Brenda Erickson is a frequent speaker, management consultant, and business development consultant with expertise in the software industry. Her passion for finding the star in each person she meets has ensured her success with clients in the United States and Canada.

Brenda, Dr. Kastner, thank you so much for being with us today on *ROADMAP to Success*.

ERICKSON

My pleasure.

KASTNER

Thank you.

About the Author

Dr. George Kastner is a world-recognized management consultant and academic leader who dedicated his professional career to excellence in academia, management, leadership, and entrepreneurial environments. His academic teaching achievements are respected throughout the world. Most recently, he devoted the past five years of his academic contribution to HULT International Business School where he teaches in Boston, Shanghai, and Dubai.

A seasoned CEO and accomplished entrepreneur, he is currently founder and CEO of First GTK, LLC, parent company to REDITUS International, Inc., and GTK I, LLC. First GTK and REDITUS Inc. are dedicated to Strategic Consulting, Talent Strategy, Executive Coaching, Strategic Implementation, and Risk Management with a focus on service organizations while GTK I, LLC manages investments in ongoing concerns for turnaround purposes, and start-ups.

Throughout his career, which encompasses a unique and dynamic mix of corporate and academic endeavors, Dr. Kastner developed visionary and innovative programs that were also practical and results-oriented. Recent consulting engagements have focused on several Latin American countries, ventures in the United States, and occasionally Eastern Europe. He has taught Executive AMP Programs and MBA Programs in Venezuela, Colombia, Dubai, China, Israel, The Czech Republic, and the United States.

With a pragmatic and vision-driven focus, Dr. Kastner has added a strong strategic content to several board positions. His rich portfolio of experiences includes generating value in service industries from education, hospitality, and health care to commercial banking, entertainment, and franchising.

Dr. Kastner has lived in six countries in the Middle East, Europe, North and South America and has worked in twenty-two countries. He has taught in six countries and has fluent knowledge of four languages and working knowledge of two more. He currently serves on the Board of three firms, in Venezuela, Colombia, and the United States. Dr. Kastner earned his Engineering degree in 1971, Cum Laude, his MSc degree with distinction in 1973, and his PhD in 1980.

George Kastner

First GTK LLC.
1418 Meadows Blvd
Weston, FL 33327
305-218-5659
gtkastner@reditusinc.com
www.firstgtk.com

About the Author

Ms. Brenda Erickson is a speaker, coach, and management consultant based in the Washington, D.C., area. She has the unique ability to see the value and practical application of new ideas and she uses this expertise to coach and counsel entrepreneurs to grow their businesses from vision to reality.

As an executive, she has led and inspired teams to deliver exceptional business results in product development, executive management, and sales. Her strong relationship management underscores a reputation for integrity, inclusiveness, and collaboration. She is a champion of diversity and adept at working with multicultural teams. Ms. Erickson established the Canadian subsidiary for SAS Institute, the largest privately held software companies in the world. She built and led the organization to double growth, year after year for six years, before returning to the United States to work with growing software firms selling into commercial and federal government markets.

Currently, Ms. Erickson is Vice President, Programs for the itSMF National Capital Group where she is responsible for promoting the value of Information Technology Service Management. She consults with software companies entering the federal market to design and develop business programs.

Ms. Erickson is a graduate of the University of Georgia and studied computer science at UNC–Chapel Hill, where she worked with researchers in Biostatistics and Population Studies and attended graduate school at Duke University. (Go Blue Devils!) She has a Graduate Certificate in Leadership Coaching from the George Washington University and has taught within that program.

Brenda Erickson
Erickson Consulting
Reston, VA 20190
BSE715@gmail.com

Chapter Two

Fundamental Success Principles and Strategies

Catharine Wright

DAVID WRIGHT (WRIGHT)

Today I'm talking with Catharine Wright, Founder, and Chief Change Catalyst for The Wright Group, an international performance improvement firm focused on helping leaders successfully grow their business, improve their profitability, and retain highly productive engaged and innovative employees.

She and her team specialize in two key and highly related areas: overall business performance improvement and most things HR.

Catharine's credentials include more than twenty-five years of corporate, small business, and public sector experience in business development, education, manufacturing, and retail. An MBA and Professional Certified Coach, Certified Professional Behavior Analyst, and Legacy Leadership Facilitator designations make her, in my opinion, an expert.

Catharine, welcome to *ROADMAP to Success*.

CATHARINE WRIGHT (C. WRIGHT)

Thank you, David, it's my pleasure.

WRIGHT

So what does success really mean to you?

C. WRIGHT

I have always been driven to have influence and have an effect on the world—an effect that matters and is appreciated by others. Without that, I do not consider myself a success. So, to me, success is making a meaningful difference in as many lives as I am physically, mentally, and emotionally able to achieve. Success is influencing change in the minds and lives of others. It's about helping people grow, develop, stretch and prosper. That's how I measure my own success—by how effectively I've been a catalyst for positive change.

WRIGHT

You spoke about measurement in your own terms, so how are you doing so far?

C. WRIGHT

I think I deserve a fair grade and that there is much additional success to come. After all, I've never settled for a fair grade and I intend to be contributing to the world for many years yet.

Making a difference comes in many shapes and colors. Sometimes my contribution has been sizeable in worth and minimal in effect; at other times it has been little more than a small gesture yet the result was significant. As I reflect on my many offerings and actions, I believe the smaller, more intimate conversations and actions to be most meaningful. My small gestures may not be "game changers," but they certainly leave an imprint, however small or tentative, in the "wiring" of people.

If there is one thing I'm certain of, it is that every single one of us wants to be happy. It is the one thing, and probably the only thing, that we all have in common. Whenever I make someone's day a bit happier, I'm happier.

Being successful and creating success in the world doesn't mean having to lead some grand cause neither is it measured by the dollars we spend. Sometimes, success can be measured by the quality of the questions we ask, and the power of those questions to shape thinking and behavior. I don't believe there is a better gift to give an individual than to elevate his or her quantity and quality of thought.

People are, at any given time, pretty much where their thoughts have taken them. I remember a friend likening thinking to that of a taxi ride. We get in and get taken to some place. I am today where my thoughts have taken me.

Our life is a result of our thinking yesterday and each tomorrow will be a reflection of what we think today. William Arthur Ward said, "Nothing limits achievement like small thinking. Nothing expands possibilities like unleashed thinking." What we think determines who we are. Who we are determines what we do.

Maya Angelou, in a recent show produced for Oprah Winfrey's new Master Class, said something that will stick with me forever. She talked about the numerous "clouds" she has faced in her life and of the many rainbows that have followed. You can be sure that as I journey along my own unique road to success, I'll be cataloguing untold experiences of rainbows—my own and others'.

To the degree that, on a daily basis, I influence and elevate thinking—my own and that of others—I consider myself hugely successful.

WRIGHT

You talk about the role that quality and quantity of thought plays in our successes. What are some fundamental operating principles helpful to achieving dreams and goals?

C. WRIGHT

The answer to the question depends on if I'm thinking as an individual performer or as a business owner and/or leader of people. At a personal level, fundamental principles (FPs) include:

FP 1: Master self-management. This includes managing your thoughts and your time and priorities. Part and parcel of managing your thoughts is managing your emotions. Daniel Goleman is well known for his research that shows, without a shadow of doubt, that our emotional quotient is a far better predictor of success than is our intellectual finesse.

I use a tool called the *Emotional Quotient* to measure emotional maturity or control. Whether being employed at the individual or team level, it never ceases to amaze me how well it accounts for the results achieved or not achieved.

A good question for all of us to ask is, "Would I hire me to manage me?" If the answer is a resounding "yes," you're in good shape. If the answer is "no," or a "qualified yes," you have some work to do. If you have work to do, find a professional who can give you an objective assessment to use as a starting point.

FP2: Tap into your passion. Find the one or two things that are critically important to you to achieve in your lifetime. Define what it is that would make your heart sing with conviction were there no obstacles in the way. Define it, hold onto it, and don't let go of the vision. Hold onto it like a dog with a favorite bone. Write about it, post it everywhere, make it visual, solicit support, and think about it all the time.

FP3: Develop a specific plan. Spend more time planning your life than you spend planning a vacation or a significant purchase. Break it down into manageable chunks. Define your overall goals in the shortest time space possible.

But remember, if you are weak on self-management, expect to define and redefine numerous goals and plans over the years and to continually fall short of your dreams. Planning is one ball of wax; execution is another.

Planning can be a taxing task because it requires thinking and thinking consumes energy. It is easily compared to execution because that requires focus, discipline, and the development of new systems and habits. Execution is where most people fall flat.

FP4: Track, measure, analyze, and adjust. Identify a couple of critical measures of success—both leading and lagging—and create your system and habits for measurement and analysis. You can't manage what you don't know. A game without someone keeping score won't be a game for long. Design your own personal scorecard and keep score on a daily, weekly, quarterly, and yearly basis.

If you do nothing but these four fundamental things, you will be successful. Additional things to consider are:

FP5: Collaborate. I challenge anyone to name one person who has achieved any degree of success singlehandedly. Highly successful people never get the job done alone. They always achieve their dreams with and through the involvement and support of others.

I heard a wonderful story this week about a job candidate who was being considered for hire. At some point in a conversation with her potential new boss, she was playing with a couple of icons on her smart phone screen. The interviewer noticed she had several similar looking icons, so she asked what they were. The young lady said, "Oh, those are my 'Peeps.'" Upon enquiry about what is a peep, the young lady said, "They are a collection of very smart individuals around the world that I pass ideas by whenever I'm looking for an opinion or to test an idea." Guess who got offered a job? I think we would all do well to have a collection of "peeps" at our disposal. This woman had adopted a collaborative mind-set in spades!

The key is to be smart about with whom you collaborate. Pick your partners wisely. Look for "game changers." There will be many opportunities to collaborate if you are willing and communicative. Some will be better than others. Identify the potential partners who have the biggest and most relevant networks. Think big. Thinking small won't get you anywhere of any significance any time soon.

FP6: Find one or more mentors. I have played around a bit with the idea of having a bit with a quasi-mentor, but have never developed a "real" mentor relationship. Ask six very successful people to account for their success and five of them will credit a mentor. Having a seasoned someone to help us develop our thinking and open doors is a huge asset. Like me, you can still be successful but you have to have a lot of patience and "stick-to-itiveness" because it's a much longer road. There's nothing wrong with that as long as the journey along the way is enjoyed.

FP7: Be vulnerable. Great things don't happen and dreams remain unfulfilled without thinking and doing something differently than everyone. Be prepared to be vulnerable in a couple of areas. Firstly, thinking and doing uniquely involves risk. Risk requires courage and a willingness to step out on a limb. Doing so creates a sense of vulnerability and fear that we may fall, which is exactly what we're liable to do at some point if we keep inching ourselves along the tree limb.

That brings me to the second part of vulnerability. Making mistakes is part of the territory. Be quick to apologize for any wrong doings and to admit when you don't have an answer. Instead of striving to always have answers, seek answers from those who have them and work to develop a capacity in others to find their own answers. The more we are authentic and vulnerable, the more we give other people the permission to be real. And when that happens, they respect us more, trust us more, and see us to be more credible.

Much of the work I do is with business owners, CEOs, and senior decision-makers, so my mind wants to answer your question from this perspective. Everything I mentioned for personal achievement of dreams and goals also applies here plus much more. At the risk of over simplifying, here are a few additional critical success principles (SPs):

SP 1: Partner with a coach who will help you create mastery around performance excellence.

SP 2: Adopt a model or framework that fits your needs and serves to keep your focus razor sharp, your discipline and perseverance unbending, and your ability to execute unparalleled with your past and your competition. Co-opt your coach into creating the systems and structure for keeping you in the game, developing skill mastery, keeping score, and holding you accountable for results.

SP 3: Make a big deal of celebrating the small and sizeable successes along the way. Laugh often and encourage laughter in the workplace—it will pay off in spades. Research short bouts of daily laughter in the workplace double competency scores.

SP 4: Constantly assess and readjust. When it feels right, find a new coach with new skills and perspectives better aligned with where you are at that time. Create a new game and stay in practice.

I have developed a Performance Touchpoints™ model that goes a long way to improving game results. It can be shared with a coach and used as a frame of reference for achieving success in one's own unique way.

WRIGHT

You spoke about your Performance Touchpoints Model, I'm curious about that; what is it exactly?

C. WRIGHT

The model is simple. Essentially, it is: Assessment plus Behavior equals Consequences. In short-form: A + B = C.

Assessment is Critical to Success

Assessment is to "success" as water is to fish and technology is to teenagers. Not undertaking assessment in a timely manner is akin to missing an essential ingredient for living life. Selected appropriately, assessments provide invaluable insight into hiring, promotion, and succession choices. Without the benefit of good data and intuition, teams and organizations take on dysfunctional characteristics, with the oxygen being sucked out of them daily.

Assessment needs to occur on multiple levels and on an ongoing basis. Sometimes it needs to be rigorous and at other times a relatively simple thinking-knowing outcome. The more critical or complex a change or decision, the higher the level of rigor.

Top performers work hard to develop insight into self. The better they know themselves, the better are they able to isolate their critical performance enhancing opportunities. They spend valuable time within themselves sifting through their best thinking and options. About what are they most passionate? Why this and why now? Why me—what makes me suited to this endeavor and better able than others? What effect do I want to have on the world? How do I want to show up and be? What are my specific goals and timeframes? Who do I need to involve? How will I measure success?

They also have honed, and continually work at honing, their ability to assess the world around them. On this front, they ask themselves and others, "Who can I expect to be key influencers and possible raving fans? What effect do I have and can I have on others—especially those critical to my success? What do I know about my target market's needs?" These name just a few common queries.

The questions are varied and endless so they zero in on the essential questions needing answers. They source out reliable assessment tools and processes that help them formulate answers to their questions and chart their courses of action.

Many of these questions are germane to organizational-level assessment as well. You probably already get the idea. The questions take on the flavor of "What does this organization exist to do—what is our compelling purpose?" What is our vision of greatness? What will be or are currently our fundamental values and operating principles? How will we, or do we, stand out from the crowd and demonstrate our uniqueness? How well do we know and understand our customers and their emotional experiences and needs? What are our key performance indicators? How will we measure and communicate individual, team, and organizational successes? And so on.

Alongside these standard everyday-type analyses is the need for much additional assessment. Included among these are diagnoses that shed light on organizational/cultural readiness for change, business success performance and positioning, potential and current talent capabilities, the degree of customer satisfaction and loyalty, leadership effectiveness, and employee engagement scores.

Creating a clear picture and understanding of prevailing attitudes is a central principle of any assessment stage. I'm talking about attitudes and expectations at every stakeholder level. Obvious examples include shareholders, leaders, employees, customers, venders, industries, marketplace, and society in general.

We can't manage what we don't know and we are less likely to move toward that which we cannot see clearly. Underpinning our ability to create clarity and increase certainty of actions and outcomes is the quality of the information used to make decisions. Efficient and effective assessment and analysis processes significantly improve the quality of decisions and their outcomes.

Behavior is the Breakfast of Champions

If it seems like there is a lot of work to be done within the assessment stage, your perception is right. While the work done there will make a huge difference in terms of the clarity and speed within which success is achieved, the real work starts with shaping and managing behaviors in the workplace—your own and that of others. If you and your team are not doing the right things right, prepare to struggle more and longer than necessary.

The assessment stage is designed to define the right things that need to be done. The challenge, at this point, is to develop behaviors and habits that ensure the right things get done in the most profitable and effective way possible. This is easier said than done. In fact, there is probably no more daunting task to humankind than that of incredibly effective self-management.

Employees bring to the workplace well ingrained behavioral tendencies and entrenched belief systems and attitudes. Changing these takes intention, clarity, skill, patience, and a financial investment.

Managing behavior is equally about managing individual and collective brains. In many instances, it is about re-programming some neural pathways and strengthening others through repetition and practice. Shaping the context and content within each and every brain is a critical success strategy, even though most leaders don't know it yet. I'm not talking about manipulating people for ill-gain or a win-lose environment—I'm talking about win-win.

The challenge and opportunity is to develop enough knowledge and insight into the science of the brain in order to make better decisions—decisions that lead to higher levels of satisfaction, commitment, engagement, and productivity, decisions that lead to fewer mis-hires, less turnover, better investment of development dollars, lower operating costs as a percentage of revenue and higher levels of profitability, some of which end up in the hands and pockets of employees and their families and communities.

Manage the Consequences

Managing consequences is all about knowing what results you are getting from the current collection of behaviors and about understanding what is driving or reinforcing these behaviors. It's about creating and reinforcing consequences in such a way that undesired behaviors are eliminated and desired behaviors are encouraged and rewarded.

And here is the kicker. Applied Behavioral Science claims that a whopping 80 percent of the behavior we get or do is a result of consequences. If we keep doing something that fails to satisfy expectations —our own or others'—or we keep not doing what we or others know needs to be done, there is an underlying payoff that is keeping us performing at our current level. The trick is to dig into a situation and identify the payoff. It is always there.

Another interesting and related piece of science comes from the deceased guru of efficiency and productivity, Edward Deming. Deming claimed that systems and processes account for about 98 percent of the results we get. More often than not the payoff that keeps us stuck in current, ineffective behavioral patterns is found within the systems or lack thereof.

If you want different results, change behavior. If you want to change behavior, manage consequences. To manage consequences, look underneath the behaviors and find their drivers within the systems at play.

The model provides a straight-forward and easy-to-remember framework for action, observation, and planning. Each component (as in A, B, or C) has several Touchpoints which, when addressed appropriately, is where the work gets done and successful results are created.

WRIGHT

Would you give our readers some examples of the specific touch points to which you refer?

C. WRIGHT

Well, there are many, so within the context of this conversation I'll just pick out some of the highlights.

If we look first at the Touchpoints that are associated with the assessment component of the model, then they would include things like becoming very clear and vigilant about purpose, self-assessing, knowing your customers intimately, and mastering the message and its delivery.

Purpose

To go back to the first Touchpoint, which is about clarity of purpose, I say you can't become a vigilante without first becoming crystal clear about what you want to create and achieve. You must know the degree to which you are passionate, committed, unique, and able. Assess what, why, where, when, and how. Check in with yourself to make sure you are living your destiny and not someone else's dream. Never lose faith; be smart about what you do, course correct as need be, but never stop believing in yourself and your idea.

Know what "your special sauce" is to borrow a phrase from my friend and colleague, Mark Moses. Do what is necessary to provide proof that a viable market exists with an appetite and the dollars to purchase your unique brand of "sauce."

Only when you are clear about your destination can you begin to map out the direction of your journey and realize your goal with minimal casualties and set-backs along the way. Most people leap-frog over this step believing it to rob them of unnecessary time and precious energy and resources. I've been there and swirled about in a choppy sea riddled with too many options and not enough focus.

My words of advice: "Do not pass 'go' until your level of assessment and clarity here is such that your vision, values, passion, and belief system ignites a strong sense of purpose and provides the fuel for a successful launch." Trust me, it will save much time, dollars, and heartbreak—for yourself and others.

Once you've "nailed" your picture of what you are designed to become and do and about the effect or imprint you are passionate about having in the world, you are almost ready to lead with iron determination, critical insight, and harnessed optimism; but not yet.

There are still a few more assessment-related steps to complete, the first of which is to identify how success will be measured. In other words, "How specifically are you going to know when you've arrived at your destination? What are the specific results to which you will apply every ounce of energy, persistence, and wisdom in your being? What assistance will you secure and couple with a structure designed to keep you squarely focused on performance outcomes—yours and others?"

Hold out the work you do here as the torch by which you light the darkness of the night and illuminate the compass that keeps you focused in the right direction.

By the way, dreaming big doesn't mean you have to have some grand purpose in mind and to lead an army, so to speak. Pursuing a vision to reach your individual best level of performance at whatever your profession or trade is just as worthy as anything else—especially if you are clear about the positive effect you wish to have on your customers' experiences and use that as the basis for measuring your success.

Self-Assess

Before embarking too far on your journey, take time out to self-assess. This is absolutely critical. Invest in objective tools to confirm what you know, underscore strengths to be leveraged, and uncover blind spots. And yes, there are always a few blind spots.

There is a growing plethora of assessment tools in the marketplace, a few of which are better than the rest depending on the intended usage. Invest in the best with the rigor of science and current validation data supporting them.

Self-assessments will provide valuable snapshots of many things, including, among others:

- naturally-wired and adapted behavioral styles (e.g., DISC)
- primary motivators and values (Workplace Motivators)
- clarity of thought, business acumen, natural talent as it relates to a whole host of personal skills (PTSI),
- current levels of soft-skill mastery (DNA),
- emotional intelligence (Emotional Quotient),
- routine task versus planning versus problem-solving preferences, communication preferences (Task Quotient),
- leadership effectiveness (360 feedback survey)

What your assessment reports is nowhere near as valuable as the conversation you have with your coach about it. This conversation is best anchored around key conclusions and actions to be taken as a result of the assessment experience.

Customers

In order to develop and refine your strategy for fully living your purpose, you must know as well or better than anyone else what your customers want. As soon as you are on solid ground, or shall I say ice, start anticipating where "the puck is going to be" and plan yourself there. That is Wayne Gretzy's claim to fame. He said that one of his primary strategies for success was to skate to where he believed the puck was going to be rather than where it was at the time.

If you are up to the challenge, go beyond what they know they want and show them what they want. People didn't know they wanted iPhones and iPads with all the bells and whistles and apps until Apple created these products and put them in the hands of key influencers who quickly demonstrated their value.

There are some fundamental characteristics of your customers that you need to understand and address. Know what these are. For example, people generally don't buy products and services per se, but rather experiences, dreams, and transformation.

This is where Steve Jobs was brilliant. He grasped, at the most basic level—the human desire for connection, simplicity, convenience, speed, beauty and the like. As a result, he made sure everything Apple produced was designed to simplify people's everyday applications of technology, and to create a rewarding emotional experience with the Apple brand. He was dogmatic about delivering on the human need for convenience, speed, productivity, beauty, and connection.

Furthermore, because he and his team understood their customers at such a deep and intimate level, they were able to reduce their product lines down to the critical few that best delivered on stakeholder expectations. This strategy allows them to invest more energy and resources into ongoing innovation of existing products and to constantly be looking for new category "killers" and "creators."

What are your primary customers' most fundamental needs? What do they think about and wish for every day? What might they need but not yet know about? What is the nature of the transformation or change they seek? How will you create a highly interactive, emotional experience with your brand? Why should they do business with you versus any other of your competitors? Assess, assess, and assess some more until you've reached the level of knowing what is in their minds, hearts, and souls. Do enough in the beginning to launch your business with an informed start, and stay committed to ongoing decision-making based on as much objective data as possible.

To this end, annual or bi-annual customer satisfaction and loyalty surveys are a must, as is their thorough analysis and timely response. Such surveys don't have to cost an arm-and-a-leg neither do they need to consume an inordinate amount of time. Customer surveys are best outsourced to a third party. I like to make sure they are highly customized and relevant to the client.

Don't lose sight of the fact that your employees are your customers, too. Know their individual communication preferences, core motivators, strengths, and weaknesses as they relate to the critical few skills and behaviors required for superior performance, readiness for promotion, career aspirations, and views of your organization's leadership, culture, and practices.

The many assessment options identified in the previous outline on self-assessment are applicable to employee selection and development objectives. Additional value-added options include employee engagement surveys, team surveys, organizational and leadership effectiveness surveys, change-readiness assessments and coaching culture assessments.

Message

With your intimate customer knowledge, you are now ready to develop yourself as a master storyteller, using language, visuals, touch, and smells to arouse and attract your customers' emotional and logical brains.

Use powerful stories, storyboards, drawings, presentations, demonstrations, videos, and the like to convey key messages that appeal to your audience. Assess the affect of various mediums, methods, and approaches for their ability to attract attention and generate interest. Re-engineer, modify, tweak, develop, respond.

Be where your ideal client's eyes, ears, and hands are. Engage, engage, engage.

The best combination of assessments depends on your circumstances and objectives. They can be used to gain perspective on self, or to gather data at team, departmental, division, or organizational levels. Overall business assessment and analysis also needs to occur on an ongoing basis (more on this when we get to the consequences component of the Performance Touchpoints model.

All of the above were just examples of Touchpoints for the Assessment Phase of the Model. It will take longer than the time we have to provide the same level of explanation for the Behavior and Consequences components of the model, so I'll just give you some examples of Touchpoints.

Where Behaviors are concerned, Touchpoints deal with hiring right, building leadership and management bench-strength, isolating and focusing on critical behaviors, creating an accountable culture, automating simplified systems, and mastering connections.

Monitoring, measuring, and communicating are foundational Touchpoints for managing Consequences. Then there is a restarting your engine, so to speak, and a renewing of a coaching relationship or deciding it's time to engage a new coach more in line with the needs of the day.

Most people will not need to spend time on, or be ready for, every Touchpoint. It is a good idea to keep a running inventory of what has been fully addressed, what is in the development stage, and what is yet to be planned and put into motion. At any given point, it is helpful to have the road mapped and know where you are at on a journey.

WRIGHT

There is a lot of complexity to manage in order to improve one's ability to achieve his or her goals. It can seem like a daunting task. What is your secret to managing the complexity of it all?

C. WRIGHT

That's a good question. I don't know that there is any secret to it. The answer will be different for each primary behavioral style. For example, I'm a "just wade into the complexity and sort it out as I go" person. That wouldn't work at all for a more steady or analytical type. That person would have to think it all through, map it out, and develop a thorough plan for execution before even thinking of taking action.

That having been said, I think anyone would agree with the merits of pausing long enough to develop at least a basic strategy and identifying a couple of next steps and then a couple more next steps and so forth. The feeling of the anxiety that comes from a big stretch goal and the considerable yardage between current and end states can immobilize a person. One can quickly thaw from such a frozen state of mind by simply identifying a few small steps forward.

So, if there was a secret to reducing the complexity and increasing odds of success, it would be to stay in motion 80 percent of the time and to set many sub-goals with short time frames. Spend the other 20 percent of work time growing your thinking and planning competencies.

WRIGHT

Why do you think so few people achieve their dreams and/or their potential?

C. WRIGHT

Wow, that's a tough one. I'm sure the reasons are many and varied. I would say because of their thinking. Fear holds them back. Fear of failure, fear of success, fear of taking the next steps and not getting it exactly right, fear of being judged, fear of spending money, fear of stepping outside one's comfort zone, fear of change.

Fear keeps us stuck and wishful. As long as we get to stay in a fear state, we don't have to measure up, show up, and play big. We can buy into the stories we carry around in our heads that keep us thinking small. We can take short and inexpensive "taxi rides"

We don't need to "get out of our head" as some would say. Rather, we need to change what is in our head and align it with what's in our heart.

Another key reason is that they try to do it alone. They don't recognize the value that comes with hiring one or more coaches who will get them on the podium. They would rather spend their disposable dollars on vacations and cars and homes and so on. The sad thing is that when they've spent their lives and resigned themselves to ordinariness, they come to terms with how meaningless their material collections are if not balanced by having lived their dream.

Lastly, I'd say the lack of having good systems in place to ensure focus, discipline, and consistent execution. As I think about it, these reasons can all be summed up as having several bad habits that create major obstacles and barriers to success.

WRIGHT

You were talking about spending money on yourself. I can remember one time losing an argument with a man I was trying to be a good mentor to. I knew he could learn a lot from an inexpensive educational opportunity, but he was unwilling to pay any money for it. I asked him how many times he got his haircut and he answered, "every three weeks or so" and it cost $20 per. I added that together and then asked him what kind of shampoo and conditioner he used. It was fairly inexpensive and the cuts and products added up to about $400 a year. Yet, he was unwilling to spend a nickel on the inside of his head. Bad decision-making not only keeps people from realizing their dreams, but sometimes from even getting anywhere close to their potential. I think you have covered it very well.

You have mentioned a few times though the importance of partnering with a coach, how does one go about finding and selecting a coach?

C. WRIGHT

The first thing to do is create a profile of the type of coach you want to work with. For example, what experience and credentials are important to you? With what coaching style will you do your best work? Are you looking for a pure coaching model whereby the coach provides no or minimal advice or are you wanting a combination of coaching and expertise? Will you work well with a directed, to-the-point coaching style or one that is gentler and more supportive? Are you looking for someone who is prepared to challenge you and hold you accountable for results or do you want a thinking partner? Will your budget and preferences direct you to a more seasoned coach or to a lower-fee arrangement? Do you want a face-to-face arrangement or will online coaching suffice?

Once you've created your profile, it will be much easier to find a good match. Do a Google search for a coaching association and/or school in your area. Identify options and contact two or three apparent fits, based on the coach profiles, and ask to meet with him or her briefly by phone or in-person in order to discuss your needs. See how you feel and assess who will provide your best fit.

WRIGHT

So what concluding thoughts would you like to leave us with that might be helpful for those who are reading this book that would help them on their way to their goals and dreams?

C. WRIGHT

The world has changed and is continuing to change. New road maps are required because the games being played are becoming significantly different. With the dawn of each new day, the world is increasingly moving into cyberspace. Not totally, obviously, but enough of it has moved into that arena to require a re-schooling of the rules and cyber-strategies. This is a real challenge for many Baby Boomers and some Generation Xs. Given the reality of the world and the warp speed at which it moves, it is imperative for anyone aspiring to heightened levels of success to climb on the "super-wired" bandwagon or be left behind. Find and engage any twenty- or twenty-five-year-old and they'll have you wired in no time flat.

I speak of much change, and rightly so. At the same time, many of the principles and fundamentals of success that have survived the test of time still prove to be effective. Today's seeker of business success needs to understand the fundamentals and adapt them to consumer expectations—both current and future. And be clear: the road to success is no longer a journey of tweaking and improving what has worked in the past. Competition is mounting in a big way and its reach is global. Success, at any significant level today, requires the ability to get attention and stand out from the crowd.

If there are only three questions to ask and answer, let them be:

1. What is the dream I wish to live?
2. What makes me, my idea, and/or approach unique and able to attract attention and stand out from the ordinary?
3. Where can I find and engage a good coach to help me succeed?

And finally, don't forget that A + B = C.

WRIGHT

That's great advice. I appreciate all the time you've taken to answer these questions. It's been delightful. I've learned a lot and I'm sure that our readers are going to get a lot from this book.

C. WRIGHT

Thank you for formulating the questions and helping me think.

About the Author

As Chief Change Catalyst for The Wright Group, Catharine works primarily with CEOs, business owners, and senior leaders seeking change. Her unique ability to get clients to successfully complete what they otherwise would not accomplish keeps them coming back and referring their colleagues.

Catharine's expertise includes strategic planning, talent management, leader and organizational development, and leading change. Among her credentials are MBA and PCC (Professional Certified Coach) designations.

She is the author of *101 Employee Engagement and Retention Strategies* and countless articles on performance excellence. Clients regularly engage her to speak on topics pertaining to change, culture, leadership development, and talent management.

Her many accomplishments include being named a Paul Harris Fellow by Rotary International and serving her community as a director and a chair of numerous boards.

Catharine lives in Edmonton, Alberta. When not working her magic with clients, she can be found running the trails of the river valley, chasing a golf ball around a nearby course, or immersed in a good book.

Catharine Wright, MBA, PCC, CPBA
11630 Kingsway Avenue
Edmonton, AB, Canada T5G 0X5
780-701-8178
coaching@wright-group.ca
www.wright-group.ca
www.aleadersjourney.com

Chapter Three

THE POWERS OF SUCCESS

REBECCA BALES

DAVID WRIGHT (WRIGHT)
Today I'm talking with Rebecca Bales. Rebecca is an author, international speaker, and organizational consultant. She brings decades of experience in leadership and personal development. She is partner of the Americas for Lumina Learning, a global community of business consultants bringing innovative solutions and next-generation assessment tools to organizations, transforming and inspiring their people. Her recent book, *Step Up to the Plate: The Power of Passion and Determination,* helps people find the formula for personal and career success.

Rebecca, welcome to *ROADMAP to Success*.

REBECCA BALES (BALES)
Thank you, David; it's great to be here.

WRIGHT
So what is your definition of success?

BALES

To me success is based on a foundation of happiness—it's being truly and completely happy and joyful. It's loving what you do and doing what you love. In order to find this, you have to be living your life with purpose, knowing who you are so completely that you know what makes you happy, what you value, what your purpose in life is, and how you wish to go about living it. It's at that point where everything falls into place, where your decisions become easy because they line up with your life. Once you get that right I believe you experience true success. Find your passion and live it, then the rest will come.

WRIGHT

Who are the people who have served as your role models for success?

BALES

I'd have to say first off it would be my father. He had his head on straight, worked hard, and was dedicated to his faith and his family and knew what his priorities were. He was happy and content with his life.

Personally, this involves a poignant story about a monetary role model. When I was in college, I was traveling on a plane to go home for the holidays. A distinguished gentleman sat down beside me. He was an attorney and dressed in a grey business suit. I can still see him vividly, exactly what he looked like. He started asking me about what I was majoring in and what I was going to do with my life. He told me something that nobody had ever told me before. He said that my generation of women would experience for the first time in business the ability to be and do whatever we wanted and we wouldn't be limited by any kind of typical stereotypes or bound by restrictions that women had experienced in the past. That was an incredible concept for me at the time. Nobody had ever even asked me what I wanted to be in life or could be or even told me I had no limitations. Looking back on this now, I feel as though I experienced an angel delivering a stunning message. It precipitated a seismic shift in my thinking and opened up the world to me and doors that I continue to explore to this day."

Another role model who has had a profound effect on my life is Wayne Dyer. That came during a period after a very tragic event in my life. I spent several years searching for what made sense to me, spiritually and personally. I had lost the ability to find the purpose in my life. I wasn't sure why I was here or what I was supposed to be doing. I had begun to practice meditation and study how our attitudes and beliefs attract similar attitudes and beliefs, therefore affecting our life experiences as a whole. Then I came across Wayne's book, *The Power of Intention*, and it all flowed together for me. It just made total sense. It spoke to the spiritual and religious questions I had then as well as those about my life in general. It sent me down a completely new path of discovery. It was an incredible transformation for me. There have been other great books similar to his, but that was the one I found first. Now, I hope others will discover my book and that the concepts and beliefs resonate as powerfully for them.

WRIGHT

So what do you think are the biggest obstacles that people face in trying to become successful?

BALES

I think the answer is in the question. People who are struggling to become successful often focus too strongly on financial success and recognition. People who become successful are people who are passionate about what they are doing and are living lives filled with passion and determination. These are two of the four very important keys to success.

Passion is number one because you must first understand who you are and what inspires and ignites your actions. It is impossible to truly know this unless you are a person who understands your core self. Once you understand and have clarity around your core persona, you can define what personal success is to you.

This moves you into self-awareness, which is the next step to success. Self-awareness is knowledge and knowledge is wisdom. Having the knowledge of how you show up in this world and being aware of your actions and reactions is key to success in any situation. It gives you power to handle any situation.

Then you move to the Power of Choice, the third key to success. Here you make rational and logical choices, exercising your personal courage to break through any limiting beliefs you may be harboring.

Finally, you reach the fourth key to success, Determination, where you must find and exercise the mental toughness and resiliency you need to pull you through the tough times.

We all know that there are some obstacles that will present themselves along the way. Many of these we can be prepared for but many will come out of left field. I call these life's curve balls. These curve balls can either knock us out of the program altogether, or we can learn to adjust. It is in that adjustment that we find success beyond our imagination. We find it when we are not really trying for success at all but are simply trying to stay the course. Therefore, we end up crossing the finish line when our typical reaction might well have been to crater and give up. This is when many of us stop short of completing our goals. When we are in touch with our passion and what our true self means, we are able to hear our call to action. At this point, we can recognize our purpose. Once we are crystal clear on this, then we simply need to engage our inner strength and courage to make it all the way through the journey.

Some of us are born with a great deal of mental strength and toughness. However, these are traits that can be learned and strengthened. Courage and mental strength are like muscles—the more you use them, the stronger they become. Remember, we all get thrown curve balls. Success is about the accomplishment of a goal or dream. Once you can make sure that dream or goal is in line with your true self, you are halfway there. The other half is being ready for those curve balls along the way. Using your determination will carry you through to the end.

So it is your passionate inner drive, fueled with your determination and resolve, that will create your success without your focus on "being successful."

WRIGHT

So do you have personal experience of this?

BALES

I have spent years searching for who I really was and what I ultimately wanted out of my life; it's not been an easy road for me. I would say it took at least seven years.

I want to help others discover and follow the process to find out who they are, what they're passionate about, and then begin to realize their purpose in life. It doesn't have to take years; it may only take weeks, but it is an ongoing process. I consider myself a passion pathfinder and to me this is the road map to the soul. Finding your passion is where you find true success because if you find your passion, you will be successful.

WRIGHT

For me, now that I look back many years, I always thought success, in the early years, was a accomplishing a goal and I would be successful when I accomplished it. But the strangest thing happened to me. When I set a goal, as soon as I start on it, it makes me happy, and I am successful. I act as if I'm already there. Have you experienced things like that?

BALES

Absolutely. I think it's when we break down our vision of success into manageable steps, focusing on the goals and not merely the overall picture of success. Baseball pitchers do the same. They focus not on throwing a no-hitter or winning the game, but throwing a strike, getting the batter out. Success, if you win at each of these key bases will follow. When we're not trying to be successful is when we become successful. It's because you're really doing what you love to do at the time and that is what drives it.

WRIGHT

So with that in mind would you tell our readers a little bit about what drives you to be successful?

BALES

Absolutely. For me it's simple. I want to make a difference in the world, I've always wanted to help others and that has been a dream of mine ever since I was a little girl. I started out my life as a teacher and I loved the experience of helping others find the way or see the light. I transitioned over to the business world through coaching, consulting, and training, so I used similar teaching methods in the corporate mode.

Seeing the proverbial light go off for people is what makes me tick. I just love helping others see that path that took me long and difficult years to find and that's very gratifying.

Anything I can do that helps others shorten that time frame is deeply gratifying.

WRIGHT

Looking back on your professional career, what would you say would be the biggest contribution to your professional success?

BALES

I'm very clear about that. I took a values clarification exercise at another point in my life. I was not satisfied at all with my then current job. Once I took this values clarification exercise and identified what was really important to me, I understood why. I looked at the defining moments in my life and how they helped to create who I am today. At that particular moment it set me free because it gave me permission to leave the profession that I had trained for, prepared for, and invested in greatly. Getting "permission" that it was okay to leave and do something different was huge for me—it set me free.

WRIGHT

I remember when I was a sophomore in college that I started taking a course called Values Clarification. The author was teaching it. I felt the same way—as soon as I got it all together and figured it out, it became a lot easier.

BALES

It does; it just becomes your internal compass and all your decisions become easier and clearer. It really is amazing, it's profound.

WRIGHT

So in your new book, *Step Up to the Plate: The Power of Passion and Determination,* you say that passion and determination are the two most important factors in success. How do these two things relate to success?

BALES

Oh, that's a great question. I use a four-step process that I outline in my book. It's the process I went through myself. The process involves four steps that are set around a baseball metaphor. I have worked through these four steps with many of my coaching clients and workshop participants.

It starts with discovering your passion; I call it "The Power of Passion." Then you move on to "The Power of Knowing"—knowing how you show up in the world. It includes how you interact with others in three areas of your persona—your underlying self, your everyday self, and your overextended self. You then move to the third base, "The Power of Choice." Here you examine how your life is a series of your choices—even not making a choice is a choice in itself.

Finally, you get to home plate, "The Power of Determination." This step involves the mental toughness and courage you need to persevere and make it all the way. Passion and determination are the bookends to this process and I feel they are the key drivers to success. Passion is what steers your journey but determination is the fuel that drives you forward. Determination is about your inner strength, it's the resiliency, the drive, the persistence and the attitude that you possess. You don't necessarily have to be born with these, but if not, you must learn and strengthen these are things in order to be successful. Just remember you can learn and fully develop these powerful forces within you.

The first three steps: passion, knowing, and choices can get you there, but it's the last one—forceful determination—will carry you through. It will reveal itself, and in an instant make a difference between someone who succeeds and someone who gives up. It's the moment that we step up to the plate.

WRIGHT

So what made you want to write this book?

BALES

I have personally experienced the moment of getting knocked down and hearing the tapes in my head telling me that I couldn't succeed or overcome this setback. My old reaction was to admit defeat. It's that self-limiting belief that creeps up when you least expect it. I've had that moment several times in my early career and I watched as others experienced it.

One day I woke up and I realized I had control of those self-limiting beliefs and imposed restrictions. I didn't have to bow to their pressure. I could stand up and step up. In that one instant I could choose another path, push through, go forward, and make all the difference in the world. It was truly the difference in my being successful or not, and I have seen it be the pivotal point for others. It can determine whether they become successful or not. So I wrote the book about what it takes to survive, thrive, and persevere. That moment I speak of is the differentiating factor. It's that Step Up to the Plate attitude my book is based on.

It's incredible when you narrow it down to think differently in one moment, but that's what it takes—that's all it really takes. When you think you're beaten and you refuse to be beaten, you get up and you keep going. You persevere with determination and you succeed.

Once I discovered that magic moment and I saw it work for me, I started seeing it work for others. I wanted to tell everybody about it and that's why I wrote the book. Along the way, I had my doubts about being able to complete it. I even had a discussion with a very wise writing coach who told me to consider all the things to which I was committed. That expanded on my previous list of passions and goals. I made a list, slept on it, and got up the next morning and completed my book. It was in that moment that I stepped up to the plate. So it takes being committed and pushing through to make it happen.

WRIGHT

Do you still work a lot on your passion or is passion something that is in concrete from the beginning?

BALES

No, I think you always work on your passion. I think that just like your values can change, depending on the different events that happen in your life, your passions can change along the way as your life experiences affect you.

Life is ever in a state of flux, never static. Clients I work with can have huge life changes. They suddenly may have new family issues and don't want to travel with their jobs as they were before, or vice versa. So as things shift, you have to constantly regenerate that passion. Sometimes it is merely recharging; sometimes it is a change of focus. Your core values can change along with your passions. It's part of the reason I suggest that my clients revisit their passions and their visions for their life on a regular basis. Success is predicated on how we define our success, which is based on how closely we are living our lives in congruence with our vision, our passion, and our purpose.

WRIGHT

I have always been told that I had to come up with my purpose and it always scared me to death. It confused me more than anything else because I find purpose in almost everything I do. So what is the message you want people to hear so they can learn from your success?

BALES

I want them to know that they can be successful—anyone can do it. First of all, they have to understand what success means to them. Then they have to have the self-determination to know what drives them so they can claim what they are passionate about. With passion, I mean their values, their purpose, and their orientation to life—what's important to them? Is it money, is it family? What defines their filters?

Secondly, they have to know who they are and that includes their strength and their vulnerabilities. If you know who you are, you can speak your truth and you can speak it from the heart in a way that is not emotional, but factual. So they have to understand how they show up in the world. They have to know that they have choices; they can claim their own choices and be bold about their decisions. But by not making a decision, they've made a decision by default. So they may have to stand up against what others think they should do, or should be, and look at what they really want to do and who they really want to be.

Finally, it takes that determination of which I've spoken. It takes inner strength—the intestinal fortitude to pick themselves up after they get knocked down. It takes a positive outlook on life and their ability to overcome obstacles and stay the course. Those things are key.

WRIGHT

You mentioned in your book that success breeds success. How can people help other people succeed?

BALES

This is simple, too, and core to this message. They can't be afraid or intimidated by the success of others, and many people are; but they have to see success through the eyes of abundance. Success *is* abundant. It's not scarce or limited in any way. It's because success is *your* happiness—it's your level of joy and happiness for the world, so there is plenty of that to go around. If you could see me at this moment, you would see me with a huge smile; it's because this concept is what charges me. When others succeed, you should be happy for them and supportive and helpful. In that manner, we should all give each other a hand up because we don't have to see it as something that is rationed. You can't believe, "Oh, they get it and now it's gone and there isn't enough for me." That's not the case and the more someone is successful, the more success it breeds and the more we can all share in everyone's success. It's not just for a select few, it's for everybody. The way I view it is, "step up to the plate and claim yours."

WRIGHT

So I know what an author and international speaker is, but I'm not so sure about organizational consultants. Tell me what an organizational consultant is and perhaps even give an example of how you have helped an organization as a consultant enjoy more success or even reach success.

BALES

That's a great question, David. An organizational consultant is somebody who goes into an organization and works with them in different facets to build organizational culture and to help them get aligned to their overall strategy.

Most of the work I do with organizations is compatible with the direction an organization is trying to go strategically, but occasionally it involves a degree of cultural shift, such as when two companies are merging. Most of an organization's strategy revolves around its sales, marketing, technology, staying at the forefront of their industry, and "hard" skills as far as operations and timelines it needs to meet. I come in more on the "soft" skill side because an organization is a body of people and those people have to feel valued. They have to feel important to the organization; they need to feel heard in order to be as highly productive as they can be. As people understand and get passionate about their work, they can get engaged in what they're doing. The level of productivity for that organization skyrockets. So that's what I do—I help them find the path to accelerated productivity.

WRIGHT

I agree with you about the soft skills and that we're all people. As I look at my company, there are many different age groups represented here. I have heard and I read so much about the different generations and how we're so culturally diverse. Since you're a professional and work with people do you find that there is that much division in the generations and do you think they can all work together and learn from each other?

BALES

Absolutely. I think the key to generational issues is to help others understand what the needs and the drivers are for the various generations.

They are very different and if you don't understand that, you might look at a particular generation and think they're not getting on board with our work ethic, or they dance to the beat of a different drummer so to speak, and they do. They can be just as productive as any generation as long as we understand, recognize, and value what their needs are and what is driving them.

The younger generations in the workforce are just phenomenal with technical skills. They can do so many things twice as fast as some of us because of their comfort level and knowledge. If we can recognize this and learn how to spur their creativity, then they can be huge contributors to keep organizations thriving. We're going to have a real issue coming up as the Baby Boomers exit the workforce. They will leave behind a significant vacuum in experience of conservative and measured values. The balance they bring to operations and planning is of unlimited value.

I'm big on building a culture and structure that promotes mentoring within organizations. It can be a dynamic and enlightening two-way street. Because there are so many Baby Boomers and not enough Gen X'ers behind them to step in and fill the more senior positions, within many companies, it is a critical need. More importantly, Gen X'ers and younger haven't had the opportunity to developed certain skill sets to the same levels as those acquired by the departing Baby Boomers. That's going to be a challenge all companies and leaders will be dealing with during the next ten to fifteen years. How well those different generations integrate together will have a major bearing on their level of success.

Success is measured differently by different people and generational differences are a big element on the success scale, but people are all still people. So remember, find your true self so that what you are doing outwardly is in line with your heart. It is then when you will find your purpose in life. When you are aligned with this purpose, your choices become clear.

Step up and accept the challenges and choices in life, if they are in sync with this alignment. Don't worry about the success. It will come. Just be determined to live your life in total harmony with the real you. Enjoy and cherish every step of the way. The hard knocks lead us to the path we may have never seen. See the opportunities these contain. Make your life the best it can be. If not now, then when?

WRIGHT

Well, what a great conversation. It makes me wish you were one of my organizational consultants.

BALES

I'd love to; you know how to reach me!

WRIGHT

You sound like you know what you're talking about. This has been a real pleasure, Rebecca. It's always a pleasure talking with you and I appreciate your answering these questions.

BALES

It's been a pleasure to be here again, David. Thank you so much.

WRIGHT

Today I've have been talking with Rebecca Bales. Rebecca is an author, an international speaker, and organizational consultant. Her recent book, *Step Up to the Plate: The Power of Passion and Determination,* is a must read. It helps people find the formula for personal and career success.

Rebecca, thank you so much for being with us today on *ROADMAP to Success.*

BALES

Thank you David.

About the Author

Rebecca Bales is an author, international speaker, and organizational consultant. She is one of the leading experts in leadership and personal development. Rebecca has held several senior level positions in sales, organizational consulting, and enterprise solutions for Fortune 500 companies in the industries of pharmaceuticals, technology, retail, healthcare, and finance. She is a member of Who's Who in Women Leaders, World Pulse: Global Issues Through the Eyes of Women, Women for Women International, the National Association of Women Business Owners, and the National Association of Female Executives. Her recently released book, *Step Up to the Plate–The Power of Passion and Determination,* helps readers to find their inner power and live the life of their dreams.

Rebecca's background is in Human Dynamics and Psychology with graduate studies in Organizational Development from the University of Dallas. Rebecca is an adjunct faculty member for the Cox School of Business at Southern Methodist University in Dallas, Texas. She has achieved the prestigious certification as a professional mediator in Commercial Mediation from Seton Hall Law School in New Jersey and was a senior consultant for the Attorney General's Office, State of Texas.

Rebecca is the developer and creator of the award-winning experiential programs in leadership and teambuilding, Bungles® and Teamship®, which have been showcased nationwide.

Rebecca Bales
Lumina Learning US
St. Petersburg, Florida
888-827-8855
rebecca@rebeccabales.com

Chapter Four

THE CAREERS YOU LOVE MODEL FOR SUCCESS

MARLENE HALEY

DAVID WRIGHT (WRIGHT)

Today I am talking with Marlene Haley, who holds a Master of Counseling Psychology degree and has achieved the Master Career Counselor designation, one of the highest career counseling designations in North America. She is also a Professional Certified Coach and has earned this credential from the International Coach Federation. Her passion is helping executives and professionals with charting successful career paths. She is the developer of the Careers You LOVE Model and has helped thousands of people for more than twenty years. Her areas of expertise include: career planning, career testing, labor market research, job search campaigns, salary negotiation, resume writing, education planning, and self-employment.

In the business sector, Marlene assists companies by providing customized career management programs for employees navigating their careers through corporate environments. Additionally, when a company is going through organizational change, she provides outplacement programs for terminated staff to assist them in leaving the company and moving on to new job opportunities.

Marlene is a foremost authority on career development and is a frequent media advisor for television, radio, magazines, and newspapers. As an expert in career success strategies, she has made presentations at conferences, professional associations, and tradeshows. Marlene has also served as a faculty member at a university and a college.

Marlene, welcome to ROADMAP to Success.

MARLENE HALEY (HALEY)

Thank you. It's nice to talk with you, David. I'm glad to be here.

WRIGHT

You have had a great deal of success from offering career counseling to executives and professionals for more than twenty years. From your experience, what does the road map to success look like?

HALEY

Typically, when we think of people becoming successful in their careers, we think of a vertical career road map, or what some would call a "career ladder," where an individual works in a field, accepts a series of promotions, and moves up one rung at a time until he or she reaches the top of his or her chosen profession.

Achieving success using this road map is still common today, however, new road maps have developed over the last two decades because research shows that people experience an average of eight to ten career changes during their life. Consequently, I have seen three new road maps emerge.

Lateral Career Road Map

The lateral career road map to success involves people moving in their profession in a horizontal pattern, either moving through multiple corporations or multiple industries, or some combination of both. Often success is experienced by these individuals because they are exposed to the excitement of variety.

Portfolio Career Road Map

The portfolio road map is best suited for individuals who are not satisfied with just one job, so they pursue multiple full-time or part-time positions simultaneously. They might have a "day job," plus they "moonlight" with one or two evening or weekend jobs. Typically this road map is followed by start-up entrepreneurs, do-gooders who want to contribute to society, or artists trying to break into their field. This road map is appealing to individuals who want to follow their passions no matter what it takes.

Hopscotch Career Road Map

The last pattern I've seen is what I call the "hop-scotch" road map. It's usually followed by thrill seekers who see life as an adventure and see themselves as lifelong learners. Individuals "hop scotch" in and out of jobs based on their personal interests and life circumstances. From the outside it seems like career success is achieved through luck, however, upon closer investigation, I've discovered that these individuals are usually very proactive in creating a strong network of contacts. A solid base of contacts often leads to interesting career opportunities.

In terms of which road map to success is best for a person, it's important to remember that no two people make their career decisions the same way, and I believe that's how it should be. Choosing a career and a road map to success is giving yourself permission to be who you truly are.

Now, you might wonder why people need to give themselves permission to be who they are and you probably think it should be as natural as breathing. And for some folks it is. However, for many others, they get caught up in following someone else's dream for themselves or they let "practical" considerations overshadow their dreams. Of course, practical considerations definitely have merit but they do not speak to the heart. We must accept the fact that our preferences, our interests, and our desires are just not logical. They are often a mystery. We don't ask why people love chocolate, so why should we ask people why they love engineering or social work? I believe that we need to accept that when it comes to career choice, we sometimes may never know exactly why we want what we want.

People often get free advice from well-intentioned family and friends whether they ask for guidance or not. I usually inform my clients that when they get serious about a career choice, they should not be surprised if the people closest to them disagree with their decisions. Resistance from others is sometimes a positive sign that means you are defining success on your own terms and taking charge of your own career path.

I guess what I'm saying is that I believe there is no best road map for success. If a career choice feels "right" and your gut says "go," then the next step is to test it out in the reality of the job market. I think it's better for you to pursue your dreams and learn from your experiences rather than to give up on a career before you even start and then have regrets for not giving your career dream a chance.

My role as a career counselor is to believe in my clients and encourage the pursuit of their goals. Over and over again, it's been my experience that my clients can succeed even when others around them least expect it.

WRIGHT

How exactly can career counseling assist people along the road to success?

HALEY

The art of career counseling is the art of helping people to deeply hear their inner voice, access their natural gifts and talents, and find the inspiration to move themselves into action to achieve their career goals.

One of the most fundamental dimensions of career counseling is helping you discover and build skills that you most like to use. Often you know what your job accomplishments are but you get stuck trying to identify the related transferrable skills. Career counseling helps you to clearly articulate your skills and build the customized professional "career vocabulary" necessary for resume writing, job interviews, and annual performance reviews.

Once you can clearly identify your skills, the next step is values clarification. Values clarification and transferrable skills identification go hand in hand. Values clarification is a process of figuring out what's really important to you in a job and ranking your requirements. It usually involves coming up with a list of specific criteria to evaluate career options so you can make key decisions.

Giving information about labor market demand, job descriptions, retraining programs, and salary ranges is also a major component of the career counseling process. I think it's important that career counselors not just assist you with identifying your career passions, but also help you to access up-to-date knowledge about current trends. With most of the executives and professionals I work with, they get so busy with their own job that sometimes they lose touch with what's out there in the job market. With lack of knowledge, they get stuck and sometimes stay in a job too long. Getting timely, current career information can help you get moving again and back on track.

Sometimes career counselors will set up opportunities for role playing so that you can rehearse and practice skills such as interviewing for a job, asking for a raise, or confronting a co-worker about on-the-job issues. Even with savvy professionals, when it comes to talking about themselves in a job interview or asking for more money, they often experience performance anxiety, despite the fact that they are usually very competent in their field. So, the rehearsal of possible scenarios gives them the confidence to put their best self forward.

I believe that it is essential for career counselors to provide encouragement and emotional support during the career counseling process. Most of what you feel during a career counseling session is not usually stated directly, therefore, an effective career counselor will carefully listen to the feelings behind your words. As you identify your feelings, you gain access to your passions and often this helps to pull you out of your career doldrums and ignite new career possibilities.

Probably career testing and assessment is what most people think of when they think about career counseling. A trained career counselor with a Master of Counseling degree can administer and interpret both Level 1 and Level 2 psychometric assessments. These tools can help you learn about yourself as well as give you ideas about occupations you didn't even know existed. If a career counselor lacks a Master of Counseling degree, then that counselor will be very limited in what tests he or she can administer and interpret with you, so it's always best to check out credentials before contracting for services.

Helping you launch a job search campaign is another important aspect of career counseling. Of course, job hunting is very different than it was five to ten years ago because the Internet is used more than ever for job searching. So, your career counselor should assist with helping you identify the top online job posting sites for your industry and help you use social media sites for networking. In addition to providing feedback for your resume and cover letter, career counselors will also help you compose LinkedIn profiles, professional biographies, and career branding messages. Alternatively, if you don't want to conduct a job search campaign, a career counselor can help you identify feasible self-employment options and acquire business skills. In both cases, your career counselor should be helping you identify your career goals and facilitate concrete action steps and progress.

What I've noticed in recent years is that when my clients finally figure out what career they want and land a job, they often continue with career counseling so that they can ensure on-the-job success. The first ninety days of a new job is critical and, depending on your employment contract, you could face termination if you don't quickly get up to speed with your new job responsibilities or don't fit into the corporate culture. In order to help you keep your job, career counselors will assist you in developing "star performer" competencies. Typically, they will assist you with developing and honing on-the-job skills such as: leadership skills, managing time, supervising employees, enhancing creativity, managing stress, and achieving peak performance.

So, as you can see, there are many ways that career counseling can assist you with achieving success. If you want to ensure that you are working with a trained professional, be sure to do your research and ask about your career counselor's credentials. Depending on where you live, the field of career counseling may not be regulated. I usually advise checking out professional associations for a list of credentialed career counselors.

WRIGHT

In today's tough economy, how do people follow their career dreams but also survive and make a living?

HALEY

With so much attention being paid to the state of the economy these days, many companies reduce or otherwise restructure their workforce. With this in mind, workers must prepare for a very competitive job market. Job seekers must put themselves in employers' shoes and ask themselves, "What makes me so special that an employer will hire me?"

Workers are shortsighted if they think that all they need to do in today's job market is show up and perform their job duties. The real challenge is to demonstrate to employers what they will gain if they bring you on board.

I assist my clients in figuring out and clearly articulating how they will add value to an organization. So, let me now share the criteria I know recruiters and hiring managers look for when they conduct job interviews and reference checks. In no particular order, they are:

Be a driver

In today's economy, companies must react to constant market changes. That means you have to be a driving force when a company changes directions and be quick to realign yourself with new corporate goals and objectives.

Be a change agent

Be a fast adopter of new company directives and develop a strong sense of urgency. Employees who move slowly or who are resistant to change are often left behind in the corporate dust.

Be an improviser

In a tough economy, organizations constantly shift priorities to stay afloat. You must develop the ability to improvise with existing company resources and devise new initiatives while keeping an eye on the big picture. Be part of the solution, not part of the problem.

Be a contributor

Challenging economic conditions require that all employees pull their weight. Take ownership and consider how you can contribute to cutting costs, building staff morale, raising funds, increasing customer satisfaction, and building a positive company reputation. Be your own service center and refuse to sit on the sidelines waiting for someone else to do it.

The bottom line here is that the "good ol' days" are gone when companies rewarded workers for putting in long hours, earning seniority, or mastering technical skills. In a tough economy, above average employees focus on outcomes and demonstrate results.

Remember, employers will compare you to other job candidates based on your past track record. In the job market, it is your accomplishments and your references from previous positions that will move you on or get you stuck. Realize that jobs come and go but your reputation is invaluable. Your reputation is your brand. Companies can't afford to waste their resources on an employee who only does what it takes to get by. It's essential in a tight labor market that you review your work history and identify all your achievements so you can clearly articulate them to your superiors. Typically this is easier said than done because most people are too close to their work to be objective or they are too humble to notice their greatness. That's the value of working with a career counselor who can help you with this.

Finally, the most important factor to remember when you're competing in a tight labor market is that when you love your career, it is easier to go the extra mile to do whatever it takes to stay on top of your profession and prove to employers you are worth hiring and keeping. Finding a career you love is prudent because it gives you the stamina to persevere and do the extras to stay competitive in your field of work. It's just smart and sustainable.

WRIGHT

I understand that you've developed a model to help people with career decision-making. Will you tell us about it?

HALEY

After having worked with thousands of clients over the years, I developed a user-friendly model to assist clients. I call it the Careers You LOVE Model and it breaks career planning down into four steps.

Step 1
L = Learn About Your Career Assets
The knowledge of who you are must be developed before meaningful work is discovered. I use traditional and innovative career exploration activities to fuel your imagination, discover your talents, build on your accomplishments, and determine your best career choices. Some of the career counseling activities and techniques I use include: career testing, written exercises and journaling, visualizations and creative activities, specific how-to demonstrations, focusing and goal-setting exercises, and strategic action planning.

Step 2
O = Observe Current Career Trends
   I believe that information is power. To accelerate the speed of your career transition, I carefully select online and print resources to help you with career planning. Up-to-date information is necessary for analyzing current trends so that you can take advantage of today's best career opportunities. Some of the resources I use include: career directories and encyclopedias, labor market information and trends, job classification systems, company databases, industry forecasts, and salary survey reports.

Step 3
V = Value Your Inner Wisdom
   Lack of confidence in yourself to achieve your career goals will impair your efforts in having fulfilling and exciting work. As you move through career transitions, it's important to listen to your intuition or inner wisdom and ignore the voice of your inner critic. Your inner critic is always pessimistic and discouraging. I use a wide variety of career counseling tools and techniques to help you avoid self-sabotage so you can move forward with ease and confidence. Some of the negative internal blocks I help with are: fear and procrastination, low motivation and energy, anger and frustration, doubt and indecision, arrogance and pride, boredom and underemployment.

Step 4
E = Express Your Career Branding
   Career transitions are often overwhelming due to the fierce competition you may face in pursuing your career dreams. In today's tight job market, it's essential that you identify and express your personal career brand to give yourself a competitive edge and a sustainable labor market position. I have seen that when you create a powerful career brand, you distinguish yourself from the crowd of leaders and professionals with equally strong qualifications. Some of the activities I help with include: identifying your value proposition to organizations, launching a personal career visibility campaign, defining your strategic message, and positioning your career brand.

WRIGHT
   What are the winning attitudes for success?

HALEY
   I believe there are a number of winning attitudes that pave the way for success. Each one can be developed over the span of your career and sometimes you might find that at times some of them are more important

than others depending on what career stage you are in (for example, career entry, midlife, or pre-retirement).

Patience

You must cultivate patience with your own journey and avoid the temptation to compare yourself to others. If discovering a career you love was easy, then everyone would have already done it. Although it is important to be proactive with your career search, you must allow it to unfold and do not force premature conclusions, otherwise you could end up making mistakes under anxiety and pressure.

Acceptance

It's essential that you recognize and fully accept your natural interests and talents. Do not take your strengths for granted. Just because something is easy for you doesn't mean it is not valuable. When you take notice of your unique gifts, you uncover helpful clues to finding a career you love.

Willingness

You must be willing to change anything that is an obstacle and gets in the way of pursuing your dreams. You may not know the exact steps to take, but develop an attitude of willingness to do whatever it takes to find career satisfaction. Remember that when you approach your work with enthusiasm and eagerness, you usually find that it's easier to find creative solutions to problems.

Commitment

Be committed to becoming a lifelong learner in your chosen career but don't rely on your employer for professional development. Invest your own time and money in improving yourself to become the best you can be in your professional field. Always be in charge of setting the direction of your career and aim for being a leader.

Focus

Stay focused on your own success. Fully experience the present and take action toward your future. When you actively participate and engage in each moment when you are at work, you influence what's going on. Focus and personal involvement leads to owning a bigger stake in creating success.

Modesty

Strive to do your very best but don't believe that you are irreplaceable. Don't take full credit for team projects. It's acceptable to let colleagues know about your achievements through case studies, promotion bulletins, or other such tools but it's quite another matter to arrogantly brag. There is not usually room for "divas" in the workplace.

Achievement

Break down your goals into manageable, bite-size chunks. Focus on small tasks that you can and will do. Set deadlines. Savor the sense of satisfaction that comes from achievement.

Optimism

Don't put someone else in charge of your own morale at work. Although you may do your best to surround yourself with positive people, it's impossible to avoid all people who are negative. Try to extend compassion to those who are pessimistic but do not allow yourself to be a doormat. Set appropriate boundaries and take care of yourself.

Humility

Despite your best attempts to become successful, sometimes you will stumble. Seek out the advice of colleagues or a mentor. Ask for honest feedback and try to learn from the career experiences of others who come from generations different than your own. Recognize your shortcomings and get support in managing them so they don't create problems. Expose yourself constantly to new ideas and approaches.

Gratefulness

Recognize your good fortune and take joy in counting your blessings. Be deliberate in extending appreciation toward others you come in contact with when you work. Acknowledge all the leaders in your chosen career who have gone before you, and how their legacy has made it possible for you to pursue your dreams now. Remember, what goes around comes around.

WRIGHT

Given the tight labor market these days, what are the best ways for people to get jobs when they are unemployed?

HALEY

First of all, I've noticed that among the people who get laid off due to the economy, many of them see their unemployment situation as an opportunity to pause and rethink what they really want out of their career. In other words, they see their unemployment situation as a chance to do some soul searching and figure out if they want to continue with their career path or change tracks. Often they don't want to be impulsive, taking the next job that comes along and then get themselves back into a job they really don't enjoy. I recommend that if you are unemployed and you choose to take a timeout period to figure out your next career move, you should determine a specific timeframe and then stick to it, so that a couple of weeks or months doesn't turn into a year or more.

Once you know where you want to go with your career and you've defined your goals, then the next step is to launch a job search campaign. It's been my experience that most people are not strategic in their job hunt. There are many job search methodologies you can use and it's critical to use only the ones that are best suited for your specific job objective, otherwise you are wasting your time and money.

So, one of the first exercises I ask my clients is how much annual salary they want in their next position. Then I ask them to calculate their earnings on a monthly, weekly, daily, and hourly basis. From there, they can figure out the real cost of every month they are unemployed, every week they are unemployed, every day they are unemployed, and every hour they are unemployed. My clients report that this number crunching exercise motivates them to stay strategic and not waste time on unproductive job-hunting methodologies.

Some of the most common job hunting methodologies that I've seen job seekers use include:

- Executive recruiters
- Internet job postings
- Social media Web sites
- Professional journals
- Resume/cover letter mass mail outs
- The telephone "Yellow Pages"
- Cold calling employers
- Private employment agencies
- Networking
- Volunteering (e.g., board of directors)
- Post-secondary alumni services
- State/federal unemployment services
- Newspaper ads

Choosing which job search methodologies are best for you depends on a number of factors including: your occupation, industry, sector (private, public, non-profit), level of education, years of experience, and ideal job level.

Unfortunately, I can't tell you how many times I've met clients who were completely frustrated with job hunting only to find out they were using the wrong job search methodologies. Unfortunately, by the time they came to see me they were experiencing what I call "job search burnout" and felt exhausted, as well as desperate. So, it's critical from the outset of a job search campaign that you define a specific job goal *and* the best job search methodologies. Don't get caught in a negative job search cycle of unproductive busyness.

If the circumstances around your becoming unemployed was stressful or if your termination was a shock or if the last time you conducted a job search was longer than five years ago, it's important to make sure that you don't aim too low in your job search. Believe it or not, I have seen many times when people go out for an interview and they return happy even though they did not get the job! I think this is because they really didn't want the job in the first place since they felt it was beneath them. So, you should always aim for a job you want at the level you want, then go after it with all you've got. In the end, genuine interest and excitement in a job you love will often impress a prospective employer and you'll increase your chances of getting a job offer.

Another factor that should be considered when you are unemployed and looking for what you want to do with your career is self-employment. If you are out of work, and you can't find a job anywhere, many people use their unemployment situation to turn their dream of starting a business into reality. If you've ever wondered about becoming a consultant, an independent contractor, or a freelancer then you might think, "It's now or never." I recommend that you spend time figuring out what kind of business to start and ask yourself some key questions:

Key Questions to Ask If Considering Self-Employment:

- What have you always dreamed of doing?
- What transferrable skills and knowledge could you bring to the business? What new skills and knowledge would you need to learn?
- Can you start the business during evenings and weekends and then expand your hours?
- Is there a product or service that is missing in your community? Is there a product or service in your community that could be improved? How would your business be different from existing businesses in your community?
- Have you invented something that you would like to take to market?
- What would your ideal customer/client look like?
- What goals would you have for the company (are they specific, measurable, realistic)?

- How do you feel about marketing and selling to prospective clients/customers? What skills would you need to learn to feel more comfortable?
- Do you have a supportive network of mentors, colleagues, and friends who can help you compensate for your business weaknesses or lack of experience?
- What would it take to get started (finances, equipment, employees, etc)? What risks are involved? How much profit could you make? Are you willing and capable of writing a business plan?

When I work with clients thinking about self-employment, I usually recommend that they do an Entrepreneurial Assessment. The results of the assessment show how your answers compare to proven, successful entrepreneurs. It's a quick and helpful way to find out if you have what it takes to make it as a successful businessperson.

The last approach I want to mention when people are trying to find a job in a tight economy is retraining. Going back to school is a huge investment in time and money, and when I say money, I mean money for tuition and money in lost earnings if you attend full-time studies. So, it's not a decision to be taken lightly. I recommend talking to a campus advisor and asking a lot of questions. Take notes and compare programs at different educational institutions.

Key Questions to Ask If Considering Retraining:
Career and Academic Services

Does the institution help students get jobs after graduation? What career services are available to students (assessment, resume writing, interview rehearsals)? Can students get references from professors? What percentage of students find work in their field? What academic services are available (tutoring, essay writing, exam preparation, etc.) and what is the cost?

Accreditation and Reputation

What type of accreditation does the institution hold? When was it granted and when is it up for renewal? What are the credentials of instructors? What is the maximum number of students in each class? How many students have successfully graduated from the program?

Fees

What are the fees for tuition, books, computer software, library usage, etc? What tuition increases are projected in the next few years? What are the costs if a student starts but chooses to leave the program before completion? What type of student financial aid is available?

Sometimes people make a lot of naïve assumptions about how retraining will assist them with dealing with their unemployment situation. For example, many of my executive and managerial clients wonder about doing a MBA, thinking that the degree will resolve their unemployment situation. My recommendation to them is to make a list of five to fifteen ideal employers and then use LinkedIn to network into these companies to talk to the hiring managers and ask how much weight they give candidates who have an MBA. Many have been surprised at the varied answers they receive and often it depends on the occupation, industry, and sector.

The bottom line is that you want to know this information *before* you invest your time and money into going back to school and not just make uninformed assumptions.

WRIGHT

What are the most common mistakes people make while traveling along the road to success?

HALEY

The road to success is most often not straight. As most people know, it's usually bumpy and has a few twists and turns.

Low self-esteem is like a traffic loop that causes career confusion on the road to success. When you allow yourself to let your self-esteem get low, you end up seeing yourself as smaller than you are and you believe that all career counseling tools and techniques will work for everybody *except* yourself. You usually isolate yourself and wrestle with your career problems under the delusion that you are the only one who has such complicated career problems and concerns.

A victim mentality is like a big obstacle you need to cut through on the road to success. When you see yourself and career through the lens of a victim mentality it interferes with your self-empowerment because you avoid taking responsibility for how your career is turning out. You get caught up with blaming others and you don't learn valuable lessons from past mistakes. Usually you continue making mistakes but the consequences get more severe.

A desire for "the big easy" is a sure fire way to get hurt by speed bumps on the road to success. Often in a desperate attempt to mimic the fast-forward movement of career success, you act impulsively and eventually you end up backtracking to your original confusion because you were so shortsighted. You want the quick fixes and the shortcuts without having to do all the hard work of figuring out who you truly are and what career you really want. Remember, you reap what you sow.

Indulgence in distractions is like worthless detours on the road to success. When you allow yourself to procrastinate with distractions, you inadvertently lose faith in yourself. As you lose the connection to your career priorities, you feel disoriented and you constantly get lost. Common distractions include running out of time at the end of the day for career planning and job-hunting activities, oversleeping and overeating, or helping others more than yourself. Ultimately you indulge your fear by clinging to what's familiar.

When you catch yourself making these common mistakes, it's important to get back on the road again and start anew. I recommend that you take some time to define an immediate, attainable goal related to your career. Next, find someone, perhaps a friend or a career counselor, to hold you accountable for breaking down your goal into specific tasks with deadlines. Lastly, take time to celebrate all your small steps of progress with acknowledgement and fun little rewards. Make a firm decision that you and your career really matter, and that you deserve success.

WRIGHT

Are there any roads to success that clients should avoid and not take?

HALEY

First of all, I believe that no matter what road a client takes to achieve career success it can be valuable if it can be used to learn from mistakes.

That said, there is one road that has negative consequences, not only on your career, but also on your relationships with others and your well-being. It's the road of workaholism. Unfortunately, workaholism is prevalent in our society and it's insidious because it's an addiction that often gets rewarded by companies through promotions, higher salary, and praise. Outwardly, you seem successful but inside you are left hollow and empty.

Workaholism is an obsessive-compulsive disorder and it is not the same as working hard. Workaholics crave attention and they seek it out in the workplace. Often they are overachievers, have control issues with delegation, and are not good team players. They also use work as an avoidance tactic to escape from dealing with anxiety, low self-esteem, or intimacy issues with significant others. Typically they ignore feedback from bosses, colleagues, and family members because they are in denial.

Some of the symptoms of workaholism include: working too much overtime (including evenings and weekends), taking little or no vacations, and sacrificing quality time with family and friends. On the job they tend to under-perform despite putting in longer hours. It's the scenario where they seem busy but they are not necessarily productive.

I usually recommend that clients seek therapy to treat this addiction. As well, many have found that the twelve-step program, Workaholics Anonymous, has been valuable in getting their life and their health back on track. Probably the biggest regret workaholic clients report is the lost time with loved ones due to toxic lifework balance. As with all addictions, workaholism gets worse with time so seeking help in the early stages can save you many years of unhappiness.

WRIGHT

I notice that you call yourself a Master Career Counselor. Will you tell us more about that?

HALEY

Master Career Counselor is a professional designation that is granted by the National Career Development Association. It's one of the highest designations in North America that one can achieve in the career counseling field. In order for me to earn this designation, I had to complete a master's degree in Counseling Psychology, with a supervised practicum and years of post-master's experience in career counseling. As well, I had to complete university coursework in six competency areas that included: career development theory, individual/group assessment, individual/group counseling skills, information/resources, diverse populations, and ethical/legal issues.

Along the way to becoming a Master Career Counselor, I've had the good fortune of being mentored by some of the leading experts in the field including Dr. Norman Amundson and Dr. William Borgen. I am very grateful to them for the opportunity to be their research assistant while I pursed my master's degree. I was involved with many research projects including: the study of career counseling techniques, the psychological effects of job insecurity on employees, the psychological impact of unemployment on youth, and a comparison of termination procedures for laid off workers.

When I did my undergraduate studies (I have a Bachelor of Arts in Sociology), I experienced firsthand the benefits of career counseling from Nancy Kendall who was a university campus career counselor. She was my first career counselor and she exemplified excellence in demonstrating to me what an effective career counselor must embody. In fact, the university later established a professional association award in her name for exceptional and unwavering service.

Looking back over the years, my work has also been influenced by volunteerism. I've been on the board of directors for a national counseling association and I've participated in committee work. But probably some of the most rewarding volunteer work I've done was with Mother Teresa's

Sisters of Charity in the United States, Canada, and Mexico. When I finally met Mother Teresa in 1989 at her mission in Tijuana, I saw firsthand the importance of kindness in the service of others. Mother Teresa once said, "We can do no great things, only small things with great love." Her powerful example has always inspired me in my work as a career counselor.

WRIGHT

Do you have any final words to help our readers achieve success?

HALEY

It's important to not give up on yourself. I believe you must find work you love. Recently, I've been thinking about how short life is and, on average, how much of it we spend working. So, I did some calculations and if we consider that an average working week is forty hours, then that equates to 1,960 hours per year if annual holidays are deducted. That's 22.4 percent of our lives, not including any overtime that we may be required to complete. Now, let's assume that the average person begins his or her working life at age twenty-one (after post-secondary education) and retires at sixty-five. That's a career that spans forty-four years. If we use the same forty-hour working week, we arrive at a figure of 91,250 hours!

Since your work is going to probably encompass a large part of your life, the way to find satisfaction and be productive is to do work that you find personally rewarding. So, if you have not found work you love, you must keep searching. Never lose hope. Be courageous. Be gentle with yourself and keep searching. Most of all, listen to your heart and I believe that it will lead you to a career you love.

About the Author

Marlene Haley has a unique background in career counseling and coaching that informs the assessment and guidance she offers her clients. She is the developer of the Careers You LOVE Model that turns the seeming complex process of career decision making into four easy-to-understand steps. Now, with more than twenty years of professional career counseling experience, she has designed customized career planning and job search programs for thousands of executives, managers, and professionals.

In today's challenging economy, companies turn to Marlene to develop outplacement programs for terminated employees. Her insights and recommendations about the labor market and her practical job search recommendations assist unemployed individuals to quickly land new jobs.

Marlene is a frequent media advisor and regularly contributes to newspapers and magazines, as well as television and radio. She has also served as a faculty member at a university and a college.

Speaking on topics related to career management and transition, Marlene has made presentations at conferences, tradeshows, professional associations, networking clubs, and women's groups. "Enthusiastic" and "inspiring" are the two words most often used by audiences who come to hear her speak.

Marlene holds a Master of Counseling Psychology degree and a Graduate Diploma in Counseling Psychology. During her graduate studies, she was a research assistant to two distinguished professors, Dr. Norman Amundson and Dr. William Borgen, who are leading experts in the field of career development. As a university research assistant, she conducted research on multiple topics related to career development including: the study of career counseling techniques, the psychological effects of job insecurity on employees, the psychological impact of unemployment on youth, and a comparison of termination procedures for laid off workers.

As a firm believer in lifelong learning, Marlene has earned multiple credentials and designations throughout her professional career including one of the highest career counseling designations in North America,

Master Career Counselor, from the National Career Development Association). Marlene's executive coaching credentials include: Professional Certified Coach (International Coach Federation), Advanced Certified Executive Coach (College of Executive Coaching) and Certified Professional Coach (College of Executive Coaching). To stay up-to-date with career and job trends, Marlene has completed specialized certifications: Certified Job and Career Transition Coach, Certified Job and Career Development Coach, Certified Business Development and Marketing Coach and Certified Professional Resume Writer. She is also a member of Career Directors International.

And yes, she loves her career!

Marlene Haley, MCC
Master Career Counselor
Careers You Love, Inc.
888-602-2974
www.careersyoulove.com

Chapter Five

Discover Your Inner Resource

Dr. Deepak Chopra

DAVID WRIGHT (WRIGHT)

Today we are talking to Dr. Deepak Chopra, founder of the Chopra Center for Well Being in Carlsbad, California. More than a decade ago, Dr. Chopra became the foremost pioneer in integrated medicine. His insights have redefined our definition of health to embrace body, mind, and spirit. His books, which include, *Quantum Healing, Perfect Health, Ageless Body Timeless Mind*, and *The Seven Spiritual Laws of Success*, have become international bestsellers and are established classics.

Dr. Chopra, welcome to *ROADMAP to Success*.

DR. DEEPAK CHOPRA (CHOPRA)
Thank you. How are you?

WRIGHT
I am doing just fine. It's great weather here in Tennessee.

CHOPRA
Great.

WRIGHT

Dr. Chopra, you stated in your book, *Grow Younger, Live Longer: 10 Steps to Reverse Aging,* that it is possible to reset your biostats up to fifteen years younger than your chronological age. Is that really possible?

CHOPRA

Yes. There are several examples of this. The literature on aging really began to become interesting in the 1980s when people showed that it was possible to reverse the biological marks of aging. This included things like blood pressure, bone density, body temperature, regulation of the metabolic rate, and other things like cardiovascular conditioning, cholesterol levels, muscle mass and strength of muscles, and even things like hearing, vision, sex hormone levels, and immune function.

One of the things that came out of those studies was that psychological age had a great influence on biological age. So you have three kinds of aging: chronological age is when you were born, biological age is what your biomarker shows, and psychological age is what your biostat says.

WRIGHT

You call our prior conditioning a prison. What do you mean?

CHOPRA

We have certain expectations about the aging process. Women expect to become menopausal in their early forties. People think they should retire at the age of sixty-five and then go Florida and spend the rest of their life in so-called retirement. These expectations actually influence the very biology of aging. What we call normal aging is actually the hypnosis of our social conditioning. If you can bypass that social conditioning, then you're free to reset your own biological clock.

WRIGHT

Everyone told me that I was supposed to retire at sixty-five. I'm somewhat older than that and as a matter of fact, today is my birthday.

CHOPRA

Well happy birthday. You know, the fact is that you should be having fun all the time and always feel youthful. You should always feel that you are contributing to society. It's not the retirement, but it's the passion with which you're involved in the well being of your society, your community, or the world at large.

WRIGHT

Great things keep happening to me. I have two daughters; one was born when I was fifty. That has changed my life quite a bit. I feel a lot younger than I am.

CHOPRA

The more you associate with young people, the more you will respond to that biological expression.

WRIGHT

Dr. Chopra, you suggest viewing our bodies from the perspective of quantum physics. That seems somewhat technical. Will you tell us a little bit more about that?

CHOPRA

You see, on one level, your body is made up of flesh and bone. That's the material level but we know today that everything we consider matter is born of energy and information. By starting to think of our bodies as networks of energy information and even intelligence, we begin to shift our perspective. We don't think of our bodies so much as dense matter, but as vibrations of consciousness. Even though it sounds technical, everyone has had an experience with this so-called quantum body. After, for example, you do an intense workout, you feel a sense of energy in your body—a tingling sensation. You're actually experiencing what ancient wisdom traditions call the "vital force." The more you pay attention to this vital force inside your body, the more you will experience it as energy, information, and intelligence, and the more control you will have over its expressions.

WRIGHT

Does DNA have anything to do with that?

CHOPRA

DNA is the source of everything in our body. DNA is like the language that creates the molecules of our bodies. DNA is like a protein-making factory, but DNA doesn't give us the blueprint. When I build a house, I have to go to the factory to find the bricks, but having the bricks is not enough. I need to get an architect, who in his or her consciousness can create that blueprint. And that blueprint exists only in your spirit and consciousness—in your soul.

WRIGHT

I was interested in a statement from your book. You said that perceptions create reality. What perceptions must we change in order to reverse our biological image?

CHOPRA

You have to change three perceptions. First you have to get rid of the perceptions of aging itself. Most people believe that aging means disease and infirmities. You have to change that. You have to regard aging as an opportunity for personal growth and spiritual growth. You also have to regard it as an opportunity to express the wisdom of your experience and an opportunity to help others and lift them from ordinary and mundane experience to the kind of experiences you are capable of because you have much more experience than they do.

The second thing you have to change your perception of is your physical body. You have to start to experience it as information and energy—as a network of information and intelligence.

The third thing you have to change your perception on is the experience of dying. If you are the kind of person who is constantly running out of time, you will continue to run out of time. On the other hand, if you have a lot of time, and if you do everything with gusto and love and passion, then you will lose track of time. When you lose track of time, your body does not metabolize that experience.

WRIGHT

That is interesting. People who teach time management don't really teach the passion.

CHOPRA

No, no. Time management is such a restriction of time. Your biological clock starts to age much more rapidly. I think what you have to really do is live your life with passion so that time doesn't mean anything to you.

WRIGHT

That's a concept I've never heard.

CHOPRA

Well, there you are.

WRIGHT

You spend an entire chapter of your book on deep rest as an important part of the reversal of the aging process. What is "deep rest"?

CHOPRA

One of the most important mechanisms for renewal and survival is sleep. If you deprive an animal of sleep, then it ages very fast and dies prematurely. We live in a culture where most of our population has to resort to sleeping pills and tranquilizers in order to sleep. That doesn't bring natural rejuvenation and renewal. You know that you have had a good night's sleep when you wake up in the morning, feeling renewed, invigorated, and refreshed—like a baby does. So that's one kind of deep rest. That comes from deep sleep and from natural sleep. In the book I talk about how you go about making sure you get that.

The second deep rest comes from the experience of meditation, which is the ability to quiet your mind so you still your internal dialogue. When your internal dialogue is still, then you enter into a stage of deep rest. When your mind is agitated, your body is unable to rest.

WRIGHT

I have always heard of people who had bad eyesight and really didn't realize it until they went to the doctor and were fitted for lenses. I had that same experience some years ago. For several years I had not really enjoyed the deep sleep you're talking about. The doctor diagnosed me with sleep apnea. Now I sleep like a baby, and it makes a tremendous difference.

CHOPRA

Of course it does. You now have energy and the ability to concentrate and do things.

WRIGHT

Dr. Chopra, how much do eating habits have to do with aging? Can we change and reverse our biological age by what we eat?

CHOPRA

Yes, you can. One of the most important things to remember is that certain types of foods actually contain anti-aging compounds. There are many chemicals that are contained in certain foods that have an anti-aging effect. Most of these chemicals are derived from light. There's no way to bottle them—there are no pills you can take that will give you these chemicals. But they're contained in plants that are rich in color and derived from photosynthesis. Anything that is yellow, green, and red or has a lot of color, such as fruits and vegetables, contain a lot of these very powerful anti-aging chemicals.

In addition, you have to be careful not to put food in your body that is dead or has no life energy. So anything that comes in a can or has a label, qualifies for that. You have to expose your body to six tastes: sweet, sour, salt, bitter, pungent, and astringent because those are the codes of intelligence that allow us to access the deep intelligence of nature. Nature and what she gives to us in bounty is actually experienced through the sense of taste. In fact, the light chemicals—the anti-aging substances in food—create the six tastes.

WRIGHT

Some time ago, I was talking to one of the ladies in your office and she sent me an invitation to a symposium that you had in California. I was really interested. The title was *Exploring the Reality of Soul*.

CHOPRA

Well, I conducted the symposium, but we had some of the world's scientists, physicists, and biologists who were doing research in what is called, non-local intelligence—the intelligence of soul or spirit. You could say it is the intelligence that orchestrates the activity of the universe—God, for example. Science and spirituality are now meeting together because by understanding how nature works and how the laws of nature work, we're beginning to get a glimpse of a deeper intelligence that people in spiritual traditions call divine, or God. I think this is a wonderful time to explore spirituality through science.

WRIGHT

She also sent me biographical information of the seven scientists who were with you. I have never read a list of seven more noted people in their industry.

CHOPRA

They are. The director of the Max Planck Institute, in Berlin, Germany, where quantum physics was discovered was there. Dr. Grossam was a professor of physics at the University of Oregon, and he talked about the quantum creativity of death and the survival of conscious after death. It was an extraordinary group of people.

WRIGHT

Dr. Chopra, with our *ROADMAP to Success* book we're trying to encourage people to be better, live better, and be more fulfilled by listening to the examples of our guest authors. Is there anything or anyone in your life who has made a difference for you and has helped you to become a better person?

CHOPRA

The most important person in my life was my father. Every day he asked himself, "What can I do in thought, word, and deed to nurture every relationship I encounter just for today?" That has lived with me for my entire life.

WRIGHT

What do you think makes up a great mentor? Are there characteristics mentors seem to have in common?

CHOPRA

I think the most important attribute of a great mentor is that he or she teaches by example and not necessarily through words.

WRIGHT

When you consider the choices you've made down through the years, has faith played an important role?

CHOPRA

I think more than faith, curiosity, wonder, a sense of reference, and humility has. Now, if you want to call that faith, then, yes it has.

WRIGHT

In a divine being?

CHOPRA

In a greater intelligence—intelligence that is supreme, infinite, unbounded, and too mysterious for the finite mind to comprehend.

WRIGHT

If you could have a platform and tell our audience something you feel would help them and encourage them, what would you say?

CHOPRA

I would say that there are many techniques that come to us from ancient wisdom and tradition that allow us to tap into our inner resources and allow us to become beings who have intuition, creativity, vision, and a connection to that which is sacred. Finding that within ourselves, we have the means to enhance our well-being. Whether it's physical, emotional, or environmental, we have the means to resolve conflicts and get rid of war. We have the means to be really healthy. We have the means for being economically uplifted. That knowledge is the most important knowledge that exists.

WRIGHT

I have seen you on several primetime television shows down through the years where you have had the time to explain your theories and beliefs. How does someone like me experience this? Do we get it out of books?

CHOPRA

Books are tools that offer you a road map. Sit down every day, close your eyes, put your attention in your heart, and ask yourself two questions: who am I and what do I want? Then maintain a short period of stillness in body and mind as in prayer or meditation, and the door will open.

WRIGHT

So, you think that the intelligence comes from within. Do all of us have that capacity?

CHOPRA

Every child born has that capacity.

WRIGHT

That's fascinating. So, it doesn't take trickery or anything like that?

CHOPRA

No, it says in the Bible in the book of Psalms, "Be still and know that I am God"—Psalm 46:10.

WRIGHT

That's great advice.

I really do appreciate your being with us today. You are fascinating. I wish I could talk with you for the rest of the afternoon. I'm certain I am one of millions who would like to do that!

CHOPRA

Thank you, sir. It was a pleasure to talk with you!

WRIGHT

Today we have been talking with Dr. Deepak Chopra, founder of The Chopra Center. He has become the foremost pioneer in integrated medicine. We have found today that he really knows what he's talking about. After reading his book, *Grow Younger, Live Longer: 10 Steps to Reverse Aging,* I can tell you that I highly recommend it. I certainly hope you'll go out to your favorite book store and buy a copy.

Dr. Chopra, thank you so much for being with us today on *ROADMAP to Success.*

CHOPRA

Thank you for having me, David.

About the Author

Deepak Chopra has written more than fifty books, which have been translated into many languages. He is also featured on many audio and videotape series, including five critically acclaimed programs on public television. He has also written novels and edited collections of spiritual poetry from India and Persia. In 1999, *Time* magazine selected Dr. Chopra as one of the Top 100 Icons and Heroes of the Century, describing him and "the poet-prophet of alternative medicine."

Dr. Deepak Chopra
The Chopra Center
2013 Costa del Mar Rd.
Carlsbad, CA 92009
info@chopra.com
www.chopra.com

Chapter Six

A Journey to a Place Called There

Cheryl Washington

DAVID WRIGHT (WRIGHT)

Today we're talking with Cheryl Washington. Cheryl is an education/social entrepreneur and management consultant with a tenacious spirit, passion for people, and a zeal to serve the underprivileged. She has been a career educator for twenty-six years and an entrepreneur and management consultant for more than five entities with a combined budget of twenty million dollars. She attributes her success to a God-inspired vision, her servant leadership style, and management expertise. Inspired mentors and role models have challenged her to blaze a trail, to dare to be different, and to reach outside the box. Her favorite pastime is turning problems into opportunities.

Cheryl, welcome to *ROADMAP to Success*.

CHERYL WASHINGTON (WASHINGTON)

Thank you very much, David.

WRIGHT

So, given your background and experiences, how do you spell success?

WASHINGTON

Success is an attribute of a person who has received great counsel. My favorite motto is, in the multitude of counselors there is safety. With wise counsel, determination, and courage, a person is able to achieve and produce with success by first being prepared and equipped in the right season of life. "When you are planted in the right place, in the right season, your roots are deep and things just seem to happen!" "Everything your hands touch becomes of success." So success comes by way of being ready, having the character to handle success, and being willing to serve other people and empower them with the things you have inside you.

Second, wise counsel coupled with prudent actions, ground a character to sustain success. And, thirdly, a willingness to serve others by imparting and empowering them for success is success waiting to happen. Success is, therefore, spelled out in an outward showing of:

- Blessing (fruitfulness)
- Prosperity (value)
- Happiness (fortune)

WRIGHT

Obviously many doors have been opened for you. How did you overcome the obstacles and break through the barriers that blocked your way?

WASHINGTON

I believe that people should work together as a team because when you team with people, it makes your dream come alive. I believe in strategic alliances, I believe in partnerships, and I believe in building capacity. In doing so, it's not all one person who creates or makes things happen—*together* we make the difference.

Teamwork strengthened me to overcome obstacles and break through the barriers; teaming with people made the dream come alive. I believe in strategic alliances and partnerships. I believe in building capacity; in doing so, it is not just one person who creates or makes things happen. "Together we make the difference!" (*Shekinah*, 1999)

WRIGHT

How has being a double minority in many of the cities you impacted attributed to your success?

WASHINGTON

I just believe in being in the right place at the right time during the right season. Being a double minority as female and an African American has opened many, many doors for me based on the fact that it just happened to be a season where diversity was what was going on in that place at that time and they needed more minorities. I just happened to be there at that particular time. Right timing eliminates wrong action.

Being a double minority has its advantages. In a season and time when diversity is being highlighted and gender and race are given more attention than normal, minorities tend to flourish, just because they happen to show up at such a time! The clarion call for more minorities or women positioned me for greatness and for purpose. Many doors were opened to me. There was a need for people with my gifts, talents, gender, and race. I just happened to be in the right place, at the right time. Now, I can say like Queen Esther, "Perhaps I have come to the kingdom for such a time as this!"

WRIGHT

Will you share how inspired vision and wisdom guided you to greatness?

WASHINGTON

Well, I do believe that any vision connected to people is an inspired vision—when it is clear. Then I pray for wisdom in order to be able to implement the vision, of course. I do believe that any vision that is inspired and is given to you and that has people connected to it also has provisions that have already been appointed to you before the vision is even implemented.

Vision, gives sight, structure, and discipline for the mission. "Without a vision, people cast off all restraint" (Proverbs 29:18). They perish (fail) and not prosper (achieve). An inspired vision always has people attached or connected to it. And, wisdom is the road map or action plan to accomplishing any mission and authenticating any vision.

Both inspired vision and wisdom have ordered my steps and directed my path for success. I was disciplined by godly principles, I practiced ethical behavior, and I exhibited moral leadership and character in everything I did to accomplish the mission and vision put before me. There were periods when the vision was tested for authenticity by barriers and challenges. Revisions were made to make sure I was following instructions, and provision had to be discerned accurately and with caution. Because of discipline, structure, and order that was outlined in the vision and acted upon with wisdom, challenges became opportunities and barriers became new markets and ground for potential business success.

WRIGHT

Where do you find the courage to conquer ground that others dare not go?

WASHINGTON

The spirit of a conqueror believes he or she can do all things through Christ who strengthens them (Philippians 4:13):

- mountains become insurmountable and not bridges waiting to be crossed
- barriers become blockades and not ground to be possessed or markets to be penetrated
- challenges become problems, not opportunities undiscovered
- goals go unaccomplished and dreams become sleeping giants

WRIGHT

So what part does passion play in your endeavor to be different and reach outside the box?

WASHINGTON

My passion is my drive. I believe that having a passion for something means that you have more than just a thought about it—you have a feeling that is very much a burden to some extent, with a "must do" agenda. My only motive is to do something about what I am thinking. For me, that is reaching outside the box to: uproot traditional patterns and practices that have been proven failures, disrupt the status quo, and restore the free-will and choice needed to innovate and make a difference in life. Passion is that fire that ignites the flame to:

- fire up my dream and make it reality
- act fervently to bring about change
- impact the lives of others, transform systems, and contribute something of value to my society and the world

WRIGHT

Will you elaborate for our readers what drives your success and how you maintain that pace while sustaining a profit?

WASHINGTON

Yes, very carefully and cautiously. What normally drives me is my passion and love for people. I love to serve people and help them meet their needs. "I believe I have not come to be served, but to serve" (Mark 10:43). As a servant leader, I try to do just that. Therefore, because I'm driven by my passion, I'm always looking for an opportunity to meet another's need; and there are many needs in society that are not met, obviously. So, when I see a person getting ahead in life because of something that I was able to contribute to his or her life, it encourages my passion and drives me to go even further. Supplying others' needs and being a resource for others drives my success. This brings many social benefits for the giver and receivers, adds value to lives, and makes for healthy profits. Maintaining that pace becomes as natural as breathing and sustaining a profit is the legacy built by replicating a practice that benefits more than self. To me, this is an example of sharing and caring.

WRIGHT

As a servant leader, whom do you serve and how do you serve to ensure success is achieved?

WASHINGTON

As an educational/social entrepreneur and management consultant, I serve my clients, students, and partners by teaching, training, mentoring, and advising. When I am sharing valuable information, my desire is to please and add value. To my partners, I am a "trusted advisor." To my students, I am a "supplier and technician." To my clients, I am added value. Success is achieved when those I serve are satisfied, gain, prosper, and in turn, make recommendations that keep me in business.

WRIGHT

What would you say contributed to your success personally and professionally?

WASHINGTON

Personally, I have had the opportunity to travel around the world and to many of the states in the United States. As a result, I have an increased awareness of international issues and I have a global perspective. In addition, experience in life has taught me many things and brought me in contact with a variety of people and cultures.

For example: Living abroad in Turkey and Hawaii has taught me how to respect other cultures and appreciate the freedoms I have in my country and culture. Being under martial law while serving on a tour of duty in the Air Force with my former husband in Incirlik, Turkey, and having to live for two years bound by curfews and cultural norms as an American adult, helped me to identify with the real comforts of freedom and liberty offered in the United States and by Christ. I received one of the greatest revelations of all time. There are parts of the world that are not free. This let me know that it is time to be more than successful; it's time to reach for significance by helping others be freed up for success.

Also, having personal spiritual insight gives me purpose and a call. My beliefs and convictions have guided and protected me through many challenges, crises, and victories. "Righteousness [really does] exalt a nation" (Proverbs 14:34a). To many, this may mean being correct or an expert; to me, it means being upright in character and noble in my actions. When we stand for what is right, a nation or people or group is lifted up and raised to a "higher standard."

Professionally, I have prepared myself to be marketable in a competitive society. I have taken advantage of opportunities to be educated, replicated, and dedicated.

For example: I have been positioned in education for a purpose! Twenty-six years of loyal service as a career educator proves my loyalty and shows that I am committed to a cause bigger than I. Having a social responsibility to uphold the integrity of the profession, I have been instrumental in helping to raise the standard for public accountability and financial transparency in the public education system. I have bloomed where I was planted.

When it was revealed that the Texas public school system was in trouble because of funding and failure, I chose to carefully evaluate the system, accept the facts, and rather than cover them, I sought an opportunity to make a change. I chose to stay in Texas and stand and fight for the social justice of all Texas students, which was my moral imperative, and effect change in the system. Dedicated to my students and state, I got tired of hearing the negative and set out to produce the positive by becoming an entrepreneur of learning who dared to be different and pioneered a move to create a new school system. I helped turn a failure upside down and around and made the word "failure" spell "success"!

WRIGHT

So how exactly have you invested your many talents to ensure a return on your investments?

WASHINGTON

Well, I endeavor to invest my talents in people. I do this by making a deposit in people and their lives. Again, I am a people person and endeavor to impact the lives of people. I share with others what I know and who I am. Those who receive with good intentions what I share with them are empowered and can therefore empower others, leaving a legacy for generations to come.

WRIGHT

Is there one particular person in your life to whom you give credit for helping to launch your dream and spur you to action?

WASHINGTON

There are many who have added value by making a rich deposit in my life. However, my father is given the credit for influencing my life and showing me how to dream big. He was a hard worker, faithful husband, and a daddy who qualified to be a good father.

For example: Every evening when I was growing up, I recall sitting at the dinner table and talking about our day. My father's favorite words were: "You can do anything you set your mind to, just have gumption!" When report card time rolled around, he would review them with a magnifying glass and then state: "You may be something one day with these grades" or "This is not education material." We knew what he meant.

He encouraged excellence and discouraged mediocrity and sloth. He didn't believe there was a generation gap, just rebellious children who chose not to listen to wise counsel. That's why I believe wise counsel is the formula for success.

When my father passed on, I looked for his attributes in those who fathered me spiritually and motivated me, and mentors (faith, family, and tenacity).

WRIGHT

Being a pioneer and having a path different from many, how do you describe the legacy of success you leave behind?

WASHINGTON

I have found over the years, having an entrepreneurial spirit and blazing a trail for others, that I was chosen to "dig the ditches" and to "till the soil," so to speak. Others can follow in my footsteps to success and they won't have to fall in the same holes. "A Good Man leaves an inheritance for his children's children." By transferring this entrepreneurial spirit into the next generation, many will receive the seed to plant new foundations, dare to be different, and implement change. They will know their genealogy and forefathers who paved the way and made it possible. And, with great honor and fortitude, I believe they will do all in their power to continue this story for those who follow behind.

WRIGHT

Who are some of the people you trust to give you counsel and how are you prepared and equipped for the journey you are on?

WASHINGTON

I only receive counsel from those with proven track records. Godly counsel keeps me. Wise businessmen or businesswomen who have attained success and profited from the wise counsel of others in their lives are those I choose to learn from. They have been in the field and know the do's and don'ts of the profession or business. And though I don't want to be a copy or clone, I know the value in standing on the premise of a solid foundation. Those roots are deep. I act as a branch that continues to grow from a foundation that is rooted and grounded in good works!

WRIGHT

A wise man told me one time that if I were walking down the road and saw a turtle sitting up on a fence post that I could bet he didn't get up there by himself.

WASHINGTON

Oh that's good. No one is an island. We all have to start from somewhere and have a starting point.

WRIGHT

So who helped you along the way? I know you've talked about teachers, but who formed the person you are today?

WASHINGTON

God shaped me and formed me for a purpose. Many have crossed my path by divine design and helped me by opening doors, believing in me and my vision, and bringing out of me what I could not see.

Spiritually, my leaders in the ministry have held me accountable to biblical principles and values. Professionally, mentors have empowered and encouraged me to conquer, and personally, the crises I have experienced have taught me many valuable lessons that I can pass along to others.

WRIGHT

How would you title a message for others who hope to accomplish at a level of greatness?

WASHINGTON

I would title it "The Best is Yet to Come." When people are encouraged to do their best to create and make a difference, I would encourage them to never forget those who have inspired them to move forward. In their teachers is something that is now a part of them. What they have learned will expand their vision and increase the vision they now have.

WRIGHT

So what can be written to describe your life of success for others to study?

WASHINGTON

My passionate pursuit to serve others drove me to success because self-sacrifice, sharing, and caring leave great rewards.

WRIGHT

Those are great words.

WASHINGTON

Thank you.

WRIGHT

So lastly, what's up for Cheryl Washington in the future?

WASHINGTON

I'm looking forward to continuing to work with people and expanding my businesses and opportunities to create. I believe that my proven success of laying the foundations of many nonprofit and for-profit organizations has opened the way for other people to not only create opportunity for themselves, but to expand on what we have created. Entrepreneurs produce after their own kind, so I see the spirit spreading in the young and old, male and female. I see a future of entrepreneurs and intrapreneurs ready to make a change in our now stagnant economy, to offer social benefit, value, and wealth that will strengthen our economy and create new businesses, new jobs, and new ways of doing things with better results.

I see myself somewhat as a midwife sometimes as I help people to give birth to their dreams and not give up on them. Sometimes I see myself as a surgeon, waking the sleeping giant that is inside each of them and making it happen.

To sum it all up, I just want to make a difference in the lives of others so that they can make a difference—period!

WRIGHT

What part has faith played in your life?

WASHINGTON

A tremendous part. Faith has been my substance, activator, and power to shake things and make things. By faith, I have been able to see:

- obstacles as bridges that need crossing
- barriers as pathways to the future
- mountains leveled, uprooted, and moved
- people in need of great opportunity
- Each person as God's gift, each to the other
- Miracles never seen before performed before my very eyes

WRIGHT

Well, what a great conversation. I've really enjoyed it and learned a lot. I'm sure that our readers will also.

WASHINGTON

Thank you so much for allowing me to share my heart and my passion with you. I hope it will blaze a trail for many to follow and turn on the light in many lives.

WRIGHT

I appreciate you taking all this time to answer these questions. This will be a good chapter for the book.

WASHINGTON

Well, thank you.

WRIGHT

Today we've been talking with Cheryl Washington. Cheryl is the Founder and CEO of four nonprofit organizations and one for profit organization, created to help educate people and economically develop communities. She has grown from one entity with twenty-five consumers to five entities with sixteen satellite operations in ten cities, eight counties, and two states in the United States. She attributes her success to her passion for people, entrepreneurial spirit, and servant attitude.

Cheryl, thank you so much for being with us today on *ROADMAP to Success*.

WASHINGTON

Thank you, David, once again. God bless you.

About the Author

Cheryl Washington, founder and CEO of Shekinah Learning Institute, is an educational/social entrepreneur with management expertise in organizational change and development. Having established the foundation for sixteen charter school campuses, an educational foundation, an early childhood learning center, and consulting firm, Dr. Washington is an inspiring community leader who seeks allies to create opportunity and wealth, transform organizations, and add value to benefit the lives of the disenfranchised. She has been proven successful in each endeavor undertaken. From her humble beginnings as a law enforcement official and through many lessons learned, she has attained the rank of a successful minority businesswoman who not only produces, but reproduces by replicating her successes in others, thereby leaving a legacy.

Cheryl A. Washington
Shekinah Learning Institute
Deja' Discovery Learning Centers
Legacy Educational Foundation
Kingdom Impact Consulting, LLC
12470 Woman Hollering
Schertz, Texas 78154
(210) 945-2207
Electlady47@aol.com
www.shekinah-edu.com

Chapter Seven

BE LEGENDARY

JAMES CARTER

DAVID WRIGHT (WRIGHT)

Today I am speaking with previous collaborative author James Carter, the Founder and CEO of Be Legendary. Be Legendary is an idea that will change the world one action, one person, one moment at a time.

Be Legendary has worked with a diverse clientele, from corporate and philanthropic entities, down to the everyday individual, enabling leaders, teams, and organizations to reach their legendary potential.

James, welcome to ROADMAP to Success!

JAMES CARTER (CARTER)

Thank you, David. I appreciate the opportunity to offer my own road map.

WRIGHT

Now that you mention it, what is your road map to success?

CARTER

Before I begin giving you details about my particular road map, I want to first define our destination—success.

The success I am describing is the ultimate success we have in life—our legacy. What are we leaving behind? How do you leave behind a legendary life? And where do you start?

Creating that legendary legacy is the success I am speaking about—the destination on my road map. However, you cannot have that legendary legacy without Being Legendary throughout life. So I will concentrate on what you can do to be legendary every day of your life

WRIGHT

Okay, that's great to know for our readers. Tell us about your road map.

CARTER

I also want to be absolutely clear—what do I mean when I say "Be Legendary"? I mean having the courage to take action based upon your core beliefs to make a positive difference in the world around you.

Be Legendary is:
> *Not* about being better than anyone else.
> *Not* about glory or fame.
> *Not* a goal to achieve.

Be Legendary is our own personal evolution. It is the discovery and rediscovery of the very best of who we are, and who we can be.

WRIGHT

I can't wait to hear more about your road map!

CARTER

A few years ago I began researching "Legendary" people—Mother Teresa, Nelson Mandela, Gandhi—to see how they accomplished so much in life, were able to leave such an incredibly legacy, and what they have in common. If there are commonalities, can they be learned?

It was and incredible process as I studied all of these amazing people and was continually inspired by what was possible.

Then one day I was surfing the Internet looking for information on legendary people I may not know. I found an article with the most amazing story. It goes like this:

The Janitor Story

A few years ago, a young reporter noticed his little town had completely filled up with people one day—the town was packed with cars and people were everywhere. Every extra bedroom had a relative or two in it, hotel rooms were booked, and restaurants were packed. He checked the calendar. No holiday, no festival, no parade. What was going on?

He began asking around and quickly found out that everyone had come into town to attend a funeral. So he began asking more questions.

After talking to more than a dozen people, he heard a similar story—they were attending the funeral of a man they barely knew and most had only known for a short time. And yet these people had travelled from all over the world when they heard the news of this mystery man's passing. In fact, almost ten thousand people had come to town that day to pay their respects.

Who was this funeral for? Was it someone who changed the country? A movie star or musician? Someone extremely wealthy?

As it turned out, the man had worked in this small town, in the same place, for forty-five years. He worked in a middle school and these were all students who had passed through the school in those forty-five years, most only knowing him for three.

The reporter then naturally asked what this person did at the school. Was he a principal, a favorite teacher? No he was not. He was, in fact, the janitor at the school.

Somehow, without any direct authority, this man was able to affect thousands of young people and leave such an effect that they left their lives and family for a few days and journey to see him.

It's almost staggering to think of what he accomplished. But if almost ten thousand people actually attended the funeral, just imagine how many were not able to make the trip!

After reading the article, I was amazed at the influence someone like that can have. Several days later I had an epiphany that was like seeing the first star come out after sunset. This man, this janitor, was legendary! But very much like after seeing the first star, I began seeing everyday legendary people everywhere! And now I had a number of people I could speak to about what they have done, how they have done it, and why.

Of course, a common denominator was that not a single one of them would accept the idea that he or she was legendary!

Stop and think for a moment. Picture in your mind a legendary person in your life like the janitor. We *all* have at least one person in our lives like this. While we talk about Be Legendary, I want you to keep that person in mind and see if they fit.

WRIGHT

I can think of a couple of people who are simply amazing and seem to infect everyone around them with positive energy and yet, are just like you and me.

CARTER

Exactly! If you look around for more people like that, you will begin to see them everywhere, just like I did—stars after sunset.

Well, through the process of speaking with so many legendary people, both famous and non-famous, I realized they have all mastered three areas of their lives. To make it simple, we call this the ABC's of Being Legendary:

> **A**wareness
> **B**eliefs
> **C**ourage

WRIGHT

Will you be taking us through the ABC's as part of your road map?

CARTER

Absolutely. As luck would have it, they *are* the road map!

So let's begin with A, which stands for awareness. There is a constant battle for our awareness. Many entities are trying to get us to pay attention—advertisements, commercials, politicians, even the news. Unfortunately, the easiest way to grab and hold our attention is by getting us to focus on negative "stuff." Not only do we have the media throwing negative images, videos, and stories at us constantly, we have all been trained since we were very young to focus on the negative.

WRIGHT

We have been *trained*?

CARTER

Yes, look at our education system. Beginning in first grade, children get their homework back with red marks all over, highlighting what they have done—wrong. Our educational system helped us to be acutely aware of what we were doing wrong.

What might happen if we highlighted all the answers children get right? How different might our education system be?

But our training begins even before we enter our education system. A few years ago, researchers put recording devices on five-year-old children. They found that as much as 90 percent of the time, communication surrounding these children was negative:

> How bad things are,
> Who is to blame,
> What was done wrong and
> What not to do.

From the time we were small children, we were taught to be more aware of the negative. This continued through our lifetime up to and including today. We are experts at being critical and analytical, exposing faults, and debunking arguments. We have been taught to find problems and fix them, then repeat!

This alone is not a bad thing. In fact, it is an incredibly powerful tool and a strength many possess and use very well. However, if we use this all the time and we use nothing else, it becomes a weakness.

As I said before, seeing legendary people was like seeing stars after sunset. At first, I was trained to see other people's mistakes and errors. Once I began to focus on the great things people were doing, I began to see it everywhere and a starlit sky emerged. And you know what? If felt *good!* I began a few years ago to retrain my awareness and intentionally see more of the great things people are doing.

That does not mean I don't see the negative. I do! I simply don't spend any energy focusing on the negative. This takes practice at first, but becomes easier because it feels good.

We are now seeing many people shift, as I have, and focus on what we really want—to see a world filled with amazing people doing amazing acts and creating legendary lives.

One key to your shaping your awareness is to understand what you *want*. Focus on what you want.

Let me give you a couple of examples of what I am speaking about.

Sports psychology is a great example, as they have actually been focusing on awareness and what you want for some time.

In an experiment, people were taught how to bowl—knocking down ten pins with a large, heavy ball. They were divided into two groups and videotaped. One group was shown videotapes of their successes. The other group was shown videos of their mistakes. Who do you think improved?

WRIGHT

Well, I am guessing the group shown successes improved.

CARTER

You are half right. Both groups improved! However, the group shown their successes improved *twice* as much as the other group. This is a key point. Focusing on the negative and what you get wrong achieves results. However, focusing on what we want, and our successes, achieves much more.

This idea is now used in every sport and in every coaching situation and we understand now what affect our vocabulary has on us as well.

In golf, coaches teach students to imagine *and say* to themselves, "hit the ball in the fairway," instead of "don't hit the ball into the trees."

So the words we choose are critically important to our success and a key part of our awareness. Words reinforce our thoughts.

The golfer who pictures the fairway but says to himself, "Don't hit the ball into the water," only *really* mentally hears, "Hit the ball into the water." Where does the ball go? You know the answer—right where he told it to go and in the water.

You may see now that consciously controlling our awareness is critical.

The research with the five-year-olds and our education system clearly shows us how we have been essentially *trained* to see the negative and when we focus upon that, how easy it is to miss the opportunities to Be Legendary.

So then, the question is how do I retrain my awareness? You can begin to control your awareness by carefully selecting what you are paying attention to:

- Are you looking at your successes versus mistakes?
- What do you automatically see in other people?
- What vocabulary are you using? Are you using positive vocabulary?

You don't need to *stop* doing everything, but begin making small changes to reduce negative messages and emotion in your life.

WRIGHT

For now, for argument's sake, let's just assume that you were consciously controlling your awareness. What is next?

CARTER

I am so glad you asked because that is exactly where I was going. This brings us to B, or Beliefs. In a classic study that is now called the Pygmalion Effect, researchers told teachers that certain students had unusually high potential for success in school. The children were, in fact, selected at random. Several months later, the chosen few were far surpassing their classmates. Why? The teachers gave the high potential students a little more attention, a little more encouragement and these were in line with the teachers' expectations.

The students own self-image had changed based upon the teacher's belief. The *belief* of the teachers had become the student's *reality*. In other words, *beliefs* create *reality*.

The application for this is everywhere. There is very little about human behavior, including our beliefs that are set in stone and unchangeable. So if beliefs create our reality, it is incredibly important to know which are most important to us and spend time on them.

Here is the critical question to think about: what are your beliefs? And are those beliefs truly your own? Are they something you adopted from someone, typically our parents? Or were taught?

I cannot stress how important this is if you want to lead a legendary life. You will not recognize opportunities to act unless you first know which are valuable. Take the time and write down what your deepest values and beliefs are and I think you will surprise yourself at what you find. We simply don't spend time thinking about them and yet, our beliefs drive everything we do.

We have created what we call the Legendary Intent. Our Legendary Intent is created by completing a simple, yet powerful, sentence: "If I accomplish nothing else in this life, I will—"

WRIGHT

A challenging statement. Can you give me an example?

CARTER

Yes, it is a challenging statement. Another way to think about it is to picture your headstone at your grave. The completion to this sentence could be on your headstone. Let me give you an example.

I worked with an executive recently who was struggling with the morale of her company and specifically, her core group of executives. She had a core belief that "joy" was incredibly important in life. After some introspection and coaching she realized her Legendary Intent was: "If I accomplish nothing else in this life, I will create joy in the lives of those around me."

She decided that if "I created joy in the lives of those around me" was written on her headstone, she would be thrilled with that.

She had a strong belief that her humor was great strength. Looking at her executives, she realized that neither she, nor her staff, laughed very much at work. Using her Legendary Intent as a filter, her "daily mission" was to find one opportunity to make someone laugh every day—just one. What she found was that there were far more opportunities than she ever realized and just like stars after sunset, she began to see them everywhere.

Just a few months later, the culture in her staff had completely changed and, indeed, the informal culture of the company was changing. Everyone was taking cues from her!

WRIGHT

Wow, that is incredible. So knowing our Beliefs and using that to create our Legendary Intent creates a filter through which we see the world. Is that right?

CARTER

Absolutely. We are essentially creating new lenses to filter in all the things we want. We will still see the negative things, but once you begin seeing this new world, you will want to keep the lenses on!

WRIGHT

So I am betting that since we covered Awareness and Beliefs, the A and B, that Courage is next!

CARTER

Right you are! When we know our Beliefs and have our Legendary Intent firmly in place, we essentially have a filter through which we see the world. We become Aware of opportunities to act. There is only one thing left to ensure action—Courage.

There are many different kinds of courage. Typically, we think of a physical action like soldiers in wartime. But that is just one kind of courage. Let me tell you a story as an example of one kind of courage.

Very recently, while looking for a non-profit partner for one of our philanthropic programs, we ran across a young man named Kyle Weiss. Kyle went to Europe at thirteen to see the FIFA World Cup and met a number of fans from Angola. He came home deciding to ship cleats and soccer balls over to Africa.

However, someone said, "Wait, don't they need fields?," and FUNDaFIELD (www.FUNDaFIELD.org) was born. Kyle and his brother Garrett recruited thirty other young people in junior high and high school and helped them see why they should care about other kids their age on the other side of the world. They all raised money the hard way, many times one cupcake at a time.

What is truly remarkable is that as a young teenager, Kyle had travelled to Africa, negotiated with local politics, construction companies and staff, and schools where they built the fields. He dealt with local corruption, facilitated community meetings, and communicated with international organizations to make the fields a reality.

Now eighteen and just graduating high school, Kyle has been to Africa seven times and built eight fields—all in different countries. He has also developed leadership within FUNDaFIELD so that when he goes to college this fall, the organization will stay strong and continue to build fields.

Do you see the Be Legendary pattern in Kyle's actions?

1. **A**wareness – He became aware there was a problem for children in Africa to play soccer without shoes, a field, and even no balls.
2. **B**elief – He believed he could have an effect upon the problem
3. **C**ourage – He says it really was not courage, he was just doing what he does.

Most of us stop at the Awareness area—we see and/or become aware of a problem or challenge and let it go at that. But because of Kyle's passion for soccer and strong belief that every child should be able to play, courage was not really a factor—it was almost a given. It was just something that had to be done. Without knowing it, Kyle was living his Legendary Intent. I cannot wait to see what he accomplishes moving forward.

WRIGHT

Obviously an amazing person—young or not! I see the courage it must have taken for him to even fly over to Africa.

CARTER

While Kyle's story is filled with obvious courage, there is one aspect of courage that that is incredibly challenging and is not obvious—telling yourself the right story. He could have not acted because he told himself a different story:

- "I am too young to make a difference."
- "No one will listen to me because I am a kid."
- "They will think I am just some American with money telling them what to do."
- "I will do something after I graduate from college."

Have you said something like that to yourself? I have. It is easy. And self-defeating. These are limiting stories and keep us from taking action when that is exactly what we need and want to do.

We run an activity with executives to help them experience how easy it is to not tell ourselves the right story. In this activity, partners pair up and are told to draw a picture of each other in sixty seconds.

During the sixty seconds you can hear them laughing and saying things like:

"I am *so* sorry."
"This is *terrible*."
"Please don't be offended!"
"How awful!"

Why? Why are they awful? Because their experience automatically compares your sketch to the Mona Lisa, right?

I think we can agree the picture I draw of my partner is *not* a da Vinci! But should I really be comparing myself to da Vinci? Can I only be proud of my sketch if it compares to a professional artist?

The same is true when it comes to legendary people. I meet and interview legendary people (who I believe are legendary). When I suggest they are legendary (by our definition above), they all say the same thing, "Not me! Someone else maybe, but not me." Not a single person has said they were legendary. And I have met some truly *legendary* people. Humility is a common characteristic of legendary people.

Think of the janitor. If you walked up to him and said he was legendary, what do you think he might have said? He would have thought it was ridiculous!

Do you know what first-graders do after I ask them to draw a picture of their partner? They stand up, proud as can be to show off their pictures:

"Look at mine!"

"Mine is *awesome!*"

"SaaWeeet!"

And they clap and cheer for each other's drawings, each one of them a da Vinci. They have not learned they are not artists, yet.

Remember, Be Legendary is not about being the best, or even better than someone else. Be Legendary is you at your best and having the courage to act upon your Legendary Intent.

What is the right story to tell yourself? "This is the very best drawing I can do in sixty seconds with the artistic skill that I have. I am proud of it."

Have the courage to hold your artwork up high, have the courage to tell yourself the right story, and have the courage to believe and say, "I can be legendary, too." When you do that, you are harnessing your courage in a way that makes taking action very simple.

WRIGHT

The ABC's of Be Legendary is a fantastic model for creating the life you want. I am wondering how, in our busy lives, do we possibly remember to follow the ABC's and take action?

CARTER

Consider the U.S. penny, the smallest form of currency. Pennies are the most common man-made item on Earth. There are more than 130 billion pennies in existence today and 6.5 billion in circulation—in our pockets, in cash registers, and even laying on the ground.

There are so many pennies that many times we don't even see them. If you are like me, when I *do* see them on the ground, I am so busy I don't even take the time to bend over and pick them up. And why not? Because they simply are not valuable enough.

But they do have value, don't they? What is each penny worth? One cent—1/100th of a dollar. If you add up one hundred cents, you'll get a dollar. And dollars can add up.

I will take those 6.5 billion pennies! Just dump them on my driveway and I will roll them and everything!

And if I were to look through the 6.5 billion pennies carefully, I would find tens of thousands of pennies that are actually worth real money—more than a penny and in most cases worth $10 or more.

In fact, the most valuable penny in circulation today is valued at $35,000. I don't know anyone, not billionaires, who would walk by a $35,000 penny.

How do you find a valuable penny? Three things:

1. You have to be Aware of the pennies.
2. You have to know what a valuable penny looks like (Legendary Intent – what is valuable to you) and Believe that every penny has value.
3. You have to act – take the extra two seconds it takes to pick up the penny and risk people possibly thinking you are crazy (Courage) for picking up pennies.

So what do these valuable pennies look like? I have no idea. I really don't! What interests me is how pennies are like acts that make a difference. An act that makes a positive difference in the world is just one act—one penny. Some acts are more valuable than others—a valuable penny—but still just one act. It is the accumulation of pennies, and acts, that is important, not any single act.

There are around 6.5 billion pennies in existence in the world today. There are around 6.5 billion people on Earth. In essence, we are all just a penny. The difference is, we get to decide what our value will be!

The legendary people you may be thinking of in your lives are more valuable than one penny. But these people cannot do it alone.

Your life is essentially a collection of pennies, a collection of actions. Spend time thinking about your actions, your pennies, and become more aware of them, their value and why, where do your beliefs fit in, and did it take courage to act. Also, have the courage to give yourself the credit you deserve. Celebrate your successes! If you do, I think you will find your current collection of legendary actions is far greater than you might think.

It is my greatest hope that people will read this and every time they see a penny, they will think of Be Legendary and take an action to make a difference.

WRIGHT

Do you have any common acts that people do so that we can begin immediately?

CARTER

Oh, there are literally thousands of *great* acts out there. You can look at our Web site, www.BeLegendary.org for stories and videos of everyday people leading legendary lives. Google "acts making a difference" or something like it and you will find great ideas.

One of the blogs that I follow is by Marie Wikle, the creator of Spreading Joy. It is really inspirational and keeps me going. She is truly amazing and started with nothing except a desire to spread joy.

However, each of us has an amazing opportunity to consistently affect people every day in a meaningful way.

What am I talking about? Conversation. Conversation is one of the single greatest contributions you can make. Talking to others about their beliefs and sharing your own. Creating space to disagree and re-evaluate your own values and be open to expanding your awareness is critical, as long as it is authentic. You can talk about the weather, if you want, or something else trivial. Or you can have a deeper conversation around something more important and develop relationships that you otherwise could not do.

It may be a bit uncomfortable in the beginning because we are not practiced at it. We are used to surface communication and talking about the minutiae of our day—our boss and other trivial discussion. Get through that. Take a risk, have the courage, and have a real conversation. Share a legendary story of your own or someone else's and ask if they have seen something like that lately. You can have great conversations that are also very comfortable.

I challenge you to have great, authentic conversations. Each one of them is important and valuable.

WRIGHT

Many of our readers are businesspeople. How would an executive or manager bring the spirit of Be Legendary into their organization?

CARTER

Most of the work we do is in exactly this arena. While companies hire us to come in and help them, there is a great deal that a single leader can do to create a legendary workplace.

The idea is to connect a person's heart and mind to his or her job and to the company. This may seem daunting, if not impossible, but it is completely achievable. And best yet, this is also what people want! We all want to work in a place in which people support one another, develop deep and meaningful relationships, and know that their daily life has meaning. Help them focus on what they want.

Let's look at each of the ABC's and I will briefly provide some suggestions you can take:

Awareness – Have a conversation with each of your staff and help them understand what they *really* want. What do you (staff person) want? Use our Legendary Intent model to help phrase questions:

If you wanted to accomplish only *one* thing today, what would it be? Why?

If you could only have *one* thing in this job, what would it be? Some suggestions are: job security, great teamwork, projects that challenge you, and so on.

What is the *one* thing that you want to learn while you are here to take to your next job, either in this organization or in the next?

There are many questions you could create and should want to know the answers to from your staff.

Next, of course, is "How can I (the manager) help you achieve those answers?"

Beliefs – You can do this in a larger group and in a very fun way. We have some activities that work for this, but the goal is to discover what are the individual beliefs of the people in the room? What are the common core values and beliefs?

You can have everyone put a single belief or value on a sticky note and use a wall, projection screen, or flipchart to begin grouping them together.

It is absolutely amazing to see what the common core values and beliefs are in the group and how much everyone shares with one another.

Next is to look at the groups one at a time and connect them back to the job they do. Even to the tasks done on a daily basis. It may not seem obvious in the beginning, but if you keep up discussion, you will find connections between the beliefs and the organization.

Finally, what we (management) can do more of to emphasize our beliefs within the group. For example, if family is a core value or belief (very common), what opportunities can managers be watching for to create the feeling of family at the workplace?

Courage – As a leader, you need to show your courage through vulnerability. Always go first—always.

While you are asking questions in A and B above, be a complete participant. Don't hold back and place yourself above your staff. You need to risk first and let others see your courage. Also, as a leader, you need to become an expert on trust—on how trust is developed and destroyed.

Both A and B above require taking a risk. If your staff does not trust you, it would take an enormous amount of courage and a large risk to answer your questions. The answers may not be what you want to hear.

Keep in mind, your shift to a legendary workplace will not occur overnight. Remember the example of the executive I mention earlier. It took a few months, but she was able to create a legendary culture among her staff. In turn, they began doing the same with their staff. The actions of one leader were leveraged throughout the entire organization.

WRIGHT

I see that you have a very interesting and unique graphic for your logo—a snail walking away from its shell. What is the significance of the snail?

CARTER

This our logo of Be Legendary. Do you see courage?

If you ever see this image, you will know the person has the inward goal of Being Legendary and you can support him or her.

I believe when enough of us are acting like our snail—strong beliefs, courage, and awareness of what we are leaving behind, we will see a tipping point in society that will transform the world as we know it.

I know this because it has happened in our lifetime. Our world changed on September 11, 2001. There was an unintended consequence no one could have predicted when the twin towers fell. For a short time, the world was incredibly connected, incredibly kind, open, and honest.

We *all* wanted to feel connected to one another. You could see this everywhere you went. I was in New York City a couple of months after 9-11 and when you walked down the street, people looked you in the eye. People opened doors for one another. It was legendary and incredible!

And then one day it was gone.

So where did it go? Why did we let that connection slip away? It was because we were reactionary and not *intentional* in our action. Living a Legendary Life is intentional.

When enough of us live Legendary Lives, we will feel that connection again. It is already happening in some communities around the world. It can, and is, happening everywhere.

This is the destination we all want on our road map.

Remember when I asked you to think of someone legendary in your life? This person is legendary to you, right? Do you think he or she considers himself or herself legendary? Probably not, which makes the person even more legendary. Regardless of what the person thinks, he or she *is* legendary, whether the person likes it or not because you think he or she is.

The janitor was on the legendary list of more than ten thousand people.

Oh, by the way, you are on someone's list, too. You already *are* legendary for someone! Be Legendary for yourself, too.

WRIGHT

Thank you, James. I appreciate all the time you've spent to talk with us about your road map to success—Be Legendary.

CARTER

My pleasure, as always, David.

About the Author

James Carter is the Founder and CEO of Be Legendary, a socially inspired team and personal development company.

James has created emotional learning and philanthropic experiences for thousands of participants through executive retreats and large meetings. James' passion lies in helping each person feel valuable as an individual who is part of the whole. Clients consistently report that his energy, passion, and unshakeable belief in giving back to the community are the key factors in their decision to work with Be Legendary.

James is currently authoring *Be Legendary, the ABC's* while running his company, Be Legendary. He makes his home in Northern Nevada with his wife, Christina, and daughter, Isabella.

You can find out more about Be Legendary at the contact information below.

James Carter
Be Legendary
Reno / Lake Tahoe
800-513-8759
www.BuildingTeams.com
www.BeLegendary.org
www.JamesLCarter.com

Chapter Eight

JOURNEY TO ACHIEVEMENT

MELANIE WHITE

DAVID WRIGHT (WRIGHT)

Today I'm speaking with Melanie White. Melanie is the founder of her own tutoring business with a fifteen-year track history of helping students succeed while making the learning experience fun. She is also a writer and creative productivity consultant for numerous business and speaking professionals. Her goal is to help her clients succeed by providing them with the highest quality products and services available.

Melanie, welcome to *ROADMAP to Success*.

Tell me, what does success mean to you?

MELANIE WHITE (WHITE)

So many people, especially in the United States, equate success with money or power. They think if you are someone with a prestigious position like a corporate CEO or the President of the United States, then you have obtained success. I bought into that success model for many years, thinking that if I could have a large house or afford to go on vacation whenever I wanted, wherever I wanted, then I would be successful.

But, believe it or not, this type of success is limited because it doesn't account for relationships and personal development. I know that many people think my unmaterialistic point of view is too wishy-washy. These are the same people who believe enough money and power will get you anything you want in life. After all, you can buy a trophy spouse, someone who looks good and really appears to love you—until you run out of money. The real question is whether you can have a really rewarding, close relationship with someone who is only interested in you because you make a lot of money or have a powerful position. While the person you "bought" may look great on the outside, can you honestly say that he or she would stay with you and stand by you if, all of a sudden, you lost your position and power?

Think, for a moment, about the end of your life, when you are lying on your deathbed. Who is there with you? Who really cares about you, and who is just waiting for you to die to see what you left for them in your will? In the end, it is the people you love and who love you who are much more important than any material possessions you have accumulated over the course of your lifetime.

I remember a time I got to go on a cruise free of charge because I was doing some writing for a comedian performing on board. While the trip was great, I missed my husband. On one particular night, I was watching a beautiful sunset over the ocean, and I realized I had nobody there to share it with me. I couldn't turn to someone and say, "Wow, isn't that amazing?" It made me sad.

Along with developing great relationships with other people, success, for me, also means personal development. I love learning, and I think it is important for people to have meaning and purpose in their lives. If you have a reason to get out of bed in the morning, if you are pursuing something you are very passionate about, then you are much more likely to be happy. I guess, ultimately, I equate being happy with being successful. For me, that means taking care of my health along with my spiritual growth, not to mention engaging in work projects that I find rewarding.

And as far as material success goes, I believe that all people need is enough money to pay their bills and provide for their family's basic needs of food and shelter. I believe education is also a basic need, crucial to human development.

WRIGHT

We hear a lot of people talking about the importance of setting goals. Do you have specific goals that you think are crucial to a person's success?

WHITE

I believe goal-setting can be very beneficial. Knowing what you want to achieve allows you to determine the necessary steps to get there. Often people will make five-year goals and then break them down year by year, then month by month, then day by day.

For example, let's say five years from now, you want to be sixty pounds lighter. That means you need to lose twelve pounds a year or only one pound a month. That's a very achievable goal. You just need to start making small changes to your diet like substituting water for soda, cutting out the chips you eat or the candy bar you get from the vending machine every day at work.

Or maybe you want to be earning $100,000 per year in five years. Let's say you currently make $50,000 per year. That means you want to double your income in the next five years. That means you have to make an additional $10,000 per year for each of the next five years. That's less than $1,000 per month in the first year, $2,000 per month in the second year, and so on. Now you just have to sit down and brainstorm ways you can do so, hopefully while also pursuing your passion.

Maybe you want to start a band that plays on nights and weekends. You could paint pictures or start a writing or tutoring business. You can also explore the numerous online options available for people who want to earn extra money. Whatever you decide to do, make it something you enjoy since you will probably be sacrificing your precious free time to achieve your lofty financial goal.

Just be careful to not make all of your goals financial. You want to have some balance in your life. Don't get me wrong. It's good to have financial success, but you also need to have successful relationships, be healthy, and grow as a person. By doing so, you will be amazed at the progress you can make toward a well balanced life and how much you can actually achieve in all the areas of your life.

WRIGHT

The title of this book is *ROADMAP to Success*. Do you think individuals need a road map in order to succeed?

WHITE

I do, because if you don't have a plan, then you can get lost. Without knowing which way you need to go, you are just wandering around aimlessly with no direction, so basically you are just spinning your wheels. When you know what road you want to take, you have confidence you are moving in the right direction.

The good thing about having a map is that you usually have many choices that will get you to your destination. You can take the fastest way, the shortest course, the scenic route. Each one will get you there; it just depends on what your priorities are.

People often take an interstate highway, even when the distance is longer because it allows them to drive faster. By doing so, they feel that they are making quicker progress toward their destination. For many, the quickest way is the best way because they feel that they have made progress and achieved something in a shorter period of time than it might have otherwise taken them. These are the types of people who seek out mentors and learning materials that will help them shorten their learning curve.

Other people look at the map and decide to take the road that is the shortest distance, even if it takes a little longer and they have to leave the interstate to get there. For these people, driving the fewest miles or taking the least number of steps to get them to their goal is psychologically comforting. They don't want to feel that they wasted their efforts or went out of their way to reach their destination. These individuals are more about efficiency than speed. They want the maximum return from whatever investment they make.

Still others prefer the scenic route. These people want to enjoy the ride and don't particularly care how long it takes them to get there. Although these people eventually reach their destination, it is more about the process or the road trip than it is about how long it takes them or how far they had to go. These people don't tend to be as driven, but they find great rewards in getting the most out of the trip.

Just remember that you usually have many choices of roads, but they all lead to the same destination—success.

WRIGHT

What if, despite all your efforts to follow the road map, you still get lost?

WHITE

Don't worry. It's likely that at some point on the road to success, you won't know where you're going. Being lost means not knowing where you are. The important thing is to not give up on your goal and to realize that you are simply experiencing a delay that might keep you from reaching your destination at the time you expected, but you will still get there.

It's important not to panic when you are lost. It's reassuring to remember you can always retrace your steps and find the road you missed. You can even go back to the beginning and start all over again if it is necessary. Remember, every failure is a learning opportunity. You know what you shouldn't do the next time because it sent you in the wrong direction or down the wrong path. And if you didn't learn the first time, you will keep getting the same lesson until you do learn.

Have you ever known people who had one failed romantic relationship after another because they kept getting involved with the same type of person? Either they eventually learned their lesson and finally found their way to true love, or they kept spinning their wheels and have never succeeded in having a loving relationship with another person. Relationships are a good example of how we keep getting the same lessons over and over again until we finally learn—or don't—depending on our willingness to finally get the message.

You also need to be willing to stop and ask for directions when you get lost. Some people have a hard time swallowing their pride and admitting they need help. But everyone in life depends on other people. Truly strong individuals know they need help and don't mind asking for it. They realize that they can ask others to share their knowledge, and by using that information, they can cut down on the time they are lost and can find the best road to help them reach their destination. But be careful to ask someone who actually can help you. If you ask the wrong person, that individual might just give you bad directions, and you will be just as confused as before you asked them for help. So be sure you are asking someone who has a lot of knowledge in the area or at least someone who has an accurate map to help you on your road to success.

WRIGHT

Often people experience obstacles on their path to success. Melanie, what do you do when you encounter roadblocks?

WHITE

I come up with an alternative plan. That's all you can do, really. It would be naïve to think that you aren't going to experience any problems when you are trying to succeed. You are. Some can be anticipated, but others are totally unexpected. So what you need to do when you start out is to try to determine what obstacles you might experience.

Let's say your goal is to pay off all your credit card debt in the next year, and you are $5,000 in debt. You come up with a plan to pay $600 per month, which takes care of the principal plus the interest.

Some of the obstacles you might anticipate are what you should do about the months when you have extra expenses—car registration and inspection, relatives' birthdays, Christmas, etc. Some of these expenses are set and can't be changed, but some of them are variable. Maybe you could cut down on the budget you have had in the past that is designated for things like gifts and entertaining.

Other obstacles come completely unexpectedly. So, continuing with the credit card example, perhaps your car breaks down or your roof begins to leak, and you are faced with expensive repair jobs you didn't anticipate. What do you do then? Well, if you don't have any savings, it seems that you have no choice but to put the necessary expenses on the credit card you were trying to pay off. While this could be the case, you may have other alternatives. Perhaps you can set up a payment plan with the repair company or divert your anticipated income tax refund for these expenses. You can also look into a loan that would cost less than the interest on the credit card you are trying to pay off. If all else fails and you have to put the additional expense on your credit card, you should then be mentally prepared to pay more on it each month so that you can still pay it off in a year. If your current income and budget don't allow you to do that, you need to look into either cutting other expenses or making more money or both.

You can always come up with another plan if you are open minded and willing to think creatively. There is always a solution to any problem and that includes any obstacles you experience on the road to success.

WRIGHT

Sometimes people get sidetracked when unexpected events happen. What would you say is the best way to handle detours to success?

WHITE

People have to take detours all the time, and even though taking another road may be inconvenient, you still eventually reach your destination. You have a couple of choices when you have to take a detour. You can either follow the prescribed detour route that most of the cars are taking, or you can look at a map and see if there is a different alternative route you would like to try.

Following the prescribed detour route is a good idea if it isn't convenient to look at a map at that moment in time. Perhaps the road is dark, and you don't have any light available to you right then. In other words, you can't think of an original idea that would be better than what someone else has already done. There's nothing wrong with seeing what other people are doing and following them. In fact, sometimes that's the best, most efficient way to go. After all, if other people have had success doing something a certain way, it's much easier to follow their lead than to try and reinvent liquid paper. You can always add your unique personality to the mix. If you want to be an information marketer on the Internet, you can follow the same basic success formula that works for the gurus making the most money, but add your special twist to set you apart from your competitors.

Alternatively, you may prefer to get out your map and find another way to go. You may find a back road that takes you to your destination more effectively, especially if there is a lot of traffic on the detoured road. Going a different way takes a lot of courage and a willingness to have faith that you can find a better way. Many of the world's greatest explorers and inventors have done so. Just be ready in case you find yourself on a dirt or gravel road that looked good on the map but turned out to be a really difficult drive. It doesn't mean that the side road won't get you there; it just may not be as easy as taking the road everyone else is driving. But you can be inspired by people like Robert Frost in his poem "The Road Not Taken" who said he "took the road less traveled by, and that has made all the difference."

WRIGHT

What about pit stops? How do you know when it's time to take a break?

WHITE

Before you are burned out and don't care anymore. So many people, especially Americans, have been instilled with an extreme work ethic that insists that the only way to succeed is to work really hard. And while I would agree that hard work can be beneficial, it is not healthy when you start neglecting your friends and family. It's also bad to ignore your basic needs for healthy foods and enough rest. Spiritual renewal is also very important.

Nobody is the Energizer Bunny. People can't just keep going and going and going. But so many of us feel guilty about slowing down. I know when I decide I need to take a short nap during the middle of the workday, I don't want my husband telling anyone who calls about business that I am sleeping. I have the perception that doing so will make the person calling think I am lazy. Instead, I prefer that my husband tell callers that I am not available and to take a message for me. In Europe, I hear that it is quite common to take an afternoon nap to rest and refresh for the remainder of the day. That certainly beats our custom in the U.S. of having mid-afternoon junk food snacks or stimulants like caffeine that might cause us to have a bad night's sleep. Yet there is still a stigma here in the United States about "goofing off" by resting.

And what about weekends? Are you able to take a break then or are you still going full speed ahead? I personally often work on weekends and have just started taking Sundays off for rest and relaxation. That's because I'm just now learning the important lesson that stopping to rest makes me more productive. Yet many people still only stop when they absolutely have to because they have to go to the bathroom or grab something to eat or lay down for a few hours of sleep. But this type of journey is very stressful, and being stressed out can really take its toll, causing people to be become ill. And let's face it, if people are sick, they can't concentrate on working. All they can focus on is getting better.

So I definitely think it's important to take breaks and have a few pit stops on your journey to success. Just don't stop more often than you need to. Then you will lose your momentum and could get permanently sidetracked, keeping you from ultimately making it to your destination.

WRIGHT

Melanie, you hear a lot about the importance of mentors. Who do you think success travelers should take with them on their journey?

WHITE

I think if you want to succeed, you should surround yourself with people who believe in you and what you are doing. Now, these people aren't necessarily the same as mentors. But it is very important that you have people who support you and say positive things about your efforts. If you happen to be around those who aren't supportive and give you reasons why you won't be able to succeed, you are very likely to start buying into their negativity and believe what they are saying. You will begin to doubt yourself and your abilities. And once you quit believing you can succeed, you lose momentum and are much more likely to give up and think yourself crazy for ever trying something so foolish. It's a self-defeating, downward spiral, one you don't want to fall into. As a result, it is best not to tell negative people about your goals, especially if they happen to be family members that you know you will have to associate with in the future. Otherwise, just try to eliminate negative people from your life, and instead, surround yourself with those with those who will support you.

As far as mentors go, I definitely think that associating with someone who has succeeded in a similar endeavor to the one you are undertaking can be very helpful. They can give you helpful advice that will make your learning curve much shorter. In this way, you can cut down on the time it takes you to ultimately reach success. Just choose wisely when you are selecting a mentor. Make sure it is someone you admire who truly wants to help you instead of someone who just wants you to pay for his or her time. While it's okay to compensate your mentor for his or her help, it shouldn't be the only thing your relationship is based on. Consider whether you think your mentor has your best interest at heart or whether this person is just using you to fatten his or her bank account. Take your time looking for the right mentor because when you find the right person, you will discover that this individual's help will be invaluable to you.

WRIGHT

Why take a road trip at all? Wouldn't it be easier to fly?

WHITE

You learn so much more when you go through the entire process and don't try to take shortcuts. Sometimes the journey is just as important as the destination. And think of all the sights you will see along the way that you wouldn't get to see if your head was in the clouds. There are landmarks and scenery that you discover on the road, things you learn that you never knew before and things that are invaluable to you.

Taking the road trip will give you the knowledge and experience to make a similar trip in the future. It will lay the groundwork for all your subsequent journeys toward success. Maybe later on in your career, after you have taken several road trips, you will be ready to fly, but in the beginning, you should be making the most of your opportunity to travel the path that will ultimately lead you to your destination of success.

WRIGHT

Okay, Melanie, you've successfully reached your destination. What do you do next?

WHITE

Think about where you want to go next. Plan your next trip; think about your next journey. Set your next goal. It's important in life for everyone to have a purpose, and by figuring out what you want to do next, you give yourself something to look forward to and something else to accomplish.

The worst thing you could do is rest on your laurels. While it's good to reward yourself for reaching your goal, it's just as important to evaluate what you want to do next. You can use the knowledge you have gained in achieving success to help you formulate a plan for your new endeavor. Doing so will help you to keep challenging yourself and will lead you to greater and greater accomplishments.

WRIGHT

Melanie, thank you for taking the time to talk with us today. Is there anything you would like to add?

WHITE

Only that I wish everyone reading this book good luck on their journeys to success.

About the Author

Melanie White is an entrepreneur with more than fifteen years' experience running several businesses. With a passion for helping people succeed, Melanie teaches classes and consults privately with people who want to develop both their own individual skills and talents as well as their business ideas.

An award-winning writer, Melanie has published numerous print and web articles as well as plays and jokes. In fact, she has even had some of her jokes told by Jay Leno on *The Tonight Show*.

Melanie is also an accomplished speaker who inspires people to create success, so they can ultimately achieve their highest potential.

Melanie White
214-607-4842
mwspeaking@mac.com

Chapter Nine

LIVING A VIBRANT LIFE: THE POWER OF DREAMS

MARC DRIZIN

DAVID WRIGHT (WRIGHT)

Today we're talking to Marc Drizin, He has spent his entire professional career helping companies better understand and improve employee satisfaction, with bottom line results. Speaking engagements, a series of books, and numerous articles have all featured his data-driven approach to employee engagement. Then, a series of family events caused him to take a hard look at his life and his dreams.

Today, Marc is not only helping companies stay attuned to employees' wants and needs with a refined approach, he's a passionate Dream Manager, helping individuals improve their lives one dream at a time.

Today we'd like to welcome Marc Drizin to *ROADMAP to Success*.

MARC DRIZIN (DRIZIN)

Thank you, glad to be here.

WRIGHT

Marc, what is a Certified Dream Manager and why did you become one?

DRIZIN

My journey began on Super Bowl Sunday in 2006. After fifteen years of turning down invitations to join my friends in Las Vegas for Super Bowl weekend, my lovely wife finally urged me to go. We arrived on a Friday and enjoyed the next couple of days eating, drinking, and gambling—basically doing what middle-aged men do when they are in Las Vegas. I'd elaborate, but as you know, what happens in Vegas stays in Vegas.

We stayed up very late Saturday night, and into Sunday morning. At 5:30 AM, I heard a banging at my hotel room door. It was my best friend, Willie, telling me that my dad had left a message on his cell phone because he couldn't get through to me on mine. "Let me In Marc, this is important!" Willie said. I got of bed, opened the door, and Willie came in, sat down on the edge of my bed, and he handed me the phone. The next thing I know, I hear the voice of my seventy-three-year-old dad screaming into the phone. "Marc, are you there? Marc, I can't get your mom to wake up! Marc, where are you? Marc, I need your help!" Then there was silence.

I called my dad right back, but there was no answer on his phone. I called my older brother who lived about fifteen minutes away from my parents' house. My brother told me that Dad found Mom not breathing. He was able to do CPR. He called the ambulance and they had taken her to the hospital. "I think you'd better get home right now," my brother told me. I called my wife and explained what was going on and then called the airlines to see about getting an emergency medical flight back home to Indianapolis where I would pick up my wife and drive the two hours to Cincinnati. It turned out to be the longest two hours of my life.

At the hospital, I saw my dad sitting next to my mom, who was in a coma. I knew in that instant that my mother was already gone and I had been firmly planted in the sandwich generation, responsible for my own children and now having the responsibility for my dad's future as well.

Sixteen days and two different hospitals later, Mom finally died. Every Sunday for the next two years, I drove to see my dad in his nursing home, stopping by the store to pick up things he needed or wanted. I would also pick up lunch at Red Robin and bring him a big, greasy cheeseburger and onion straws. When the weather was good, we'd sit outside. We'd eat in his room if it was cold or raining. He would ask about my work, his grandkids, and what was going on in our lives. He would tell me stories about his life and times with my mom. He would crack jokes and make light of his situation. Week after week, month after month, I drove the two hours down I-74 to spend time with my dad.

One day my dad and I were eating our cheeseburgers—the barbeque whisky kind, his favorite. We were making small talk discussing life in general. Out of the blue, my dad said, "Marc, are you living your dreams?"

I laughed, and said, "Sure Dad, I'm living my dream, just like you are."

He took another bite of his burger and asked again, "Are you living your dreams?"

Although I didn't understand why at the time, I realized that this question would somehow matter to me sometime in the future. Like any young child talking to a parent about life, I looked around his room, looked up to the ceiling, looked down to my feet, and in a quiet voice said, "No, Dad. I'm not."

Then he asked me a question that would change the direction of my life, "What are you waiting for?"

Now, I'm a professional speaker. I talk to thousands of people every year. I've authored three books, conducted press interviews, and spend most of my time on the phone, working with customers and clients, but here at this moment, like a five-year-old I was speechless. My dad noticed my discomfort, made a joke about something, and then went back to talking about nothing. Nine days later we received a call from the nursing home that my father had fallen out of his bed twice and was being taken to the hospital with what they thought was a broken hip. I knew from friends and family who had an elderly relative fall and break a hip that I was receiving a gift from God. I only had a few more days with my dad. One more drive to Cincinnati, another stay at the hospital. Five days later, the call from his nursing home came. In the same bed, in the same room, in the same hospice where my mom died, Dad finally met her in heaven.

Three months later, I received a call from a friend who had seen my dad's obituary in an old newspaper she still had in the house. Vicki gave her condolences and began to talk about life. It had been almost thirty years since we had last spoken. We found that we had things in common, including being involved in coaching and mentoring mid-level and senior level executives on interpersonal skills, management style, and employee engagement, although she was now a full time mom bringing up three children. We agreed to talk again soon.

A couple weeks later, she called me and told me about a book that she wanted me to read. "Marc it's a self-help book. I think you'll like it," she said. I told her that the last self-help book I remember being in my house was *I'm OK–You're OK* and frankly, after my mom read it she wasn't okay, and we weren't okay. I said, "Thanks, but no thanks. I'm not really interested." She said, "I'd really like you to read the book."

In our next conversation, she asked me again about the book. This time she said, "Marc it's kind of a human resource book."

I said, "I don't even like rereading my own human resource books. I'm not interested in reading somebody else's."

She said that she really believed I would enjoy it. I declined, but assured her that I appreciated the offer. Two weeks later the book arrived in my mailbox with a simple yellow sticky note on it with two words: "Read it! "

I put it in my briefcase, figuring I would read it during my next business trip because I am always looking for something to read on a plane.

I was on my way to a speech in Cleveland when she called asking me how I liked the book, the one I hadn't started reading yet but was taking up space in my briefcase. She said, "Marc do me a favor and just read the first ten pages of the book. If you don't like it, give it away to somebody else on the plane." By this point, I felt pretty guilty so I agreed and began reading the book while we were still on the runway.

Just five pages into the book, I realized what a mistake I had made by not reading it earlier. The book was *The Dream Manager,* by Matthew Kelly. The book explained how helping employees reach their dreams creates a more engaged workplace, increasing employee satisfaction, engagement, customer retention, and business success—a book about my business, but through an entirely new lens.

I read Matthew's companion book, *The Rhythm of Life,* and knew immediately that becoming a Dream Manager and helping people improve their lives one dream at a time was what my dad was asking about nearly a year earlier.

After spending an amazing afternoon with Matthew in Cincinnati, and then two days in his Dream Manager certification program in Chicago, I became a Certified Dream Manager in June 2009. Today, I have the honor and privilege of helping individuals, couples, employees, and companies dream like a kid.

WRIGHT

Is there a difference in the way children dream and adults dream?

DRIZIN

I like to tell people that kids dream big because their needs are small, and adults dream small because their needs are big. If you ask a young child what the child wants to be when he or she grows up, you'll get quite the list: "I want to be an astronaut, the president, a cowboy, a ballerina, a mom, a painter, an architect and an airline pilot"—all at the same time. The sky is the limit with kids because they don't have the life experience to know otherwise. Adults are much less likely to dream big. In fact, many determine whether they can achieve a dream before they can even write it down.

One of the saddest parts of my dream workshops is when I ask my "Dream Catchers"—the people I help—about their wildest dreams. My question to them goes something like this: "If time and money weren't an issue, and you knew that you could not fail, what would you do? What would you dream?" Out of all the categories of dreams we talk about during these sessions, adults struggle most with this question because they've been told over and over again what they can't do, what is not achievable. I tell my Dream Catchers that if they have given up on their dreams, it's a short walk to disappointment. George Bernard Shaw perhaps said it best when he said, "You see things and you say, 'Why?' But I dream things that never were and I say, 'Why not?'" Today, I am blessed to be able to help others ask "why not?"

WRIGHT

Will you explain how the Dream Manager process works? How do you help your Dream Catchers achieve their dreams?

DRIZIN

The Dream Manager process can begin in a number of ways. Some of the people I work with have attended a four-hour workshop I conduct where they are encouraged to list their one hundred dreams in various dream categories. Others know of my work through my blog, my corporate Web site at MarcDrizin.com, my newest venture at VibrantLifeIndy.com, Twitter, or even my Facebook presence. Sometimes, I'll strike up a conversation with somebody sitting next to me on a plane or drinking coffee at Starbucks. The subject always comes up when I'm working with my clients on improving workforce engagement, what I like to call my "Plan A" business.

Whether on a formal or informal basis, each engagement with an individual, a couple, a team, or a company begins with a simple question, the same question my dad asked me: "Are you living your dreams?" In the vast majority of cases, no matter whom I'm working with, the answer is "no." I then ask that follow-up question that changed my life, "What are you waiting for?"

In the more formal process, the Dream Catcher and I meet on a monthly basis for about an hour. Each session follows a similar structure. First we review the participant's progress over the last month. The Dream Catcher and I examine areas of challenge related to the four pillars of dreams—physical, intellectual, emotional, and spiritual, or what I refer to as PIES. We then discuss any homework assignments from the previous meeting and what has happened in the last thirty days that has changed, updated, or impacted their dreams. We work together for at least a year on the fulfillment of their dreams and their living a vibrant life.

No matter how we work together, it all starts with listing their first one hundred dreams, writing them down in a dream journal or a dream notebook. In our business lives, we often are asked to write a business plan. How many of us have ever written down our life plans, our ambitions, our goals, and our dreams? By writing dreams down on paper, selecting a few to be the target dreams, and then categorizing those to be accomplished in a year, one to three years, and longer than three years, much of the hard work is already accomplished. Just like a business plan, I work with individuals to ensure that these target dreams pass what I call the RUMBA test. Are their dreams are reasonable, understandable, measurable, believable and attainable?

Over the remaining sessions, we spend time working together to bring their dreams to fruition. Sometimes that means focusing on how current finances impact dreams and their completion. In some cases, we have them create a simple formal budget. We look at how their personality impacts their ability to change dreams to goals, because goals are just dreams with a deadline. We even explore how their time management or lack of it impacts their ability to reach, or not reach, their dreams.

For some Dream Catchers, the process is simple and straightforward. They do a lot of work on their own without being prompted. With others, we have to build up a relationship based on trust over time. As a Dream

Manager, I don't have a vested interest in any particular dream one of my Dream Catchers has. It's my job to help them achieve it. I usually end a dream session by reminding my Dream Catcher that the best way to predict your future is to go out and create it.

WRIGHT

Marc, I know there are different dream categories. Are some dreams more important to people than others?

DRIZIN

Sure. In the formal Dream Manager process, there are a dozen categories, including the four we already mentioned: physical, intellectual, emotional, and spiritual dreams. Others include material, professional, adventure, legacy, and again financial dreams. For most individuals I work with, three dream categories seem to rise to the top: adventure, financial, and legacy dreams.

Adventure dreams tend to revolve around travel, most people's best memories. In fact, if you ask people to tell you about their favorite or happiest memory, it usually involves going on vacation or a trip with friends, family, or other loved ones.

My greatest adventure dream was spending two weeks in the Amazon with my older son Josh, when he was thirteen. It was nearly ten years ago, and we spent a week in an ecolodge, and the other hiking the Inca trail to Machu Picchu. Interestingly, this was a combination of a dream I had written as a classroom assignment when I was fifteen—a list of fifty things I wanted to do before I die, what most people today would call their "bucket list."

Financial dreams are very common. Most people want less debt or more money in the bank. However, financial dreams also play a part in nearly every other dream category. Dreamers may want to go back to school to achieve a new degree or profession, so money plays a role. Someone may want to write a book, which is a creative dream, but the person will need to set aside some time. Having extra money in the bank is important during that time period when he or she may not be working as much. Still others may want to drive a new sports car or buy a house on the beach. Extra money in the bank is seldom the basis of a financial dream.

Legacy dreams take us to a different place, often to what we leave behind after we die. The phrase "you can't take it with you" is true, but what we can leave behind to our spouses, our family, our children, and our community makes a huge difference in what we choose to do today. Caring for the environment, teaching our children the importance of giving back, and "paying it forward" by creating an endowment for a college or a church in our will are all ways that people accomplish their legacy dreams. When it comes to the future, no dream is too small.

WRIGHT

Have people in America stopped dreaming?

DRIZIN

I truly believe that people in America haven't forgotten how to dream, they just have little or no confidence that their dreams can be achieved. The dreams I focus on are not the dreams and nightmares people have at night when they are asleep. We're talking instead about the daydreams that people have during the day when their eyes are wide shut. Adults spend so much time thinking about what is wrong in their lives—a lousy job with a boss who doesn't appreciate them, estranged relationships with old-friends and family, mounting debt, concerns about their children and their future, war, or disease, you name it.

Certainly in a tough economy, with millions and millions of people out of work, with long-term unemployment that is at its worst since the Great Depression, with gridlock in Washington pushing more and more people to the fringes, and seemingly never-ending war and conflict around the world, it sure is easy to believe the worst. When you can't see the forest through the trees, when we are bombarded daily with negative news on television, the radio, newspapers, and magazines, it's understandable that people don't dare dream. Why be disappointed again? Is it any wonder that people feel a sense of powerlessness when it comes to their own personal dreams?

As a Dream Manager it's my job to help cut through that mind-clutter to show that dreams can be accomplished just by taking one little step, and then another, and another. As Johann Wolfgang von Goethe said, "Whatever you can do, or dream you can, begin it. Boldness has genius, power, and magic in it." Begin it now.

WRIGHT

When you and I were growing up, there was this thing called the American dream. How has the American dream changed?

DRIZIN

The idea of the American dream is actually set out in the second sentence of The Declaration of Independence that states "... all men are created equal, that they are endowed by their Creator with certain unalienable rights, that among these are Life, Liberty, and the pursuit of happiness." The phrase "the American dream" was coined by a gentleman named James Truslow Adams in 1931 in his book, *The Epic of America*, James wrote, "... life should be better and richer and fuller for everyone, with opportunity for each according to ability or achievement..." regardless of social classes or circumstances of birth. He goes on to say, "The American dream that has lured tens of millions of all nations to our shores in the past century has not been a dream of material plenty, though that has doubtlessly counted heavily. It has been a dream of being able to grow to fullest development as a man and woman, unhampered by the barriers which had slowly been erected in the older civilizations, unrepressed by social orders which had developed for the benefit of classes rather than for the simple human being of any and every class."

Martin Luther King, in his letters from a Birmingham jail in 1963, actually rooted the Civil Rights Movement in the Black quest for that same American dream. Dr. King said, "We will win our freedom because the sacred heritage of our nation and the eternal will of God are embodied in our echoing demands... when these disinherited children of God sit down at lunch counters, they were in reality standing up for what is best in the American dream and for the most sacred values in our Judeo-Christian heritage and thusly carrying our whole nation back to those great wells of democracy which were dug deep by the founding fathers in their formulation of the Constitution and the Declaration of Independence."

Although some people think that the American dream is all about a bigger house, a faster car, nicer clothes, and fancy jewelry, my passion for helping people live a more vibrant life has shown that the American dream is much like what my parents, my grandparents, and my great grandparents wanted from America. They saw the American dream as the opportunity to create a better life for their children than they had when they were young. I believe the American dream has changed little since the founding of our country. What has changed is our belief that we can achieve those dreams. And I'm doing my part to help my dream-catchers live a life unimagined.

WRIGHT

Do you think that we as a society are beyond dreaming? Is it just hokey to dream these days?

DRIZIN

I do believe that there is a large segment of society that cuts across all demographic segments and believes that dreaming is just for kids. They believe that life is too fast, too chaotic, too difficult, and too impersonal for dreams.

I have been arguing with a client for months about doing a simple dream workshop with his IT and engineering folks. He suggests that these people spend all their time thinking in numbers, equations, measurements, and computer code. He is certain that these employees would laugh at the mere thought of spending time dreaming. How wrong he is.

People want to believe in a future that is better than the life they live today. They hope that their children are given opportunities for a life they themselves could have not imagined. They want to create a better version of themselves. In short, they desperately want to dream and lead a vibrant life. We do live in a fast-paced world. People are more insulated from each other than ever before. They don't even go to shopping malls anymore; instead, they buy products online. People e-mail each other instead of picking up the phone or chatting with a neighbor across the fence. Families don't talk over the dinner table anymore; they text each other on their mobile phone, even when sitting right across the table.

The power of dreams is not just in the completion of a dream. Oftentimes when a dream is realized, we recognize that the dream itself was not all that important in the first place. It's the journey, the hope, the wonder, the excitement that goes along with the initiation of reaching the dreams that makes a difference in people's lives. My own life included.

My wildest dream—the dream that I would pursue if time and money weren't an issue and I knew I could not fail—will be accomplished one day. I know it. I feel it deeply in my soul. My dream is like that of many people born in the 1960s at the height of the space race with the Russians. Someday, somehow, I will go up into space, look through a rocket window, and see the Earth like a marble in the sky. Is it crazy? You betcha. But someday I know it will happen.

If anything, with all of the horrors we face in living each day, dreams are a respite—a way to break out of who we are today, and what we want to be in the future. Dale Carnegie wrote, "Most of the important things in the world have been accomplished by people who have kept on trying when there seemed to be no hope at all." This is the world of dreams and why I am so blessed to help people achieve their personal goals and ambitions.

WRIGHT

Why does it come so naturally to some to identify and chase their dreams, while it comes so difficult for others?

DRIZIN

Some of this is the classic glass half full, versus glass half empty paradigm. If you grow up unable to see the world beyond your neighborhood, if you aren't told every day by people you love and respect that nothing is impossible, and if you believe you are stuck with the hand that you are dealt, if you are without the ability to pull yourself up by those proverbial bootstraps, you'll never be able to dream.

Part of my greatest joys as a Dream Manager is helping someone accomplish their dreams, however large or small they may see to them, or seem to me. One of the most difficult dream categories is the emotional dreams, trying to repair relationships with a loved one or a family member.

One of my friends came to my first dream session. She was deeply affected by our discussion of emotional dreams in the workshop. I could tell it by her body language, the expression on her face. A few weeks later, we were having lunch in a local restaurant. She began to cry, and neither the food nor the service was bad enough to have enlisted that response. When I asked her what was wrong she said, "Marc, as I was driving home from your dream workshop, I took a hard look at one of my target dream—one that I wanted to accomplish during the next twelve months. I picked up the phone and for the first time in six years called my mom to say hello. It was the first time in six years that I have talked with her. I asked if I could come to dinner that night and have her meet her two-year-old granddaughter."

This call wasn't a hard thing for my friend to do, but over the years, "life got in the way" making a relatively simple act more and more difficult.

As I sat at the table listening to her story, I realized that this is the power of dreams.

As adults, we are often weighed down with baggage we have accumulated over our lifetime. Small disagreements fester into large-scale fights, even though we don't remember what the original issue was. Words we spoke in anger or in haste reverberate louder and louder as the years go on. What tasks we once thought would be simple to accomplish in our youth have proven to be more challenging as we grow older. Some people thrive on hardship, it makes them work more intensely to accomplish their goals and more thankful for what they have. Others react the opposite way—they draw inward, stop taking chances, and get themselves stuck in that proverbial "rut." In either case, and for all those people "in between" the two extremes, accomplishing goals and dreams creates a better, more vibrant life.

I was personally blessed by parents, teachers, and mentors who never told me I couldn't do something if I was willing to work hard, put my mind to it, and make the sacrifices that I needed to. They laid the groundwork for me to have the careers as a consultant, author, and speaker that I have enjoyed for the last twenty years. They gave me the courage and confidence to fail, and on occasion I have succeeded in failure. Someone once said that the men who try to do something and fail are infinitely better than those who try to do nothing and succeed. That's the nature of the dream work. That's the avocation that I'm blessed to do with my Dream Catchers in my growing business, Vibrant Life.

WRIGHT

Why has business been so reluctant to embrace something so powerful?

DRIZIN

As we all know, business is about numbers, balance sheets, metrics, ledgers, forecasting, return on investment, and what "the street" thinks. Although many companies pay lip service that employees are their most important asset, those same employees are shown on a company's profit and loss statement as an expense, not an investment that will pay itself back over time. If leaders in a company want to improve the balance sheet, they look at firing ten percent of the staff. If they need to get productivity up, they go about it by working the employees even harder. And in many cases, "what gets rewarded gets done" so this pattern continues.

A lot of today's managers are adept at better, cheaper, faster. Many of them have been promoted up through the ranks because of their ability to get more out of less, to cut the fat, to run a lean organization. But when you look at the best companies, those that are leaders in their industry, what you find is that those companies with leaders who care about their employees and show it through their daily interactions with them, come out ahead nearly every single time. Employees want to work for companies with strong, capable senior leaders who see their workers as the single most important competitive edge they have, especially today when most products and services are commodities, meaning that customers have a choice. Employees want to be treated like individuals, not as an employee ID number. They want to work for an ethical organization whose leaders care about their short- and long-term development, even if that means they may decide to go to work somewhere else in the future.

These employee-centric beliefs take faith. Return on investment isn't immediate. It's like preventative healthcare. We all know that if you can help someone lose weight, quit smoking, and exercise more, the payoff in terms of decreased medical cost in the future can be staggering. But some business owners and managers and many stockholders want to see an instant return. They don't want to wait to see a better future, they want it now.

WRIGHT

How would companies benefit if they were able to harness the power of employee dreams?

DRIZIN

That's simple. It really does go back to how strongly I was touched by the Dream Manager concept. For my entire professional career, it has been my business to help companies attract, motivate, and retain top talent. I've wanted to find those things that make employees want to stay with an organization as opposed to feeling that they've got no other choice but to stay. Companies benefit by helping their employees reach their dreams because of the power of engagement.

When employees believe their organization cares about them as people, not just a source of productivity, they will act in ways that benefit their organization both short- and long-term.

Employees who are engaged with their organization stay longer and recommend their organization as a great place to work, driving down the cost of recruiting and training. Engaged employees work harder and are much more likely to go the extra mile for customers, increasing customer satisfaction, retention, repeat purchase, share of wallet, and share of market.

By helping employees achieve their dreams, whether it be buying a home for the first time, putting away a little money in a college fund, giving them the opportunities to volunteer at their favorite charity, rewarding their performance by sending them on a dream trip, or training and developing them to attain a better job, today's businesses will see an improvement in their bottom line by helping employees lead a more vibrant life.

WRIGHT

We hear a lot about the dream deficit. Will you explain what that is and why it's so critical?

DRIZIN

There is a dream deficit for both individuals and their employers. As we talked about before, many people have great difficulty dreaming. In most cases, it's not because they don't have the imagination to see a better future for themselves or for their families, but because they don't think their dreams will ever come true. If you don't see the possibility that you can achieve your goals and your dreams, the likelihood for you to dream them in the first place declines pretty quickly.

It's the same thing with today's businesses. Businesses hope to succeed, to stay in business for this month, next month, and future years for the benefit of shareholders and their various stakeholders. Companies have found it difficult to dream of a better future because in today's economy, both here in the United States, as well as worldwide, the pie isn't getting any bigger. Less people are spending less money on goods and services, so the only way to get ahead in today's business environment is not to get a bigger piece of a larger pie, but to actually grab a bigger piece from one of your competitors.

So today's companies are forced to look, not a year into the future, five years into the future, ten years into the future, but they're interested in seeing what happens in the short-term, sometimes in as little as the next twenty-four-hour cycle. Individuals, couples, companies, and teams all have a huge dream deficit. They've forgotten not only how to dream better for the future, but they've lost faith in the ability for those dreams to come true.

Dreams are what set us apart. The aspirations we have for a better time to come, the ability to provide our children and our children's children with a better future than we see today is critical to our ability to lead a happy life and our ability to create a future unimagined, not only for ourselves, but our loved ones, our companies, our culture, and our future.

WRIGHT

Today we have been speaking with Marc Drizin. He has been helping us better understand and harness the power of dreams,

DRIZIN

Thank you.

About the Author

Marc Drizin has spent his entire professional career helping companies better understand and improve employee satisfaction with bottom line results. For decades, his data-driven approach to employee engagement has taken him to employers and speaking engagements around the world. In recent years, reluctant membership in the "sandwich generation," and personal hurdles that included the deaths of his parents, prompted Marc to take a hard look at his own dreams and pursue them with abandon. Today, Marc is not only helping companies stay attuned to employees' wants and needs, he's a passionate Dream Manager, helping teens and adults improve their lives by accomplishing one dream at a time.

Marc Drizin
Vibrant Life
3440 Golden Gate Drive N.
Carmel, Indiana 46074
317-752-7508
marc@vibrantlifeindy.com
marc@marcdrizin.com
www.vibrantlifeindy.com
www.marcdrizin.com

Chapter Ten

THE SUCCESSFUL LIFE YOU DESERVE

DR. ELISE STEVENSON

DAVID WRIGHT (WRIGHT)

Today we're talking with Elise Stevenson, PhD, who is the Founder and President of Chrysalis Counseling Centers, Inc., established in 1993. Chrysalis Counseling Centers, Inc. serves individuals throughout the Northern and Central Virginia area helping children, adolescents, and adults in their life challenges. Elise is a licensed psychotherapist, psychologist, masters addiction counselor, and holds several clinical certifications, including cognitive behavioral therapy. She is also a diplomat of the American Board of Forensic Counselors. Elise received a BA in Psychology, a master's in Social Work, a master's in Business Administration, and a PhD in Psychology. She has been featured on a variety of radio shows and has been interviewed by local investigative reporters for several major television stations and for various newspaper articles.

Elise's vision has involved creating caring centers and community-based programs to create healing in the lives of others in order for them to have a loving, nurturing, and successful life. She attributes her success to her faith in God.

Elise, welcome to *ROADMAP to Success*.

ELISE STEVENSON (STEVENSON)

Thank you. It is my pleasure to be here.

WRIGHT

I know you've heard many definitions of success, but how do you define success?

STEVENSON

Yes, there are many definitions of success with a majority of individuals equating success with money or material objects. I know that many people I work with define success in terms of achieving wealth, climbing the corporate ladder, or socializing with important people.

Using this definition, one could argue that a drug dealer who makes a million dollars is a very successful person. Due to the negative affect the individual would make on the lives of others, I would not view this as a good definition of success. In addition, if the drug dealer was arrested and imprisoned, as a society we would not define this as a successful individual.

On the other hand, Ralph Waldo Emerson defines success to include finding "the best in others; to give of one's self; to leave the world a bit better . . . to know even one life has breathed easier because you have lived—this is to have succeeded."

In my clinical practice, I've treated hundreds of people who have achieved wealth, climbed the corporate ladder, and socialized with important people (those our society defines as being successful) who are not happy individuals. As we have witnessed, or maybe even experienced, we can be professionally successful without experiencing contentment. What they thought would make them happy—to have the million dollar home or the house on the beach or the most expensive BMW—didn't fill the void that was in their heart. Of course it is wonderful to have life's finest things but those items are merely icing on the cake. To make the cake, other vital ingredients are required.

Most people would define success as accomplishing something they desire, but what I have personally experienced, as well as seen time and time again in my therapeutic work with others, is that those individuals who are people-focused, instead of self-focused, lead more fulfilling and satisfying lives.

Success should not be measured by your belongings, the job you have, or the car you drive, but by the person you are, your values, and your beliefs. Material goods come and go. For example, a hurricane could come and destroy your beautiful beach home, your expensive BMW could get totaled by a careless driver, the company of your top management job could go out of business leaving you jobless, but developing loving and nurturing relationships gives you a sense of serenity no material things can ever provide.

It is important to emphasize the need for your primary relationships to be loving and nurturing. You can have many close relationships with dysfunctional individuals and experience a miserable and unsuccessful life. So who you associate with influences the person you become and whether you will be successful.

For many people who have lived in emotionally harmful relationships, it can be exceptionally frightening for them to allow themselves to be emotionally vulnerable in experiencing a loving and nurturing relationship. Most individuals I have treated have experienced many painful relationships that included emotional, psychological, physical abuse, and/or sexual abuse, so the thought of allowing themselves to get close to another human being is the last thing they want to do. It can feel much safer to keep busy acquiring possessions or working hard or drinking the pain away, because no one wants to experience the pain of being hurt again.

When we have been hurt, we find ourselves creating walls between ourselves and others. We can become critical of ourselves and feel unworthy of being loved, or we can develop exceptionally high expectations of others as another way to avoid getting close to other caring people.

A successful person cares about others and learns to care about themselves. A successful person is not concerned about making money but about developing himself or herself into a person who is valuable to others. Albert Einstein wrote, "Try not to become a man of success but rather try to become a man of value." It is important to note, however, that this frequently leads to making money because people will pay for value. Success can be measured as the encouragement we give to others that improves the quality of life to another human being.

So, in summary, success is learning to love ourselves and others as growing individuals and accept love from others.

WRIGHT

Wouldn't it be nice if while you were younger—in junior and senior high school—there were courses on relationship-building and decision-making?

STEVENSON

Most definitely. Our schools are so focused on teaching skills in reading, math, science but little focus is placed on the single most important part of our development—our relationships with others. I'm glad to see that schools are now offering psychology classes in high school.

Just as we learn how to read and write, having healthy relationships is also a learned behavior. We are learning more and more through our life experiences about the importance of emotional intelligence, which can be defined as learning how to relate successfully toward others around us. For example, if a person feels he or she is superior to others (false self-worth, also known as narcissism) the person will lack the ability to empathize with others, limiting his or her ability to experience healthy relationships. We naturally grow physically, but in order to grow successfully in life, we also need to grow emotionally, mentally, and spiritually as human being.

WRIGHT

So what would you say would be the biggest contribution to your professional success?

STEVENSON

The biggest contribution to my professional success has been my relationship with God, because He has always given me the strength to get through many challenges I've experienced. Many times throughout my career I've realized that the biggest resource we have is God. He has always given me the support and resources when I've needed them throughout the life of my business. I have found that repeatedly the biggest resource I have is God. When I would ask God for His strength, guidance, and support, He would always provide the resources needed and give me guidance to help continue to push forward.

Frequently the challenge is making sure we are looking in the right direction. Many times I have heard people say they prayed but God did not listen. God always listens. He may decide that another path will create more success—a different kind of success than what we expected.

For example, youths frequently tell me in my clinical sessions, "My parents don't listen to me." In some cases, this is the case; but in many instances, the parents may state, "I hear you want to go out and play after dark, but it isn't safe."

God created us and know what we need. He knows our desires to be successful and has given each individual special talent that can be used to help others and our society. It is hard to realize our weaknesses but He is always with us through life's challenges. God actually put resources in front of me and as I leaned on His strength and wisdom, He would put the next steps in front to continue. He's the one who ultimately gives us the strength to endure each challenge we face here on Earth.

WRIGHT

Who would you say are the people who have served as your role models for success?

STEVENSON

I would definitely say that my parents have been excellent role models in showing me the important components in living a successful life. My own parents have lived in conditions of poverty and had to work exceptionally hard in challenging situations. They both grew up on cotton farms and experienced the uncertainty of life every day. They have inspired me the most. As children, they both worked well before the sun was up, rising by 4 AM to feed the animals and do other farm duties before walking miles to school. Upon arriving home from school, they would continue to work hard for many hours after the sun set.

As youths, my parents did not have electricity so they completed their homework by candlelight. My mother was so determined to live a successful life that she would stay up later than her parents permitted, seeking to further her education by reading every minute she had an opportunity. She knew that if her father caught her, she would receive a switching but she was determined to succeed in her studies.

Growing up on a farm taught my parents the value of hard work and money, as well as how to live a faith-filled life. They learned that hard work alone does not lead to success. Their relationships with others and their faith in God to take care of them through droughts and other life struggles led to their success. They taught me to always remember that God is with us and wants us to be successful in this life. My parents have always been admirable role models because they taught me to always stay determined, never give up on the challenges that lie in front, and always remember that God is there with me.

My parents never allowed others to tell them what they could or could not accomplish. They never allowed anyone or challenging circumstances to stop them from accomplishing their goals.

This has been very important to me because I know people can make discouraging comments like, "You will never be successful, you'll never be able to get a degree, you won't amount to anything," and so on. I learned long ago not to listen to negativity from others because they do not know what I am capable of accomplishing. And they do not know what you are able to accomplish. How do others know what path God has for your life?

WRIGHT

What do you think are the biggest obstacles people face in trying to become successful?

STEVENSON

I feel the biggest obstacle people face in becoming successful is self-defeating thinking. I am sure that many people who have been listed in the book *Believe It Or Not* were told they would not be successful as well. Self-defeating statements, such as "I can't do it" or "Nobody cares about me," are detrimental to your success. Don't get into a place where you feel defeated thinking that you won't be able to pass a class, or get the job you want or make any friends or have a successful marriage. Maybe you failed a class, lost a relationship, or a home. Don't go global and then think, "I'm a failure and will never be successful."

Make a commitment to yourself to stay steadfast in your goals. Keep positive and optimistic people around you. You can't allow the fear of the unknown, the fear of being embarrassed, or the fear of failing at completing the task to stop you. In addition, don't listen to negativity or other people's critical remarks because this will prevent you from being successful. Others do not know what you are capable of accomplishing. No one knows what you are capable of accomplishing except God Himself. Always remember to stay focused on your goals and you will be successful.

When I initially started in the field of counseling, I worked with clients who had severe mental disabilities including those whose IQ's were as low as twenty.

One man I met, who has left a lasting impression on me, would always smile and embrace the challenges he experienced in his life. His parents, at a young age, had placed him at St. Elizabeth's Hospital, which was his home for fifty years until he was deinstitutionalized to a group home to live out the rest of his life. Every time he met someone new, he would greet the person with a big smile and say, "Hello," as he gently touched his hand on his or her shoulder.

Another client with an almost identical background, same age and IQ, and who grew up with the man I just mentioned at the same psychiatric hospital, lived in constant fear. He approached life so differently. The other man was always fearful and would go to the corner of the room or into his bedroom when others, even those he had known for years, would enter the home.

I know from their clinical histories that both of these individuals experienced severe neglect and abuse. It is impossible to measure the psychological effect the abuse and neglect had on them, but the difference was that one lived in the present embracing life and his relationships, while the other man lived in continuous fear.

A more recent client, who grew up in the 1950s, shared her story with me of the severe abuse she experienced as a child. After her parents divorced at age three, she was shifted between relatives until her father remarried at age five. At age six, her stepbrother attempted to molest her and threatened to kill her at gunpoint. When she informed her parents, her stepmother called her a liar and prohibited her from entering the home. She lived on a porch that was lined with windows and had no insulation and no heat.

"I had no blankets or sheets so I made my old coat into my blanket," she told me. "A nail on the wall was my closet. My dad would get me two outfits for school and one pair of shoes. If the shoes got holes, I would use cardboard to fix them. I washed my clothes by hand in the tub, but did not have basic items such as a toothbrush." She reported that her bed was full of bedbugs because the mattress had been retrieved from the dump.

My client stated that she had written a letter to her grandfather asking him for money so that she could buy some blankets. "He did send me money and I bought blankets, but my stepmother took them away and lied to my father saying she had not taken them. I was not allowed to eat any food unless I was called in for dinner, which rarely occurred. I was forced to stay in my room on the porch and could not enter any part of the house. If I snuck a can of vegetables out of the kitchen, I would be beaten so relentlessly by my stepmother that I would pee in my pants."

She described her father and stepmother as severe alcoholics with frequent physical altercations occurring within the home. "I never received Christmas presents under the tree. When I woke up, there would be a single present by my bed that I knew was from my father. I was not able to celebrate Christmas with the family being restricted to my room on the porch. I never was hugged or kissed by my parents."

At the age of fourteen, she left home and resided at various friends' homes. "My life was an everyday survival. I cried a lot during my childhood many tears of pain."

She went on to say, "I believe people come in your life for a reason, and I have had a lot of very special people come into my life. I used to pray for God to please take me away from this pain, but I am so glad that He didn't at that time. I now have things in my life that I am so happy for, which make up for the past. I do not dwell on my past. Even now, when I meet people they think that I had a good upbringing because of my friendly attitude. My stepmother did not win even though she beat me down because she did not beat me out of a good life." Even though my client, Connie, was diagnosed with MS in 1973, she stated, "I realize that I am blessed for each day I spend on this Earth and for all the special people in my life. I have so much love in my heart that I could cry when I think about it all. I have so much love and peace in my heart."

Many of us hold onto the past and feel that the past is going to define our future. In order to be successful, we need to let go of painful life experiences. Our past does not define the future. It only informs you of what has previously occurred. If you are focused on looking back at your past, you will not be able to see what is in front of you. We need to realize instead that we don't know what the future is going to bring, otherwise we will limit ourselves to reach our full potential. It can be very exciting to see all the many blessing that can come if we chose to embrace each and every day.

WRIGHT

So how do you know what you need to be successful?

STEVENSON

What you first need to be successful is to develop a positive outlook on your life. You also need to continue to realize that there is so much in life that you can learn. In addition, it is important to identify people in your life who are supportive and are people you feel are emotionally safe.

Identifying resources is also extremely important in being successful. It's not feeling as though you know it all or feel you need to know it all. I see this as an area that prevents many people from truly being successful because when they feel that they know it all, then there is nothing more for them to learn. Realize that each person you meet can teach you something. It doesn't matter if the person is in a low income bracket or living on the streets, each one has learned different lessons in his or her life journey.

Successful people are always looking at situations from a positive point of view. If you are having a very bad week and so many negative events have occurred, you can easily feel defeated. You might say to yourself, "Since today was such a bad day, then tomorrow can't be any worse." And if the next day is also a bad day, you can say to yourself again, "Since today was such a bad day, then tomorrow can't be any worse." This attitude will enable you to stay focused on moving through your life challenges and will assist you in being successful.

Make sure to always realize that you never know where that silver lining in the cloud might be, and the joys that you might find from the different experiences you have in life. You might discover that a person you trusted betrayed you. Don't let that experience create a fear in being able to trust another individual. If you do, then you are allowing that individual to control your life and your destiny.

WRIGHT

Would you tell our readers a little bit about what drives you to be successful?

STEVENSON

What drives me to be successful is the realization of my purpose in this world. I don't have time to be negative or associate with negative people. My clinical practice has showed me time and time again that negativity leads to depression, anxiety, and hopelessness. Every day I make sure to thank God for the blessings He has given me—the beautiful clouds in the sky, the moon that guides me back home after a long day at the office, my family and friends, heat in my home during those cold winter months, or air conditioning in the hot summer months.

My parents taught me to not put my focus on other people but rather to stay focused on the task in front of me and push through any challenges that may come my way. They never gave up on their goals and would pray to God for wisdom in their own life decisions.

WRIGHT

Do you believe that it's important to balance your success in your life? If so, how do you do it?

STEVENSON

Balancing success is important. As I stated previously, true success is building relationships with other people and creating a quality life for yourselves and others. If you are so focused on being successful in your business but neglect your family relationships, you really are not experiencing a successful life.

Being successful is prioritizing your primary relationships first. Make sure you are being kind to your spouse, your parents, your children. Then make sure you are being kind to your boss, your neighbor, the person you meet in the grocery store.

Remember, healthy relationships lead to a quality life. If you do not water the flowers you plant, don't expect them to continue to grow in your garden. Balancing success in my life is reminding myself regularly of my life's purpose of caring for the well-being of others.

WRIGHT

What is the message you want people to hear so that they can learn from your success?

STEVENSON

Having had the wonderful opportunity to work with a diverse population, I have learned so much about various life experiences. I have had the opportunity to work with a diversity of people, from those who are homeless to people who are billionaires. These experiences have assisted me in realizing what true success and happiness is and how we can achieve it.

The people I see who are most successful are those who don't become discouraged when life's storms come along. They identify resources to help them and are thankful. They also value others. Your focus is on the positive and the healthy things.

For example, if you went to the supermarket to purchase apples and you saw a rotten apple in the basket. Are you going to purchase the rotten apple? Of course not. But we make choices every day that are bad for us. We need to be more consciously aware of the choices we are making and ask ourselves, "Is this something that is going to nurture my heart, feed me emotionally, physically, mentally, spiritually? Or is this something that is going to harm my body, my mind, or harm my relationships?"

Make sure to not pick up the bad apple. The message I want people to hear is try very hard to remain a positive thinker. See the glass as half full. Whatever is concerning you today usually is a faded memory a year from now. Moods are contagious. So don't focus on the negative. Identify people who can assist in your goals, be open to listening to others, but be clear of your path. Don't let others discourage you or defeat you.

If we are positive in our approach to others, then they are more inclined to feel positive and then have positive feelings for us. That is true success.

WRIGHT

So how can people help other people succeed?

STEVENSON

We can help other people be successful by caring for them unconditionally and not judging them. When you see challenges others experience, give them support or say a prayer for them. Don't condemn them and don't think you're superior.

As I travel from one city to another from my clinical offices, I have the opportunity to observe many types of drivers. Some drivers drive fast, pushing their way between the cars. Other drivers drive too slow, hovering on the right side of the road, never crossing to the left side of the lane. Other drivers drive in the proximity of the speed limit being watchful when they change lanes to look out for other vehicles.

Ask yourself what kind of driver are you? Are you trying to push your way in front of others in order to climb up the corporate ladder faster than someone else? Are you so fearful that you allow other people to take advantage of you because you don't feel you are deserving? Are you a driver who, as you are moving forward in your life, is showing care and concern toward yourself and others around you?

You can experience success every day. When we are assisting others to improve the quality of their lives, we are successful. The positive influence you make on the lives of others will always be a way of defining success. You should not measure success by the amount of money you have made but on the positive influence you have made for the betterment of our society. This could be simply sharing a smile with someone you meet.

In terms of success, I would have to summarize it as who we are as a person. This includes how we view ourselves and how we view the world around us. It is not a hat that you put on or take off. It is learning to embrace life and finding the rainbow in yourself and others through the life experiences we encounter. If your life is successful, it will be infused with kindness, compassion, consideration, and understanding. It is this that truly makes us rich.

WRIGHT

Well, what a great conversation. I really appreciate all the time you've taken with me to discuss all these important questions. I've learned a lot here today, and you've given me a lot to think about.

STEVENSON

It has been my pleasure.

WRIGHT

Today we've been talking with Elise Stevenson, PhD. Elise is the Founder and President of Chrysalis Counseling Centers, Inc. Her vision involves creating caring centers and community-based programs where people can develop their full potential in creating the life they want and the life they deserve. By her own admission here, she attributes her success to her faith in God.

Elise, thank you so much for being with us *ROADMAP to Success*.

STEVENSON

Every day is a blessing for us and we can be a blessing to someone else every day. Be a blessing and find your blessing. You and those around you deserve it.

About the Author

Elise A. Stevenson, PhD, MBA, LMHP is the Founder and President of Chrysalis Counseling Centers, Inc., which has served thousands of individuals in Northern and Central Virginia since 1993.

Elise received her Bachelor of Arts degree in Psychology with a Minor in Music, a master's degree in Social Work, a master's degree in Business Administration, PhD in Psychology, and has been a licensed psychotherapist for nearly twenty years. In addition, she has received several certifications including Certified Cognitive Behavioral Therapist, Master Addictions Counselor, and a Certified Diplomate in Psychotherapy. Elise has provided administrative and clinical leadership for more than twenty-five years, in addition to providing clinical treatment to children, adolescents, and adults. She has been featured on a variety of radio shows and has been interviewed by local investigative reporters for several major television stations, and for various newspaper articles.

Elise's vision for herself and her company is to provide quality and competent services utilizing various therapies and techniques with empathy and compassion. Through a caring and integrative approach, Chrysalis Counseling Centers, Inc. provides supportive services that promote empowerment, recovery, and self-determination in all aspects of the individual's life.

Elise Stevenson, CEO/President
Chrysalis Counseling Centers, Inc.
605 N. Main Street
Culpeper, Virginia 22701
540-727-0770, #100
estevenson@chrysaliscenters.com

Chapter Eleven

An Interview With

Dr. Kenneth Blanchard

DAVID WRIGHT (WRIGHT)

Few people have created a positive impact on the day-to-day management of people and companies more than Dr. Kenneth Blanchard, who is known around the world simply as Ken, a prominent, gregarious, sought-after author, speaker, and business consultant. Ken is universally characterized by friends, colleagues, and clients as one of the most insightful, powerful, and compassionate men in business today. Ken's impact as a writer is far-reaching. His phenomenal best-selling book, *The One Minute Manager*®, coauthored with Spencer Johnson, has sold more than thirteen million copies worldwide and has been translated into more than twenty-five languages. Ken is Chairman and "Chief Spiritual Officer" of the Ken Blanchard Companies. The organization's focus is to energize organizations around the world with customized training in bottom line business strategies based on the simple yet powerful principles inspired by Ken's best-selling books.

Dr. Blanchard, welcome to *ROADMAP to Success*.

DR. KEN BLANCHARD (BLANCHARD)

Well, it's nice to talk with you, David. It's good to be here.

WRIGHT

I must tell you that preparing for your interview took quite a bit more time than usual. The scope of your life's work and your business, the Ken Blanchard Companies, would make for a dozen fascinating interviews. Before we dive into the specifics of some of your projects and strategies, will you give our readers a brief synopsis of your life—how you came to be the Ken Blanchard we all know and respect?

BLANCHARD

Well, I'll tell you, David, I think life is what you do when you are planning on doing something else. I think that was John Lennon's line. I never intended to do what I have been doing. In fact, all my professors in college told me that I couldn't write. I wanted to do college work, which I did, and they said, "You had better be an administrator." So I decided I was going to be a Dean of Students. I was provisionally accepted into my master's degree program and then provisionally accepted at Cornell because I never could take any of those standardized tests.

I took the college boards four times and finally got 502 in English. I don't have a test-taking mind. I ended up in a university in Athens, Ohio, in 1966 as an Administrative Assistant to the Dean of the Business School. When I got there, he said, "Ken, I want you to teach a course. I want all my deans to teach." I had never thought about teaching because they said I couldn't write, and teachers had to publish.

He put me in the manager's department. I've taken enough bad courses in my day and I wasn't going to teach one. I really prepared and had a wonderful time with the students. I was chosen as one of the top ten teachers on the campus coming out of the chute. I just had a marvelous time.

A colleague by the name of Paul Hersey was chairman of the Management Department. He wasn't real friendly to me initially because the Dean had led me into his department, but I heard he was a great teacher. He taught organizational behavior and leadership. So I said, "Can I sit in on your course next semester?"

"Nobody audits my courses," he replied. "If you want to take it for credit, you're welcome."

I couldn't believe it. I had a doctoral degree and he wanted me to take his course for credit, so I signed up. The registrar didn't know what to do with me because I already had a doctorate, but I wrote the papers and took the course, and it was great.

In June 1967, Hersey came into my office and said, "Ken, I've been teaching in this field for ten years. I think I'm better than anybody, but I can't write. I'm a nervous wreck, and I'd love to write a textbook with somebody. Would you write one with me?"

I said, "We ought to be a great team. You can't write and I'm not supposed to be able to, so let's do it!"

Thus began this great career of writing and teaching. We wrote a textbook called *Management of Organizational Behavior: Utilizing Human Resources*. It just came out in its eighth edition last year and has sold more than any other textbook in that area over the years. It's been nearly thirty-five years since that book came out. I quit my administrative job, became a professor, and ended up working my way up the ranks.

I obtained a sabbatical leave and went to California for one year twenty-five years ago. I ended up meeting Spencer Johnson at a cocktail party. He wrote children's books—a wonderful series called *Value Tales for Kids* including, *The Value of Courage: The Story of Jackie Robinson,* and *The Value of Believing In Yourself: The Story Louis Pasteur*. My wife, Margie, met him first and said, "You guys ought to write a children's book for managers because they won't read anything else."

That was my introduction to Spencer. So, *The One Minute Manager* was really a kid's book for big people. That is a long way from saying that my career was well planned.

WRIGHT

Ken, what and/or who were your early influences in the areas of business, leadership, and success? In other words, who shaped you in your early years?

BLANCHARD

My father had a great effect on me. He was retired as an admiral in the Navy and had a wonderful philosophy. I remember when I was elected to president of the seventh grade, and I came home all pumped up. My father said, "Son, it's great that you're the president of the seventh grade, but now that you have that leadership position, don't ever use it. Great leaders are followed because people respect them and like them, not because they have power." That was a wonderful lesson for me early on. He was just a great model for me. I got a lot from him.

Then I had this wonderful opportunity in the mid 1980s to write a book with Norman Vincent Peale. He wrote *The Power of Positive Thinking*. I met him when he was eighty-six years old when we were asked to write a book on ethics together, *The Power of Ethical Management: Integrity Pays, You Don't Have to Cheat to Win*. It didn't matter what we were writing together, I learned so much from him, and he just built the positive stuff I learned from my mother.

When I was born, my mother said that I laughed before I cried, I danced before I walked, and I smiled before I frowned. So that, on top of Norman Vincent Peale's influence, really affected me as I focused on what I could do to train leaders. How do you make them positive? How do you make them realize that it's not about them, it's about whom they are serving? It's not about their position, it's about what they can do to help other people win.

So, I'd say my mother and father, then Norman Vincent Peale, had a tremendous effect on me.

WRIGHT

I can imagine. I read a summary of your undergraduate and graduate degrees. I had assumed you studied Business Administration, Marketing Management, and related courses. Instead, at Cornell you studied Government and Philosophy. You received your master's from Colgate in Sociology and Counseling and your PhD from Cornell in Educational Administration and Leadership. Why did you choose this course of study? How has it affected your writing and consulting?

BLANCHARD

Well, again, it wasn't really well planned out. I originally went to Colgate to get a master's degree in Education because I was going to be a Dean of Students over men. I had been a government major because it was the best department at Cornell in the Liberal Arts School. It was exciting. We would study what the people were doing at the league governments. And then, the Philosophy Department was great. I just loved the philosophical arguments. I wasn't a great student in terms of getting grades, but I'm a total learner. I would sit there and listen, and I would really soak it in.

When I went over to Colgate and took some education courses; they were awful. They were boring. The second week, I was sitting at the bar at the Colgate Inn saying, "I can't believe I've been here two years for this." This is just the way the Lord works—sitting next to me in the bar was a young sociology professor who had just gotten his PhD at Illinois. He was staying at the Inn. I was moaning and groaning about what I was doing, and he said, "Why don't you come and major with me in Sociology? It's really exciting."

"I can do that?" I asked.

He said, "Yes."

I knew they would probably let me do whatever I wanted the first week. Suddenly, I switched out of Education and went with Warren Ramshaw. He had a tremendous affect on me. He retired a few years ago as the leading professor at Colgate in the Arts and Sciences, and got me interested in leadership and organizations. That's why I got a master's in Sociology.

The reason I went into Educational Administration and Leadership? It was a doctoral program I could get into because I knew the guy heading up the program. He said, "The greatest thing about Cornell is that you will be in a School of Education. It's not very big, so you don't have to take many Education courses, and you can take stuff all over the place."

There was a marvelous man by the name of Don McCarty who ended up going on to be the Dean of the School of Education, Wisconsin. He had an effect on my life, but I was always just searching around. My mission statement is: to be a loving teacher and example of simple truths that help myself and others to awaken the presence of God in our lives. The reason I mention "God" is that I believe the biggest addiction in the world is the human ego, but I'm really into simple truth. I used to tell people I was trying to get the B.S. out of the Behavioral Sciences.

WRIGHT

I can't help but think when you mentioned your father, and how he just bottomed-lined it for you about leadership.

BLANCHARD

Yes.

WRIGHT

Years and years ago when I went to a conference in Texas, a man I met, Paul Myers, told me, "David, if you think you're a leader, and you look around and no one is following you, you're just out for a walk."

BLANCHARD

Well, you'd get a kick—I'm just reaching over to pick up a picture of Paul Myers on my desk. He's a good friend, and he's a part of our Center for FaithWalk Leadership, where we're trying to challenge and equip people to lead like Jesus. It's non-profit. I tell people I'm not an evangelist because we've got enough trouble with the Christians we have, we don't need any more new ones. But, this is a picture of Paul on top of a mountain, and there's another picture below of him under the sea with stingrays. It says, "Attitude is Everything. Whether you're on the top of the mountain or the bottom of the sea, true happiness is achieved by accepting God's promises, and by having a biblically positive frame of mind. Your attitude is everything." Isn't that something?

WRIGHT

He's a fine, fine man. He helped me tremendously.

I want to get a sense from you about your success journey. Many people know you best from *The One Minute Manager* books you coauthored with Spencer Johnson. Would you consider these books as a high water mark for you, or have you defined success for yourself in different terms?

BLANCHARD

Well, *The One Minute Manager* was an absurdly successful book, so quickly that I found I couldn't take credit for it. It was published around the time when I really got on my own spiritual journey and started to try to find out what the real meaning of life and success was. That's been a wonderful journey for me.

The problem with most people is they think their self-worth is a function of their performance plus the opinion of others. The minute you think that is what your self-worth is, your self-worth is up for grabs every day because your performance is going to fluctuate on a day-to-day basis. People are fickle. Their opinions are going to go up and down. You need to ground your self-worth in the unconditional love that God has ready for us, and that really grew out of the unbelievable success of *The One Minute Manager*. When I started to realize where all that came from, that's how I got involved in the ministry I mentioned. Paul Myers is a part of it. As I started to read the Bible, I realized that everything I've ever written about or taught, Jesus did. You know, He did it with twelve incompetent guys that he hired. The only guy with much education was Judas, and he was His only turnover problem.

WRIGHT
Right.

BLANCHARD
It was a really interesting thing. What I see in people is not only do they think their self-worth is a function of their performance plus the opinion of others, but they measure their success on the amount of accumulation of wealth, on recognition, power, and status. I think those are nice success items. There's nothing wrong with those, as long as you don't define your life by that. What I think you need to focus on rather than success is what Bob Buford, in his book *Halftime,* calls significance—you know, moving from success to significance.

I think the opposite of accumulation of wealth is generosity. I wrote a book called *The Generosity Factor* with Truett Cathy, who is the founder of Chick-fil-A, one of the most generous men I've ever met in my life. I thought we needed to have a model of generosity. It's not only your treasure, but it's time and talent. Truett and I added *touch* as a fourth one.

The opposite of recognition is service. I think you become an adult when you realize you're here to serve rather than to be served. Finally, the opposite of power and status is loving relationships. Take Mother Teresa, as an example. She couldn't have cared less about recognition, power, and status because she was focused on generosity, service, and loving relationships, but she got all of that earthly stuff. If you focus on the earthly, such as money, recognition, and power, you're never going to get to significance. But if you focus on significance, you'll be amazed at how much success can come your way.

WRIGHT

I spoke with Truett Cathy recently and was impressed by what a down-to-earth good man he seems to be. When my friends found out that I had talked to him they said, "Boy, he must be a great Christian man, but he's rich." I said, "Well, to put his faith into perspective, by closing on Sunday it cost him $500 million a year." He lives his faith, doesn't he?

BLANCHARD

Absolutely, but he still outsells everybody else.

WRIGHT

That's right.

BLANCHARD

Chick-fil-A was chosen as the number one quick service restaurant in Los Angeles. They only have five restaurants here and they've only been here for a year.

WRIGHT

The simplest market scheme, I told him, tripped me up. I walked by the first Chick-fil-A I had ever seen, and some girl came out with chicken stuck on toothpicks and handed me one; I just grabbed it and ate it, it's history from there on.

BLANCHARD

Yes, I think so. It's really special. It is so important that people understand generosity, service, and loving relationships because too many people are running around like a bunch of peacocks. You even see pastors who say, how many in your congregation? Authors, how many books have you sold? Business, what's your profit margin? What's your sales? The reality is that's all well and good, but I think what you need to focus on is relationships. I think if business did that more and we got Wall Street off our backs with all the short-term evaluation, we'd be a lot better off.

WRIGHT

Absolutely. There seems to be a clear theme that winds through many of your books that have to do with success in business and organizations.

It is how people are treated by management and how they feel about their value to a company. Is this an accurate observation? If so, can you elaborate on it?

BLANCHARD

Yes, it's a very accurate observation. See, I think the profit is the applause you get for taking care of your customers and creating a motivating environment for your people. Very often people think that business is only about your bottom line. But no, that happens to be the result of creating raving fan customers, which I've described with Sheldon Bowles in our book, *Raving Fans*. Customers want to brag about you, if you create an environment where people can be gung-ho and committed. You've got to take care of your customers and your people, and then your cash register is going to go ka-ching! and you can make some big bucks.

WRIGHT

I noticed that your professional title with the Ken Blanchard Companies is somewhat unique—Chairman and Chief Spiritual Officer. What does your title mean to you personally and to your company? How does it affect the books you choose to write?

BLANCHARD

I remember having lunch with Max DuPree one time. He is the legendary Chairman of Herman Miller. Max wrote a wonderful book called *Leadership Is An Art*. I asked him, "What's your job?"

"I basically work in the vision area," he replied.

"Well, what do you do?" I asked.

He said, "I'm like a third grade teacher. I say our vision and values over, and over, and over again until people get it right, right, right."

I decided from that, I was going to become the Chief Spiritual Officer, which means I would be working in the vision, values, and energy part of our business.

I ended up leaving a morning message every day for everybody in our company. We have about 275 to 300 around the country, in Canada, and the U.K. Then we have partners in about thirty nations.

I leave a voice mail every morning, and I do three things on that as Chief Spiritual Officer. One, people tell me who we need to pray for. Two, people tell me who we need to praise—our unsung heroes and people like that. And then three, I leave an inspirational morning message. I really am the cheerleader—the energy bunny—in our company, and the reminder of why we're here and what we're trying to do.

We think that our business in the Ken Blanchard Companies is to help people to lead at a higher level, and help individuals and organizations. Our mission statement is to unleash the power and potential of people and organizations for the common good. So if we are going to do that, we've really got to believe in that. I'm working on getting more Chief Spiritual Officers around the country. I think it's a great title and we should get more of them.

WRIGHT

So those people for whom you pray, where do you get the names?

BLANCHARD

The people in the company tell me who needs help—whether it's a spouse who is sick, or kids who are sick, or they are worried about something. We have over five years of data about the power of prayer, which is pretty important.

This morning, my inspirational message was about an event my wife and five members of my company participated in. They walked sixty miles last weekend—twenty miles a day for three days—to raise money for breast cancer research. It was amazing. I went down and waved them all in as they came. There was a ceremony, and 7.6 million dollars was raised. There were over three thousand people walking, and many of the walkers were dressed in pink. They were cancer victors—people who had overcome cancer. There were even men walking with pictures of their wives who had died from breast cancer. I thought it was incredible.

There wasn't one mention in the major San Diego papers on Monday. I said, "Isn't that just something." We have to be an island of positive influence because all you see in the paper today is about Michael Jackson and Scott Peterson and Kobe Bryant and this kind of thing, and here you get all these thousands of people out there walking and trying to make a difference, and nobody thinks it's news. So every morning I pump people up about what life's about, about what's going on. That's what my Chief Spiritual Officer is about.

WRIGHT

I had the pleasure of reading one of your current releases, *The Leadership Pill*.

BLANCHARD

Yes.

WRIGHT

I must admit that my first thought was how short the book was. I wondered if I was going to get my money's worth, which by the way, I most certainly did. Many of your books are brief and based on a fictitious story. Most business books in the market today are hundreds of pages in length and are read almost like a textbook. Will you talk a little bit about why you write these short books and about the premise of *The Leadership Pill*?

BLANCHARD

I developed my relationship with Spencer Johnson when we wrote *The One Minute Manager*. As you know, he wrote *Who Moved My Cheese*, which was a phenomenal success. He wrote children's books, and I was a storyteller.

My favorite books were, *Jonathan Livingston Seagull* and *The Little Prince*. They are all great parables. I started writing parables because people can get into the story and learn the contents of the story. They don't bring their judgmental hats into reading. You write a regular book and they'll say, "Well, where did you get the research?" They get into that judgmental side. Our books get them emotionally involved and they learn.

The Leadership Pill is a fun story about a pharmaceutical company that thinks they have discovered the secret to leadership, and they can put the ingredients in a pill. When they announce it, the country goes crazy because everybody knows we need more effective leaders. When they release it, it outsells Viagra. The founders of the company start selling off stock and they call them Pillionaires. But along comes this guy who calls himself "the effective manager," and he challenges them to a no-pill challenge. If they identify two non-performing groups, he'll take on one and let somebody on the pill take another one, and he guarantees he will out-perform by the end of the year. They agree, but of course, they give him a drug test every week to make sure he's not sneaking pills on the side.

I wrote the book with Marc Muchnick, who is a young guy in his early thirties. We did a major study of what this interesting "Y" generation—the young people of today—want from leaders, and this is a secret blend that this effective manager in the *Leadership Pill* book uses.

When you think about it, David, it is really powerful on terms of what people want from a leader. Number one, they want integrity. A lot of people have talked about that in the past, but these young people will walk if they see people say one thing and do another. A lot of us walk to the bathroom and out into the halls to talk about it. But these people will quit. They don't want somebody to say something and not do it.

The second thing they want is a partnership relationship. They hate superior/subordinate. I mean, what awful terms those are. You know, the "head" of the department and the hired "hands"—you don't even give them a head. "What do you do? I'm in supervision. I see things a lot clearer than these stupid idiots." They want to be treated as partners. If they can get a financial partnership, great. If they can't, they really want a minimum of psychological partnership where they can bring their brains to work and make decisions.

Then finally, they want affirmation. They not only want to be caught doing things right, but they want to be affirmed for who they are. They want to be known as a person, not as a number. So those are the three ingredients that this effective manager uses. They are wonderful values if you think of them.

Rank-order values for any organization is number one, integrity. In our company, we call it ethics. It is our number one value.

The number two value is partnership. In our company, we call it relationships.

Number three is affirmation, which means being affirmed as a human being. I think that ties into relationships, too. They are wonderful values that can drive behavior in a great way.

WRIGHT

I believe most people in today's business culture would agree that success in business is everything to do with successful leadership. In *The Leadership Pill*, you present a simple but profound premise, that leadership is not something you do *to* people, it's something you do *with* them. At face value, that seems incredibly obvious, but you must have found in your research and observations that leaders in today's culture do not get this. Would you speak to that issue?

BLANCHARD

Yes, and I think what often happens in this is the human ego, you know. There are too many leaders out there who are self-serving. They're not serving leaders. They think the sheep are there for the benefit of the shepherd. All the power, money, fame, and recognition moves up the hierarchy, and they forget that the real action in business is not up the hierarchy—it's in the one-to-one, moment-to-moment interactions that your front line people have with your customers. It's how the phone is answered. It's how problems are dealt with and those kinds of things. If you don't think that you're doing leadership with them, rather you're doing it to them, after a while they won't take care of your customers.

I was at a store recently (not Nordstrom's, where I normally would go) and I thought of something I had to share with my wife, Margie. I asked the guy behind the counter in Men's Wear, "Can I use your phone?"

"No!" he replied.

"You're kidding me," I said, surprised. "I can always use the phone at Nordstrom's."

"Look, buddy," he said, "they won't let *me* use the phone here. Why should I let you use the phone?"

That is an example of leadership that's done to them not with them. People want a partnership. People want to be involved in a way that really makes a difference.

WRIGHT

Dr. Blanchard, the time has flown by and there are so many more questions I'd like to ask you. In closing, would you mind sharing with our readers some thoughts on success? If you were mentoring a small group of men and women, and one of their central goals was to become successful, what kind of advice would you give them?

BLANCHARD

Well, I would first of all say, "What are you focused on?" I think if you are focused on success as being, as I said earlier, accumulation of money, recognition, power, or status, I think you've got the wrong target. I think what you need to really be focused on is how can you be generous in the use of your time and your talent and your treasure and touch. How can you serve people rather than be served? How can you develop caring, loving relationships with people?

My sense is that if you will focus on those things, success in the traditional sense will come to you. I think you become an adult when you realize that you are here to give rather than to get. You're here to serve not to be served. I would just say to people, "Life is such a very special occasion. Don't miss it by aiming at a target that bypasses other people, because we're really here to serve each other." So that's what I would share with people.

WRIGHT

Well, what an enlightening conversation, Dr. Blanchard. I really want you to know how much I appreciate all this time you've taken with me for this interview. I know that our readers will learn from this, and I really appreciate your being with us today.

BLANCHARD

Well, thank you so much, David. I really enjoyed my time with you. You've asked some great questions that made me think, but I hope are helpful to other people because as I say, life is a special occasion.

WRIGHT

Today we have been talking with Dr. Ken Blanchard. He is the author of the phenomenal bestselling book, *The One Minute Manager*. Also, the fact that he's the Chief Spiritual Officer of his company should give us all cause to think about how we are leading our companies and leading our families and leading anything, whether it is in church or civic organizations. I know I will.

Thank you so much, Dr. Blanchard, for being with us today.

BLANCHARD

Good to be with you, David.

About the Author

Few people have created more of a positive impact on the day-to-day management of people and companies than Dr. Kenneth Blanchard, who is known around the world simply as "Ken."

When Ken speaks, he speaks from the heart with warmth and humor. His unique gift is to speak to an audience and communicate with each individual as if they were alone and talking one-on-one. He is a polished storyteller with a knack for making the seemingly complex easy to understand.

Ken has been a guest on a number of national television programs, including *Good Morning America and The Today Show*, and has been featured in *Time, People, U.S. News & World Report*, and a host of other popular publications.

He earned his bachelor's degree in Government and Philosophy from Cornell University, his master's degree in Sociology and Counseling from Colgate University, and his PhD in Educational Administration and Leadership from Cornell University.

Dr. Ken Blanchard

The Ken Blanchard Companies
125 State Place
Escondido, California 92029
800-728-6000
Fax: 760-489-8407
www.blanchardtraining.com

Chapter Twelve

As You Think You Are: Your Thoughts Create Success

KANDY GRAVES

DAVID WRIGHT (WRIGHT)

Today I'm talking with Kandy Graves. Kandy has certifications as an Emotional Release Therapist, and Intuitive Life Coach, as well as extensive training in NLP (Neuro Linguistic Programming), Speak-Out Feelings, Inner Child Work, Guided Imagery, and Visualization and Meditation techniques. She has studied and worked with a Debbie Ford trained and certified coach, she is also trained in the modalities of Emotion Code and EFT (Emotional Freedom Technique). Being the adult child of an addict, and mother herself to two addicts, she is well versed in the twelve-step recovery program and understands the importance and use of the Higher Power in the healing of generational family patterns and traditions. She also offers wellness/health coaching and currently has assisted more than one hundred clients to release a combined total of 2,135 pounds! Her weight release coaching and her many trainings and certifications represent the tools in her toolbox that she can reach for and draw from to facilitate and expedite the healing of her clients whether in the private setting or in group trainings and seminars. She offers these trainings and seminars with her Emotional Release trained husband of thirty-one years and partner in the AsYouThinkYouAre Coaching Center. Kandy and her husband, Bruce, offer relationship seminars that improve your key, core relationships, which directly affect your personal resonance and therefore your experience in life and especially with money. Kandy is an avid mountain biker and loves warm weather and being outside and connecting with nature. She loves working out at the gym with cardio and weights as well as running 5K races. She also loves spending time with her three adorable grandchildren and three adult sons.

Kandy Graves, welcome to *ROADMAP to Success*.

KANDY GRAVES (GRAVES)

Thank you very much.

WRIGHT

So why is your Web site titled As You Think You Are?

GRAVES

That particular title came to me from a verse of scripture that states, "As a man thinketh in his heart so is he" (Proverbs 23:7). At the AsYouThinkYouAre Coaching Center, I suggest to clients that they begin to notice what they're thinking about. Many are unconscious of the thoughts they are entertaining with repetition and emotion. When they become aware of what they are thinking about, they can then see a direct correlation with their thoughts and their results in life. When they can see that they and they alone are responsible for attracting and creating their experiences, I point out how powerful they are in creating what they *don't* want and that creating what they *do* want is completely possible. The law of attraction (that which I send out in the form of thought and energy is what comes back to me in the form of experience) is at work in our lives; we are very powerful creators.

WRIGHT

So what role do our thoughts play in our success in life, or in business?

GRAVES

Our thoughts play a far greater role than people realize. My clients feel better, and have hope for change in their very first session. They're able to see that when they change their thoughts, they feel differently. This "feeling better" is a vibrational change that takes place in their energy field, which begins the attraction process to more of what they want to experience rather than what they don't want. There is a great quote by Emerson that states, "The ancestor to every action is a thought." I would say also that "The ancestor to every emotion is a thought." So when you are aware of what you are thinking and that those thoughts facilitate the feeling or emotion and even the outcome in your life, then the outcome or the current experience you are having can change.

Thoughts, words, and emotions and their meanings have a resonance or calibration to them. In Dr. David Hawkins book, *Power vs. Force*, he explains that emotions and words attached to those emotions emit a frequency and they calibrate at a particular level. It's like a dolphin swimming around in a dark ocean. The dolphin emits a sound and those sounds come back to it to assist it in navigating around objects and toward food in the ocean. It's similar for us in that as we think certain thoughts, the energy of those thoughts emits a frequency or vibration as noted on Dr. Hawkins' Map of Consciousness chart. (You can see this chart on my Web site, www.asyouthinkyouare.com.) We are "sending out" that vibration. What comes back to us is that same frequency in the form of experience. The definition of the Law of Attraction is, "The Essence of that which is like unto itself is drawn." Whatever we emit comes back to us—good or bad!

WRIGHT

Would you explain for our readers what you mean by the term calibration in the context of success or failure?

GRAVES

The term calibration or resonance can best be explained by the following quote: "When we form 'heart centered beliefs' within our bodies, in the language of physics we're creating the electrical and magnetic expression of them as waves of energy, which aren't confined to our hearts or limited by the physical barrier of our skin and bones. So clearly we're 'speaking' to the world around us in each moment of every day through a language that has no words: the belief waves of our hearts."—Gregg Braden.

When we realize that the very thoughts we hold in our minds send out a beacon that literally allows us to materialize whatever we are thinking about, then we can accept responsibility for our life! We can be more deliberate in creating success in business or in our personal life.

For example, a client had been experiencing a constant struggle in generating enough business each month to pay the bills. Her husband had always been the primary breadwinner but his income had taken a sharp decline and she needed to step up and support the family. In session we were able to get to the core belief she held about her ability to provide for herself and her family. The core belief, which is the same thought held with repetition and emotion, was that she needed someone to take care of her. She was creating the lack and failure to thrive in her business, which, by the way, she was gifted in. This core belief is held in our subconscious mind.

Our ability has nothing to do with our success. What matters is what we think about that ability! She was able to break this pattern of thought and create a new neuropathway in the brain that provided the course correction her business needed, and the clients began streaming in! Similar success has occurred for clients who had blocks about their ability to be in thriving interpersonal relationships.

For example: A client came to me after her twenty-year marriage ended in divorce. Her deeply rooted belief was, "I deserve better," which we discovered in our second session together was the driving force not only in her marriage but in every relationship she was in up to her marriage at age twenty-eight. This came as a shock to her but she could plainly see that she resonated with this belief and, at her every turn, she found that her experiences were serving up this feeling of lack. She was always left to question why she couldn't be treated better. The awareness of this fact started to facilitate the change of her pattern and she began to experience healing in each encounter she had until ultimately she was able to "bring in" a man who treated her right—a man about whom she never had to say, "I deserve better" than this.

This process brings about awareness and an understanding of who you really are and knowing the truth that your origin is, in fact, divine changes your result. I assist all my clients in recognizing exactly what their thoughts and beliefs are so that a more desirable outcome can be achieved. Our thoughts are the conscious mind and our beliefs, which we are sometimes unaware of, are the subconscious mind.

WRIGHT

Why is emotional release such a powerful component in the work you do?

GRAVES

Emotional release is a vital component to clearing blocks that have to be addressed if a person is not happy with the current outcomes he or she is experiencing in life. It is through recognizing and then releasing and reframing these limiting beliefs that allows people to create consciously what they truly desire to achieve and become.

Each of us has traumatic events in our memories. We have common events such as 9/11 and we have personal and private events stored as well. These events have an electrical charge to them and are known as "Somatic Markers" in the brain. Through various modalities I assist my clients in "diffusing" the charge of the marker. It's this charge and the beliefs we hold based on these events in our lives that resonate a particular frequency and therefore bring into our conscious experience the success or failure of our lives.

I've had many personal experiences with this; I will share just one here. When I was nine years old my mother attempted suicide. I was instrumental in saving her life. This event took place on Mother's Day 1972 and was just one of many "events" that I "stuffed down" to keep from having to feel the pain associated with them.

One thing I discovered in the process of healing this marker was that I carried an immense amount of guilt. The guilt was due to a decision I made and had not even consciously realized. The truth was that I really wanted her to die that day. Her prescription pill addiction and her intense self-hate caused me so much grief and pain that I really did not want her to live anymore. This was a lot for a nine-year-old to deal with.

Realizing this and finally identifying it and choosing not to carry it anymore was one of the most freeing and liberating events of my life! I eventually replaced the guilt with love and forgiveness for myself and my mother, who was doing the best she knew how. (And so was I!)

When we can clear the emotion that causes the electrical charge, it clears our path to be able to raise our calibration so that we're no longer stuck in that lower, slower calibrating emotion. We can literally raise ourselves to a place where now our experience is much more positive and feels a lot better.

Prior to clearing this event, I had struggled with depression and seriously low self-worth and esteem. What was once unconscious thought and belief about me came to my awareness and I could now do something about it. Changing the belief about me in that event changed the course of my life!

This path of awareness and healing allows each one of us to reach our highest potential and create more of what we want in life rather than what we don't want!

WRIGHT

Would you explain the context in which you refer to generational patterns and traditions?

GRAVES

A grandmother, a mother, and a daughter are together and you ask the daughter why do you cut the end off of your ham? She says, "Because my mom always did." Then you ask the mother, "Why do you cut the end off your ham?" She says, "My mom always did it." Now you ask the grandmother and she says, "So it will fit in my pan." This is a humorous way to illustrate the pattern and how it gets passed on. We respond and function in life based on what we saw modeled for us. In these generational patterns and traditions, we are doing things on autopilot because it is what we know. If we knew better we'd do better.

I help people to see that it is their pattern of thought and response to those thoughts that produce their results in life. Awareness is the light that shines on the truth. The truth is that we are completely responsible for our outcome. *"As soon as you embrace the* gift *of Personal Responsibility fully, you stop dwelling on things outside your control and, instead, begin to build enthusiasm about growing, developing, and changing yourself"*—Brian Biro.

A client came to me because she had divorced a few months previously and although she felt very good about that decision, her ex-husband had begun dating and this caused her great heartache and pain. She didn't understand why she was feeling like this, particularly when the divorce felt so right.

We got to the core belief she held about her role in relationships. The only way she knew how to behave or act was to be in control, even downright controlling. She was in control in the divorce process but once divorced, and he began dating this became a real trigger for her because she no longer had control over him or was able to influence his choices as she once had. This was a completely new concept for her. It was something she had never recognized before but could see clearly how her mother "taught" this to her through her behavior and responses to her and others in the family. This client held a deep allegiance and love toward her mother and it was very hard for her to look at her mother in anything but an ideal light. I helped her to see that her mother was acting in a way that was also modeled for her by her parents. She got the pattern in the same way she had given it. It's easy to love someone and honor them when you can separate them from their pattern. There is no mother, even the most abusive, that wakes up in the morning and *consciously* declares, "How can I screw up my kid today?" That just does *not* happen. We have all been born to well-meaning parents who are doing the best they know how! What we know is what we learned through observing our parents and other significant participants in our life.

WRIGHT

What do you mean by the pattern imprint?

GRAVES

The "Pattern Imprint" begins at the moment of our birth into this physical experience called life! We are born whole, and good. Consider that we chose our parents and our siblings and our birth position in the family and even the time in history to be having this physical experience. This focus on "what is" without judgment allows us to take responsibility for our lives and see that each one of us has had a pattern imprinted on us. It is one of the reasons for our being here—to experience opposition and contrast!

To overcome our pattern and rise above it and learn through experience that who we really are is not contained in this physical form, but the spirit part that came into this physical experience to overcome the pattern and in so doing, become awake to the fact that everything we experience is our own creation! There is a consequence to every thought. It will bring us pain or joy. We can learn the lessons joyfully or painfully. I choose joy and teach my clients how to do the same!

WRIGHT

How does an understanding of my pattern aid in my success and happiness?

GRAVES

When you know in your response that who you really are is not what is currently manifesting, then you have hope that, life as you know it can change for the better! You have hope for truly experiencing all that you dreamed of or in some cases hope to even dream. I hear over and over again from clients that their first session with me helped them more than years of traditional therapy methods ever did. These techniques that I've experienced gave me hope and brought about change for me. What I have uniquely developed from my training and experience I now offer for others. The As You Think You Are Process facilitates pattern breaking at its best. Success and Happiness surely follow those brave enough to forge a new pathway, a new, never before done, way of thinking, responding, and behaving in their life!

WRIGHT

How is identifying somatic markers and releasing their electrical charge beneficial to my path to fulfillment and success?

GRAVES

We've already discussed the concept of Somatic Markers and their electrical charge. These exist in all of us. Some are common to us all, like the events of 9/11. It's in identifying these markers, and particularly the beliefs we took on or decided were true about us that show us where we are resonating. If a client was sexually abused as a child, there is always guilt and shame present. Regardless of our life events, *be they horrific and traumatic or not*, we have formed beliefs about who we are. These beliefs are that we are less than perfect and whole, which is not the truth.

These beliefs are held in the subconscious and emit a frequency relative to the emotion (energy in motion) held in that belief. Simply becoming aware of the belief and the emotion that is present in us begins the process of lessening the charge, which instantly changes our resonance. What we resonate is directly linked to *who* we bring into our experience and *what* circumstances we find ourselves in. After becoming aware, I use powerful modalities that change the frequency to a higher calibrating emotion like peace and joy or love. You can see that if I have any of the lower, slower calibrating emotions like guilt and shame present in me, I will bring into my experience people who resonate similarly. My fulfillment and success in this tangible, physical world is often presented in the form of opportunity. Those who are unfulfilled, unhappy, and struggling in their relationships and careers are associating with like-minded, like-calibrating individuals! Change your frequency; and you change your experiences and your outcome and your opportunities!

WRIGHT

So why should any journey to success and fulfillment in life include inner child work?

GRAVES

In understanding the Pattern Imprint, we realize that our way of responding today is directly affected by what we saw modeled for us and particularly what we decided about what we saw. Those events in our past that served to shape us into the people we are today are based on our perception of what happened as well as a family pattern of responding in a particular way.

For example: My mother was unhappy most of the time. She viewed and focused on all the lack in her life instead of the many blessings she had. As a child I watched this day after day, week and after week, and year after year. This "predisposition" toward a glass half empty line of thinking became my norm as well. So events that took place and my perception of them were almost always negative and focused in the lack of the situation or event.

This, and her drug addiction, created a lot of pain in my childhood. I remember one event very vividly where it was summertime and I was bored with nothing to do. I approached my mom about calling and asking a friend to come and play. Her response is burned into my memory. She said, "Why can't you be normal and like every other child and find something to do to entertain yourself?" My decision about what she said to me was that I was not normal.

That event once had an extremely high charge to it. I questioned my worth in that moment and because of the judgment she put on me, my orientation became one of insecurity and self-loathing. It took place at about age eight and hooked into previous events of similar experiences where I came away questioning my worth. Also, as I moved forward in life, subsequent events hooked into these and solidified my belief of my unworthiness. After all, as children we look up to and believe what our parents tell us, and we also read, feel, and match very clearly, the energy they resonate as they speak to us. We do this in order to have a sense of belonging and acceptance, albeit dysfunctional.

Today I understand and realize that it was my mother's lack mentality and her own self-loathing that she was feeling—it had nothing to do with me personally. But as children we do not have the capacity to reason and make sense of what we hear from our parents and significant others and therefore what we hear and perceive becomes truth to us.

The modalities that I practice with my clients today have also facilitated my own healing and the charge no longer exists for me. I can remember it clearly but I now know the truth—I am worthy and have worth just because I am. And sometimes little girls get bored, which is completely normal!

WRIGHT

Would you explain the cycle of creation to us?

GRAVES

Words form Thoughts > Thoughts held with Emotion and Repetition form Beliefs > Beliefs hold a Frequency or Resonance and that equals Creation—Our Outcome and Experience in Life!

In my work with clients privately and in the group setting, I emphasize the need to begin "thinking about what you are thinking about." Become the observer of your own thoughts, knowing that what you focus on will grow.

WRIGHT

Hmm, that's interesting.

So what is meant by the term "the committee," and what is a "reframe"?

GRAVES

Each of us have well-meaning people in our lives who did the very best they knew how in responding to us and shaping us and our beliefs. These people on our "committees" are parents, siblings, extended family, teachers, friends, co-workers, and bosses. *The voices of these committee members come through and often limit us when we are trying to step out of our pattern and the old familiar and predictable responses. They are present and loudest when we are trying to make changes and to live a happier and more emotionally healthy and present life.* Often the intent of the committee member is that *their own value and worth is tied into your outcome.* That is, what you do and how you do it they think is a reflection on them, which is why they try so hard to influence us in the first place.

For example, I take my clients through an exercise that helps to bring out the committee thoughts. I ask them to write down the following, "Wake up the committee" statement as many times as it will fit on one side of an eight and a half by eleven-inch sheet of paper: *"All my negative thoughts and beliefs are now dissolved. I love and appreciate myself."* Then they are instructed to turn the paper over and listen to what the committee tells them, write it down, and then together we reframe those thoughts into what they want to hear and create in their life! Here are the Committee Reframe Steps:

1. Repeatedly write the statement that is designed to wake up the committee!
2. Listen to the thoughts that come up when making such a positive statement of you. Write those thoughts down!
3. Honor the negative feelings you have for the person responsible for the thoughts. It's in accepting that these negative thoughts exist within us that will facilitate the healing of them! Trying to ignore them or denying that you have them actually strengthens them! Often there is an inner child in pain and when you honor what you are feeling, you are honoring that child and healing him or her.

4. Find out which committee member is responsible for the thought. Keep in mind that there are non-physical beings in this realm that would thwart our efforts to change as well as people you know directly that have had a voice in your life. *When these non-physicals speak to you they sound as if they are you.* Just know that your higher self—the real you—does not speak negatively about you!

   Now that you know who that person is, write him or her a letter. This is a letter you will not mail, but write the letter you must. Really let them have it! Don't hold back. Express every negative thought as clearly as you can.

   For example, if there is an intense amount of anger and Dad is the responsible person, you would start like this: "Dear Dad, What makes me the angriest in this situation is—"

   The goal here is to release the anger that is present and ultimately arrive at a place of offering love and forgiveness to that person. Remember, forgiveness is a gift we give ourselves! But don't attempt to do that until the negative emotion or emotions are *completely* honored and dealt with!

5. Tip the Scale! This is the reframe step! This is where you rewrite the negative thought into two positive statements and write it as if you were experiencing it right now, in the present tense. You will want to re-read these positive reframes often!

One of my committee thoughts was, *"ugly to look at."* My reframe of that thought is, *"I am a beautiful daughter of a loving and powerful God."* I knew immediately that this came from my mother and it was her belief about herself, not me. Yet I took it on and made it about me because as a child, I didn't have the ability to understand that it was her self-loathing spilling out and that I was just hearing her self-talk. You can see that this is true for all of us. As children, we believe what we hear. We also have our own perceptions of what we see happening to us and around us and we don't have the reasoning ability and maturity to differentiate ourselves from our pattern imprint and the voices of the committee members, particularly our parents. Once these limiting beliefs are identified and cleared, using the Committee Reframe and various other techniques and modalities, awareness is clear and concise. Just as we once created a lot of what we didn't want to be experiencing in life, we can now create more and more of the outcomes we'd longed for. With focused attention on what we do want, without getting sidetracked with the voices of our committee, we begin to "Live Life Deliberately." We find ourselves having, being, and doing! More and more of our passion and purpose fill our days and we experience Joy!

WRIGHT

How does the acceptance of what is and taking personal responsibility facilitate permanent change and lasting success in my relationships and in my professional life?

GRAVES

For every force there is an equal or greater counter-force. So as I push against anything, I am met with equal or greater resistance. In acceptance and allowing "what is" to just be, my thoughts focus not on what is wrong about this situation but what is right or what has the potential to be right and more than likely will without my pushing against it! This also creates a much better "feeling" than resistance to something ever does. It's in that better feeling space where the point of attraction lies.

What we send out in thought, word, and deed (energy) comes back to us. Life and the people in our lives are a mirror for us. I can't fix another person's situation or control them and in attempting to do this, I am creating that force, which, in turn, creates that counter-force.

We are of greatest value to those we love when we model for them personal accountability and responsibility. Offering emotional health and well-being, because that is genuinely who we are, not something we are trying to be or we are trying to have them be, is also important. This creates and opens up the space for any other person we are in relationship with to do the same. This is just as true in a business context as it is in a personal one. As an Intuitive Life and Wellness Coach, as *I am* the person I choose to be and create the life I want and live it to the fullest, I automatically create that possibility for those around me—those in my personal life and those I coach professionally.

It's in honoring and listening to the committee voices and being aware of the reason they are there in the first place that allows them to finally be heard and silenced once and for all! Think of a small child who wants a cookie. Mom is on the phone having a conversation with someone and the child begins to tap incessantly on Mommy's arm to get her attention. Tap, Tap and more tapping, "Mommy, Mommy, Mommy—" It isn't until

Mommy turns to the child and acknowledges him or her that the attempts at attention-getting stops. *"What you deny you declare. What you declare you create. Acceptance of something places you in control of it. That which you deny you cannot control, for you have said it is not there. Therefore, what you deny controls you."*—Neal Donald Walsh

What I deny—that is what I attempt or try to ignore—like committee thoughts and input in my life, I am literally declaring. I am sending out that energy, whether I am conscious of it or not! It becomes my point of creation! So when I can ultimately look at what I am trying to ignore, own it and understand it, I know that it is one of the well-meaning committee members, often people who love me and were attempting to make themselves feel better *about themselves* in the advice or counsel they were giving me, that I now become a master over it, rather than a slave to it. Sometimes, too, our *committee members' own worth* is based on *our* performance in life.

Blaming, "Be-Lames" *us!* We stop progressing and moving forward when we blame another for our situation or circumstances. There is *power* in taking accountability and responsibility for our outcome and experiences in our life. When we learn that we have created our very situation based on what we think about (our opinion), what we are thinking about (our thoughts and the committee members' input that comes to mind), we can then actively and deliberately change our point of attraction and get more of what we truly want as experience and outcomes in our life.

WRIGHT

What is meant by the term "heart and mind alignment"?

GRAVES

Simply stated, this is when our left brain (mind) and our right brain (heart) are lined up and in agreement. I will sometimes refer to the left brain as the EGO or the part of us that attempts to Edge God Out (EGO). This is the logical, linear thinking side of each of us.

The heart represents that spirit part of us that has always existed and is eternal and unchanging. It is quite literally, love. This alignment occurs when we have listened to the left brain committee thoughts and understand them and therefore quieted them by not denying them. This alignment is a space of pure joy and pure potential to create *anything* we choose! This space is the goal of each of us. There is peace of mind and peace with the entire world around us in this alignment. There is quiet and calm and love only exists in this aligned space.

We've all experienced this at least some of the time. The goal is to live more and more in this space. It *feels good!* Don't we all want to feel good or feel God? That is the goal, whether acknowledged or understood, of each of the people who find their way to me and become my clients. It is my joy and privilege to assist people to this place of heart and mind alignment. It is my joy and privilege to now live here the majority of the time. Once upon a time I did not. The contrast is stark and real. I love life and living in this space and assisting others to do the same.

I want to make note here that this place and space of heart and mind alignment is our higher self, the soul/spirit part of us, awakening to the knowledge of who we really are, which I believe to be divine offspring of the literal Creator of the Universe. When we quiet that left brain and ego enough through the Committee Reframe process, we can truly connect with God. He is the author of *all* truth and is the great facilitator of true and lasting healing. I recognize and honor Him as my healer. I facilitate others to heal, but it is only through this alignment that healing takes place and is possible.

"There is no relationship of greater importance to achieve than the relationship between you, in your physical body, right here and now, and the *Soul/Source/God* from which you have come. *If* you tend to that relationship, first and foremost, you will *then, and only then*, have the stable footing to proceed into other relationships. Your relationship with your own *body;* your relationship with *money*; your relationship with your *parents*, *children*, *grandchildren*, the *people you work with*, your *government*, your *world will all fall swiftly and easily into alignment* once you tend to this fundamental, primary relationship *first"*

—*Abraham Hicks.*
(Emphasis added)

WRIGHT
Any other thoughts on this subject?

GRAVES

"The illiterate of the twenty-first century will not be those who cannot read and write, but those who cannot learn, unlearn and relearn."

Learning about our family patterns and traditions, then *unlearning* that pattern, and *relearning* a new and better way to respond in life, is the very purpose for our being here. We are incredibly powerful spiritual beings having an earthly experience, *not* the other way around! It is in knowing who we are and our power to change and overcome *any* situation and perceived obstacle, and moreover to *create* our deepest, dream of health, wealth, and happiness that is the motive of our Creator.

If any part of what I have presented here rings true to your soul, then heed that inner stirring. Change is possible, even probable. Life will continue to get your attention. The heat gets turned up incrementally until the pain of the problem outweighs the perceived pain of the solution. Don't wait to be torched and scorched! Start overcoming, and creating what you *do want* rather than what you don't! Live life deliberately, on Purpose!

WRIGHT

This has been a great conversation, Kandy. I appreciate all the time you've taken with me this afternoon to answer all these questions. It's been fascinating; I have learned a lot and I am sure that our readers will.

GRAVES

I appreciate the opportunity, David. Thank you very much.

WRIGHT

Today I have been talking with Kandy Graves. Kandy helps people to create lives of purpose and passion through assisting them to become aware of their thoughts and thought processes, patterns of behavior, and their response. She is a pattern-breaker and her purpose and passion in life is to assist others to find and create theirs. She is the owner and operator of As You Think You Are Coaching Center and is currently in high demand to facilitate others in private sessions as well as group sessions in her self-made Deliberate Living series of classes.

Kandy, thank you so much for being with us today on *ROADMAP to Success*.

GRAVES
   Thanks David.

About the Author

Kandy Graves loves assisting others to create lives of purpose and passion through assisting them to become aware of their thought processes, patterns of behavior, and response! Her experience really started at birth, being born to a drug addicted mother and an enabling father in the early 1960s in Southern California. These childhood experiences led her into her life's work of finding healing for her and showing others that life is a joyful adventure! All the pain people feel and live through is for their good. It's in facing the pain of their past that they find their greatest strengths and greatest lessons to aid in creating a life of purpose, passion, and success! Kandy is the mother of three sons and loves spending time with her husband of thirty-one years and her three grandchildren.

She is a pattern-breaker and her purpose and passion in life is to assist others to find and create theirs! She is the owner and operator of the AsYouThinkYouAre Coaching Center and is currently in high demand to facilitate others in private sessions as well as group sessions and her self-made "Deliberate Living" series of classes.

Are you ready for more of what you want in your relationships? Are you ready for a healthier body, prosperity, and abundance in all aspects of your life? The time is now! Join Kandy on the journey toward Transformation, Awareness, and Success!

Kandy Graves
AsYouThinkYouAre
2888 Marrcrest West
Provo, Utah 84604
801-221-1533
coachkandy@gmail.com
www.AsYouThinkYouAre.com

Chapter Thirteen

WELLNESS WITHIN

MARLENE GEORGE

DAVID WRIGHT (WRIGHT)

Today I'm speaking with Marlene George. Marlene began her career in the alternative health field in 1989. Certified in Therapeutic Touch™, Reiki Master, and CranioSacral therapy, Marlene includes personal consultations and transformational forms of therapy in her wellness practice. Her approach integrates emotional, physical, energetic, and psychological strategies to achieve her clients' goals. Author, lecturer, health and wellness expert and practitioner, Marlene's road map for success begins within.

Marlene, welcome to *ROADMAP to Success*.

Where was your departure point on your road map to success?

MARLENE GEORGE (GEORGE)

The date and place of my birth began my journey to my personal and professional success. As I wrote in Chapter Eight, "Success is Your Birthright," in my book, *Your Life is Now!*, your birthright guarantees the positive energy that blossoms with each new breath, provides the impetus to grow and expand into the world with creativity, originality, and unlimited potential for prosperity.

In response to requests from clients and students, I wrote my first book to share my personal journey to a happy successful life, knowing that what

I learned will benefit others. Since then, my experience validates my belief that success is everyone's birthright.

From the first breath we take, we are aware of the truth of that statement. Awareness of our entitlement does not tell us how to fulfill our individual birthright or how to define success and what success means to each of us. Following our road map will provide clues to our destination as soon as we accept the guarantee of success delivered with our birthright.

Everyone's journey begins before birth because each of us has a right to create the life we want and achieve the success we desire. If a newborn is healthy, safe, with his or her needs met, that baby is happy. If the baby could answer a question about success, for example "Do you feel successful?" what do you think the answer would be?

Unfortunately, as soon as children can verbalize their feelings, the destruction of their belief in their birthright begins. It takes great courage to master the basic human skills of functioning in the world—walking, language, producing, creating, and surviving. For many of us, the extended dependency of human infants on adult caretakers chips away at the awareness of success as a birthright. The longer it takes for maturity and ensuing independence increases the negative influence from the caretakers.

Unless the caretakers respect the concept of our entitlement to a successful life, the duration from dependence to independence lengthens the amount of exposure to their misconceptions about their birthright. Our caretakers are innocent of negative intentions when they lecture, counsel, and encourage using the child's head to achieve rather than dependence upon their heart. Unless they are enlightened to the importance of positive energy, they consider their duty is to pass on their misguided perceptions of reality.

WRIGHT

How do you reverse years of negative conditioning that affect your clients?

GEORGE

This is accomplished by returning their focus within to their authentic selves, by getting them out of their heads and into their hearts, and by restoring their *Wellness Within. This* provides them with the fuel to drive to their own personal brand of success. By the end of my chapter, the reader will know what *real* success looks like, sounds like, tastes like, smells like, and feels like. Once readers follow my directions and apply my driving techniques, success awaits their arrival at their destination.

When my clients come to me with their challenges—a health challenge, a business challenge, or a relationships challenge—I ask them, "Imagine waking up tomorrow morning after a great night's sleep. You feel well rested, refreshed, and energized. You can't wait to get into your day to continue to build on your dreams and your success. No matter what comes your way during the day, you know that you have the skills and the tools to move forward. At the end of the day, you feel good about yourself, your business, and your life." Of course, most of them say that's exactly how they'd like to feel. That's Point B, the destination at the end of our journey.

"Feel" is the universal word at the base of everyone's expression of success. So all of this is really about how we feel inside, it's not about the outside. That's the first, last, and only really important question/answer when discussing human potential, wellness, happiness, and especially success.

WRIGHT

So everyone's starting point, point A, which is our birthright, but our baggage hinders us?

GEORGE

The moment most of us arrived on the planet, we were perfect—ten fingers, check, ten toes, check, two legs, arms, hands, feet, eyes, ears, and one adorable nose. As we mature, "life" chips away at that perfection, if not externally, then most assuredly internally.

Regardless of the appearance of the vehicle we drive, it's the power of the engine beneath the hood that propels the journey. Many of my clients look great on the outside. The package looks perfect—they sound successful, they look successful, they have money, cars, houses, fame—they have it all, everything our culture defines as "success." So, why are they in my office, on my phone, or treatment table confessing their discomfort, emotional or physical pain?

"... but I don't feel successful."
"... but I feel like a fake."
"... but I don't feel authentic."

Please notice the "feel" word again. My book devotes an entire chapter to self-esteem and self-worth. Even though nobody likes to talk about this subject, and perhaps it's because it brings up their own issues. It doesn't take long to identify those "successful" people who do not feel comfortable in their skin. How we feel about ourselves on the inside affects every aspect of our lives on the outside. Our inside feelings about ourselves affect everything—our performance at work, ultimately our successes, our relationships, personal and professional, and even our body and our health.

My personal challenges prevented the success my birthright guaranteed. For example, my own self-esteem, self-worth issues held me back from pursuing the life I wanted to live. It wasn't a critical teacher, a society that didn't value persons of my background or gender, it wasn't the socio-economic class I was born into—it was me, myself, and I. Until I was willing to do what it took to feel better about me—study, read, listen, and learn—my comfort levels remained depressed, and therefore so was my life, even if it was only my perception.

As soon as I understood the concept of feeling good as the essential first step—my point of attack on the road to my success—one by one my clients validated these insights.

After several Reiki sessions in a course of her treatment, my client Laura commented that the quality of her day depended on her boss's mood. When she walked in the door, if he was in a good mood and stayed "up," then she had a good day.

"But, oh boy, when he feels bad, moody, he shares it with me," she sighed.

"So he hands you his baggage to carry, right?" I commented. "Must you pick them up?"

I could tell by the confusion tightening her face that it never occurred to her that his mood belonged to him, not her. Allowing someone else's negative feelings to determine how we feel is never part of a job description, marriage vows, or "how-to" parenting manuals.

Over time and treatment, Laura learned new strategies to cope with her boss's mood swings so that his energy no longer affected her performance, her day, or her feelings about either. She continues to see me occasionally for a "tune-up" because she realizes how important her internal state is to her life, personal as well as professional. She continues to attend my lectures and workshops, usually bringing a friend or two with her.

WRIGHT

We all have baggage; some is incidental, as in Laura's case. But her reaction to her boss's bad moods indicates she's carrying someone else's suitcase, right?

GEORGE

Our parents accompany us everywhere we go. They packed our suitcases every day they raised us. These bags were like a "tote bag," a southern term for those things guests take with them when they leave home. In our case, our parents' "gifts" go into our travel bags and we carry them into our offices, apartments, ranch houses, and vacation places long after we've left home to pursue our lives.

Parental influence in terms of what weighs us down continues throughout our lives, on our journey, until we become aware and sort out what belongs to them, and what belongs to us. As soon as we unpack their stuff, the load becomes much, much lighter.

When we come from a normal, "happy" home, our parents' baggage is not as noticeable as when we come from a dysfunctional family. Abuse, addiction, abandonment are clearly challenges for parents as well as for their children. Even though the disadvantages in an abusive home are obvious, and the effects can be obvious, the normal family's baggage can weigh us down as heavily without any *obvious* effects.

Paul, another client, had challenges that were more tangible—it was all about money. After a lecture I presented to his company's upper level executives, Paul requested a private appointment for the following week. An attractive, intelligent entrepreneur, Paul's success was a result of his hard work, persistence, and creativity. Even though his success followed his intention, once achieved he moved on rather than build on it. After every start-up exceeded his and his investor's expectations, he'd either sell the company or get bought out by his partners to move on and start all over again. This volatility disrupted his private financial life as well. His accountant fretted over the rollercoaster balance sheets on every one of Paul's bank and investment accounts.

His story began with his after school job in an Italian neighborhood restaurant to put himself through college. His father, homeless and addicted, would show up at his work place and beg for money from Paul. The first time, his boss tolerated the intrusion. Knowing it went to his addiction rather than his support, and anxious to get rid of him before his boss could see him, Paul gave him what cash he had, and then watched him stagger out the door. His father's interruptions could have cost him his job, and the memory brought back all the shame, fear, and confusion he had felt then.

Paul's slight smile did little to mask the confusion and pain behind those memories that continued to affect how he felt about himself, his work, and his place in the world. "Every time I score another big financial victory, I'm overwhelmed with shame and guilt, and can't wait to get rid of it." He looked down at his freshly manicured hands. I watched all the tension leave his body as he sank deeper into the overstuffed chair in my office.

"Are you saying you don't feel worthy of your accomplishments, achievements?"

His answer was a knowing smile of recognition and a deep sigh of relief. He sat up, loosened his tie securing his starched white shirt, and kicked off his Italian loafers. "When can I enjoy my, my—" I watched him struggle with verbalizing his success, until he finally got the words out, "my successes?"

"Now!" was my answer.

The power of the present cannot be underestimated. In my book, *Your Life is Now**, I put forth my Nine Principles for Joyous Living. I wrote that principle into an early chapter for so many valuable reasons. So, regardless of a person's appearance, in order to feel authentic we must return to the person we were born to be before the influences of others, our negative self-talk, and before we lose our way on our journey to fulfill our birthright —success!

WRIGHT

Does self-defeat stem from someone else's baggage—their negativity—or does our own negativity delay our arrival at our birthright's destination, success? (Point B)

GEORGE

The first step is sorting out the stuff in your luggage. Determine what's true and yours, and discard what belongs to someone else. Relationship issues are dealt with in Chapter Seven of *Your Life is Now!** Regardless of the issues between two people personally or professionally, when we are in a relationship we share the responsibility for it. Since the only person we can change is ourselves, that's where we start. Unpack our bags, and see what's left.

There are so many stories. So many of us betray our birthright by not feeling worthy of the wonderful power we were born with; by not acting on the confidence we had when we learned to walk, to talk, to learn; and by *fearing* those positive feelings that get things done for us

That's right—some of us *fear* our personal *success*! That fear, that negativity, can destroy the path, delay the arrival, or force us to detour from our destination: Success!

WRIGHT

So how do positive feelings promote personal and professional success?

GEORGE

Our choices are now, immediate, in the present.
Our life is now, immediate, in the present.
Our personal and professional success is in the present, too.

So, feeling well, positive, and happy day to day, minute to minute can be a product of our choices to feel the way we want to feel. That said, we can decide to feel happy regardless of our circumstance.

Let's not waste any more time giving our power away to others. Seize the moment, choose happy, then *be happy*! Soon, the positive energy on the inside will demonstrate itself on the outside, and bring things to us—things we want, or something *better*!

WRIGHT

Is that the only way to be successful?

GEORGE

What do you mean by "success"?
Is success our Dun & Bradstreet rating?
Is success our Profit and Loss Statement?
Is success our assets, awards, titles?

Regardless of the objective assessments or measurements of accumulated ownership we point to, how often we do fall asleep at night with a smile of gratitude or satisfaction on our faces? How many days do we awaken with anticipation rather than dread, with eagerness rather than reluctance to step out of our bed and get on with our day?

When you feel good about the last twenty-four hours, it carries over to feeling good about the next twenty-four hours, and that carry-over accumulates with each day as it increases the benefits to you personally and professionally.

One of my most popular presentations that never goes out of style is "Be Happy for the Holidays." When the Christmas season rolls around, my schedule fills with people who attended the past year's presentation and now want their friends and colleagues to hear the concepts they learned and benefitted from the year before. I've given this workshop/presentation to all kinds of groups from business clubs to corporations, service organizations, faculties, private clubs, and charities. Over the years, the principle remains the same—when you lock your office or home office door for the last time in the year and if you feel good about the passing year, you open yourself for more money, more opportunity, and more happiness in the upcoming year.

It became apparent to me that what works on an annual basis is equally effective on a daily basis. In fact, I apply this shortcut every day of my life.

30 Seconds to Success Daily Practice

We have great intentions to establish daily routines to accomplish our goals. There is an entire industry based on time management, another industry on paper and digital scheduling, coaches, counselors, lecturers, and trainers. We all know that we have lived our values, we have accomplished meaningful goals, and we did so with a smile of gratitude.

When my eyes open in the morning, I review my intentions, plans, and goals for the day. I envision myself accomplishing my responsibilities to myself and others with a smile on my face and happy thoughts surrounding every action I take. Once this practice becomes a habit, it takes less than fifteen seconds to set up your day—and increase its potential for success!

The last thing at night, I take another fifteen seconds to review what I did and what I didn't do. Regardless of how much I did, how little I didn't do, or the interruptions, distractions, change of schedule that occurred to disrupt my morning intentions, I choose to feel happy and grateful for the events of the day.

- 30 seconds a day.
- 15 seconds in the morning.
- 15 seconds at night.
- 24 hours of successful living!

WRIGHT

So, those thirty seconds daily are the shortcut to success? It's like cutting off the angle between where you are now and where you want to be in the future, right?

Point A

Point B

GEORGE

Shortcuts in the linear sense don't exist. I use that term to focus my clients and audiences on the central issue of success. If there was a shortcut in terms of time and distance, what would the value of achieving it be? Regardless of our definition of success, in order to feel good about our successes we need to just feel good, we need to believe that we deserve to have it, believing it is so important.

WRIGHT

You appear to have it all—a long-term, happy marriage and loving family relationships, a successful career and a growing prosperous business. You share your knowledge, experience, and insights with others who appreciate your point of view, your information and insights. I'm sure readers want to know, how do you accomplish all of this?

GEORGE

As I wrote my book, *Your Life is Now!**, it's all about energy. When we follow the Nine Principles of Joyous Living, we learn how to determine exactly what we want, then capture the feeling of already having it. As long as we feel good about what we want and what we're doing to get it, we are on the right track. Things we want, or better things, begin to appear in our lives.

It may sound like wishes, pipe dreams, or magical thinking, but this has been my experience and I have seen this happen with my clients. As soon as we believe in ourselves and that we deserve and are worthy of it, things start turning out better for us and success comes our way.

As I said in the beginning of the interview, I'm successful when, at the end of the day, I feel good about me and I feel good about my business.

To those of us who feel like failures because we feel we didn't do enough, whose standards are we measuring ourselves by? How much is enough? So, we procrastinated. Perhaps there was a good reason to delay action, perhaps not. I'm not saying we can sit on our couch and wave our magic wand and things come our way. No, we need to take some action, too. If a specific action did not get done, one of three possibilities is responsible:

1. It was not a real priority for us.
2. We feared the size of the task or the outcome.
3. It was in our best interest to not do it then.

All of the above reasons are justified for anyone who is an authentic adult, and therefore not the cause for bad feelings on our part. When we know honestly we did our best today, that's the goal—feel good and tomorrow we'll have a better day.

WRIGHT

Do you feel there is a direct route to success—a specific series of steps?

GEORGE

As soon as the seeker of success can identify specifically what he or she wants in order to feel successful, then opportunities present themselves along the way.

Identifying what makes us feel successful is a process, *not* a direct path from point A to point B on a map. There is a strategy to identify the goals that are right for you. Simply write them down, preferably with a pen or pencil, on plain or any kind of paper that appeals to you.

Pay attention to your feelings while doing this exercise. Do you feel good when you write them down? Do you feel positive about achieving them? Do you believe you can do it, have it, and most important, can you accept you are worthy of it?

When you feel good and positive about that specific goal and feeling worthy and deserving of it, then start living as if you already have it.

So set the goal. When you write it down feel good about what you are asking for. Then imagine you are already living that life and believe it's possible.

WRIGHT

Is it possible for the seeker to know he or she is on the right path? How?

GEORGE

When we feel good, we know we're on the right path. That doesn't mean we won't detour or change directions or even reverse directions for a time. Feeling good is so important to our success. It's just appreciation. It is such a simple tool to avoid getting bogged down in something that is not working out. Let's find something, one thing, in our situation that we can appreciate and then express our gratitude. Instead of worrying what's wrong or missing or challenging, and putting energy into thinking about it, talking about it, and focusing on it. That just grinds us down. Turn around and announce how good you feel about moving toward your goal, what you're requesting, and what you want.

When I'm feeling positive, I'm always moving toward my goal. When I feel negative, angry, jealous, frustrated, I'm actually pushing what I'm asking for away from me. Since I can choose to feel good, I have the power to shift from negativity to positive feelings to further my journey to success.

WRIGHT

Has your road map been a straight line or have there been a few bumps along the way?

GEORGE

Well, if you look at any road map, have you ever seen a highway, freeway, or a road that is a straight line from departure to arrival point? No, there are curves, detours, construction, toll booths, and areas of heavy traffic in the way.

How we choose to react really determines our progress.

The Chinese symbol for crisis and disaster is the same as for opportunity. So let's choose opportunity; let's welcome it, knowing it's good for us and we respond accordingly.

WRIGHT

This road map concerns one driver, one vehicle, and one destination. Were there any mentors, guides, or helpers along the way?

GEORGE

This takes me way, way back. My ninety-two-year-old mother was very much of a believer in things working out. I learned a lot from her. I learned to focus on the positive. When I immigrated to Canada with my husband and our ten-month-old son, we immigrated to a cold country. We came here with five hundred Canadian dollars in our pocket. But there was just something in my belly—that belief in my belly—that everything was going to turn out in our favor.

Through my journey I had many jobs. The first time I was fired, it was from a corporation and I felt horrible, but what I thought was a low point was really a big catalyst for turning my life around. My self-esteem plummeted, and I became a seminar junkie. I filled my shelves with self-help books and CDs.

All those positive people were writing all those positive things for people seeking solutions, hope, and yes, success. They were the beginning of my work, my journey. Accepting their messages, charting my course on my road map began with acceptance of their work and that it was possible to apply it to me.

After healing myself, I knew I wanted to heal others. I began with learning alternative modalities—Therapeutic Touch, Reiki, and CranialSacral Therapy. Once I accepted my feelings and made positive choices, the passage eased, then expanded, and finally accelerated to my current successful personal and professional life.

WRIGHT

Your bio describes you as a holistic healer, a term that used to be considered quackery, like chiropractic. However, both modalities have been validated in the face of the skepticism present at the beginning of your career. What was the fuel that kept you driving your alternative powered car?

GEORGE

My feelings, of course. As a student of alternative treatments, I felt the power behind the modalities that helped me so much when I started my journey. As I progressed in education, experience, and understanding, I saw how many others sought alternative treatments, too.

When I started my business in '89, I knew with absolute certainty that my services worked for my clients. I felt good providing the treatments, and they improved after receiving them. I joined a few networking groups to promote my business to expand my practice. At that time, many of the groups, especially business groups, were male dominated and focused on the bottom line. My point of view as a holistic healer shifted the subject to include the importance of emotions when looking at the numbers. That was a tough one for many in the membership, then. Now, after adding transformational workshops, lectures, tele-classes, and publications to my personal counseling practice, I've noticed many others doing the same work in their own unique way.

WRIGHT

Is your work resented by traditional medical practitioners?

GEORGE

Actually, no. In fact, I was invited to an international conference on Integrative Medicine a few years ago to present alternative healing methods and how they complement traditional medical practice. Doctors, nurses, researchers, and scientists consider us the "X" factor in their patients' improved health and well-being.

The term holistic refers to treating the "whole person" rather than just individual body parts. Historically, the family doctor did just that—he or she considered all the factors in a patient's life before recommending any treatment. With the technical and scientific increase in information, traditional medicine's approach had to divide into specific areas of concern. In narrowing the focus to the symptom area, many have lost sight of the rest of the person's body, environment, emotional, and psychological health.

WRIGHT

Was the worldwide acceptance of Integrative Medicine your destination—your Point B—on your road map to success?

GEORGE

Others' acceptance of what I do has nothing to do with my success. The answer to your question is a loud, *no!* Of course, the validation is pleasing, feels good, and probably helps those in need to explore all healing modalities when in pain emotionally, psychologically, physically, or spiritually. As all human beings differ from each other, there is no "one size fits all" treatment for whatever ails a person. That aspect of Integrative Medicine should increase the amount of healing throughout the world—the best of Eastern and Western treatments are included in the concept.

My Point B was much more personal and did not require anyone else's observation, approval, or applause. I knew when I got there because it felt so good to be there. I felt good about myself, my family, my friends, my business—my life!

WRIGHT

Since publication of your ground-breaking book, *Your Life is Now!**, what would you like to add to your insights on Chapter Eight, "Success is your birthright"?

GEORGE

Wellness Within—health in every aspect of a person's being, not just the physical, guarantees success on the outside, too. *Wellness Within* creates good feelings inside and out regardless of our activities. Performing our personal and professional responsibilities need not be a chore when we allow the *Wellness Within* to affect our feelings. We express those feelings in our behavior, reflect those feelings in our environment, and enhance our performance in everything we do.

What is the point of doing what we do if we don't enjoy it? If we feel good within, are happy, and behave as if we are successful, then, *we are successful*!

When we feel good about what we're doing on a day-to-day basis on our journey, that will speed up our arrival at our destination—success. My practice—whether it's personal one-on-one treatment, participating in an interactive group environment, or facilitating a workshop or presentation—always succeeds when I work with those internal emotions on the outside, then I take action.

Sometimes we need further training, sometimes we need to relocate, reassess, or simply refocus to get to where we want to be. When those actions feel good, then they are good for us and for everyone else around us.

When we came into the world, born at Point A, we were equipped to succeed, to fulfill our destiny, to follow the road map to our individual success—Point B. The difference in my approach, and that of others in my field, is that we can feel successful at every stop, with every step, and we can watch Point B meet us along our journey.

My happiness proves to me and my clients that this service benefits both of us in our real life situations. When I waken with health challenges, relationship challenges, and work challenges, which affect every aspect of personal and professional life, I'm guided to help my clients feel good on the inside so that what they show the world reflects their internal positive outlook.

My road map to success?
Success as Our Birthright (Point A)
Creates
Success at Our Destination (Point B).
Our mirror image: wellness inside/success outside.

WRIGHT

Today I have been talking with wellness expert and business professional, Marlene George. Marlene's approach integrates emotional, physical, energetic, and psychological strategies in her private and public healing sessions. Marlene is a transformational holistic practitioner, inspirational speaker, author, and life and wellness coach.

Marlene, thank you so much for being with us today on *ROADMAP to Success*.

About the Author

Marlene George entered the alternative health field to relieve emotional, psychological, and physical pain for her clients, students, and audiences. She is certified in Therapeutic Touch™, Reiki, and CranioSacral therapy. A registered Therapeutic Touch practitioner and a Reiki Master, Marlene offers treatments combining techniques with transformational therapies for her holistic approach to assist her clients achieve complete wellness. Marlene's wellness workshops, teleclasses, private counseling sessions, and holistic healing treatments help many overcome physical and emotional challenges. Marlene is an inspirational speaker and personal coach to corporate and private groups in Canada, the United States, and exotic locations such as Mexico and Africa. Marlene George has also authored books, articles, and CDs.

Marlene was awarded the Entrepreneurial & Business Reward by The South African Women for Women Organization in 1999 for her outstanding achievement of her home-based holistic wellness services.

Marlene George
34 Norfolk Avenue
Brampton
Ontario, Canada L6X 2B5
905-796-0101
mgeorge@marlenegeorge.com
www.marlenegeorge.com

Your Life is Now! (Trafford, 2004)
Marlene George presents her "Nine Principles of Joyous Living"
Contact Marlene for your copy.

Chapter Fourteen

CREATIVE VISUALIZATION:
DISCIPLINED THINKING FOR LEADERSHIP SUCCESS

LIZ DALLAS

DAVID WRIGHT (WRIGHT)

Today I'm talking with Liz Dallas. Liz is an innovator who shares her gifts through her role as an executive coach, speaker, inventor, founder, and co-owner of The Coaching Center of Vermont, Inc. The Center is built on a unique business model that supports constant innovation. A professionally trained coach drawing on twenty years of international business management experience in product development and sourcing manufacturing, Liz has coached hundreds of leaders to create success. She and her family are blessed to live in Vermont where they enjoy village living and efforts to create sustainable life for the sake of the planet and the evolution of humanity.

Liz, welcome to *ROADMAP to Success*.

LIZ DALLAS (DALLAS)

Thank you, David.

WRIGHT

In your twenty years of corporate management experience and more than ten years of coaching leaders, what have you found is the most helpful in leading people to create success?

DALLAS

Showing up as a visionary leader and inspiring people to create better bottom line results is by far the best way that leaders can create success. But not many leaders naturally use a visionary approach in their leadership. I innovate ways to help leaders be successful and today I'll share one of my proven models that helps leaders show up with a vision that inspires people to create better success than they even imagined. I call this the AB Visionary Model and it works by applying the principles of creative visualization to get clear, to communicate with impact, and to inspire people to action.

Not only do teams in the entire organization create better results in this way, the leaders who use the model enjoy more passion and satisfaction in the difference that they make in their leadership roles. Visionary leaders stay energized and inspired by the vision so that the people around them are sure to get the very best of them. In fact, leaders who adopt a visionary approach have historically moved more people from one place to another or transformed people from being one way to another way of being. It happens faster and with greater success than with any other leadership style.

WRIGHT

So don't we all have leadership styles that suit our unique personality and strengths?

DALLAS

Absolutely, and the most important aspects of personal development are to know your strengths, develop them, and put them to use. Developed strengths can be applied to make the best use of our strategic positions. But where the difference comes in is that there are positive leadership styles and there are negative leadership styles, depending on the situation and one's ability to properly execute them. In his book *Primal Leadership: Leading with Emotional Intelligence*, Daniel Goldman named six basic leadership styles: the Commander, Pacesetter, Democratic, Affiliative, Coach, and Visionary. Listing them from the least effective to the most effective, he actually ranks Commander and Pacesetter as negative styles. Democratic and Affiliative are neutral/positive, and the two most positive leadership styles are Coach and Visionary, with Visionary being an extremely high positive leadership style.

So my sense is why not get a bigger bang for your buck and develop those two most effective styles—the visionary and the coach? What if you used your leadership position to inspire and empower all day long? We can't remember to do a hundred different things but we can remember to do two and the AB Model is the perfect tool for helping leaders do just that—inspire and empower people to move from the pain of the situation now to create what is possible instead.

WRIGHT

So how do leaders become visionary? Isn't that something you are either born with or you aren't?

DALLAS

Well, some lucky few are born with the ability to be a visionary and even a few are born with the ability to lead from that vision. The truth is that visionary leadership is a skill. It can be learned, practiced, and mastered. This is the method of disciplined thinking. Before we do anything, on some level we picture ourselves doing it. For example, if I want to grab my glass of water, I'm going to actually picture my hand stretching out and grabbing hold of that glass of water. If I know what I'm going to do with that glass of water after I grab it; I'm actually going to bring it to my lips and drink from it. Visualizing what I going to do first, I am able to accomplish the task faster. The third part of creative visualization is that if I know the personal benefit for me, I'm actually going to quench my thirst by grabbing it and taking a drink; then I'm going to execute the action that much faster, with greater impact.

So by applying these basic principles:

- Visualizing an action,
- Knowing what we're going to do after the action,

- Being in touch with the personal benefit, we can create a better leadership model. It is going to allow us to do the same thing on a much more complex level by capturing the essence of creative visualization in our everyday lives.

To help you get a sense of how this might apply to a business setting or to a leadership setting, let's draw the A to B Model so that you can have a visual of how to apply these principles. I'll invite you to take out a piece of paper and turn it horizontally. On the left-hand side of the paper, put a capital A in the upper left corner. On the right-hand side, put a capital B in the upper right corner. Then draw an arrow from A to B, but draw it so that it goes three quarters of the way across the page, leaving a space between the tip of your arrow and the B. Put a question mark right in the space between the tip of the arrow and B, because you're not sure how that arrow is going to actually reach B. Then above A, I want you to draw a thought bubble and in that bubble, draw the same capital letter B, just as you did on the right-hand side of your page.

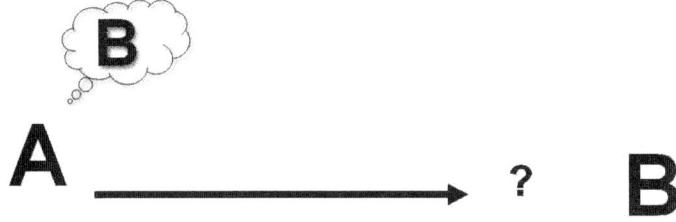

Visionary Leader AB Model

Liz Dallas, Coaching Center of Vermont, Inc.

Visionary leaders have only three jobs to do when they are "in the money." By "in the money," I mean they're doing something no one else in the organization can do. Those three "jobs" are to:

1. Create a vision—name it and articulate it for themselves,
2. Inspire people by communicating that vision a million different ways to a million different people
3. Engage and empower people to use their talents, strengths, and gifts to close that gap between A and B so that the vision is manifested by those they lead.

"A" is where people are standing now. It represents all the things we know are true about this very moment. It's the honest ugly truth, the assets, and the things we can celebrate now. The idea is to be able to slice that pie in a million different ways. You want to see "A" from your perspective, from the company's perspective, from the leader's perspective, from the perspective of people on the front line, and from your customers' perspective. Then you want to use the information you know about "A" and bring it right over to "B" where you name what you want instead.

Again, you're going to list the possibilities. What does success look like? What is the essence of living in that space when those needs are met, when that pain no longer exists as if it never existed to begin with? What you'll come up with is a list of qualities of being in the place that describes for you a place worth getting to. It may not be probable, but it will be possible. The idea is to make sure that if you waved a magic wand, what you get is worth creating.

WRIGHT

So what if a leader is detailed-oriented versus big picture? For instance many CFOs and COOs are highly effective in their roles because they're systematic in their thinking and in analysis of details. How can they lead with their strengths and still be effective at inspiring people to create better bottom line results?

DALLAS

Well, this is a good point because your CFOs and your COOs are the people who can make or break a business at any moment. It's that gift of being able to hone in on the details that have been so important to an organization up to that point; without that level of detail, this model isn't going to work.

This is not about people who can just dream big. This exercise is about the discipline of actually getting into the very specific details necessary to making where you are now ("A") come alive so that people will be engaged in their gut. They're going to feel where they are now, and it's going to likely make them uncomfortable.

Those CFOs or COOs—people who have been detail-focused in their roles—are going to have an edge because they're going to actually know the details that matter most, and they can just list those details one right after the other. They can then use those same details to describe what success looks like. One might have a big picture vision, like JFK's and put a man on the moon, but it's the details that inform people about what life will actually be like once it happens. The key to naming "B" is to really know the little details that best inform you about both "A" and "B." To further help, I ask my clients to consult their senses: what are you going to see, hear, feel, taste, and touch? I think detail-oriented people have an essential role to play in laying out what the vision looks like.

WRIGHT

So isn't visioning the same as setting the strategic direction and goal-setting, and if not, how is it different?

DALLAS

Let's go back to the AB Model and examine the arrow. This is why I had the arrow only go about three quarters of the way over toward "B," because in goal-setting, goals live at the tip of the arrow. If you think about any goal or strategy, you can probably imagine how you might get to that goal or how you might achieve it. If you can't begin to imagine it, you can probably tap into the knowledge and/or the collective imaginations of the people on your team. But somehow you can begin to figure out how to get there.

Visions are bigger than what we know how to do. You've got to push the vision piece out beyond that arrow, and you've got to be able to leave that gap of the unknown, because it's in that space of the unknown where the energy starts to build.

A visionary leader is paying attention to people's energy. You want to be able to push something far out beyond what you know, what you can predict, what you can calculate with your thinking mind into the space where you engage someone's emotional energy and inspire them, pull them to something that is better, something that still has that mystical quality to it, that you have, no idea how you're going to get there but you know when you do it will be worth it.

WRIGHT

Will you give me some examples of how this has worked with a client of yours?

DALLAS

My clients use this AB Model to be successful in leading efforts as big and as far-reaching as transformational change in their organizations. It's used in the important work of developing high performers and high performing teams and also applied to ensure wildly productive meetings and planning sessions.

Some of my clients have found the most satisfying success applying it to essential matters such as their personal preparation in making critical life decisions. I have clients take this model and put it on the wall of their office or they start meetings by drawing it out on the white board. They keep a separate file on their desktop that allows them to add to, define, and refine, honing their language so they can be more effective in communicating with it. They're constantly adding to and tweaking "A" and "B" of the Model, and it's a powerful tool that helps leaders stay connected to their commitment and intention to create success for the organization.

WRIGHT

What difference has this made for your clients and their companies?

DALLAS

The list of benefits is long and deep. Companies enjoy better bottom line results for innovation, for exceptional quality, better productivity, and greater efficiencies. They've captured new markets and they strengthen their brand by getting clearer about where they are now and where they'd like to be. They've created sales revenues beyond their expectations, and then my clients personally have been able to enjoy developing first rate teams, breaking through the glass ceiling from director to VP to the C-Level positions and they found more meaning and fulfillment in the work that they do and the home life that they live.

WRIGHT

So what do you think keeps more good leaders from figuring this out?

DALLAS

You know good leaders didn't get there by accident. Most of them have a long list of achievements and a long track record of success; but in school and in our experience we're taught to deliver results. A lot of our expertise lies around problem-solving, strategy, fixing things, etc. When you're leading with vision, strategy actually gets in the way of people's ability to inspire and be inspired.

Think about when you're trying to get buy-in from people—the place they're going to disagree with you most is in strategy. So what a visionary does is this: they're only going to draw attention to "A" (where you are now) and "B" (what's possible instead), two places that most people can agree on. People's opinions come together when describing the current situation and they can agree on where we'll be when we're finished and what success looks like. If you can connect to those two places and then go to the strategy, then people are going to be on the same page as they create success.

But I find that more good leaders often miss this opportunity because they can't let go of that strategy. Anxious for results, many leaders rush strategic, even tactical solutions. It's difficult to take the risk of leaving what has historically worked.

WRIGHT

So what would you recommend as a first step toward being an inspirational and empowering leader?

DALLAS

To start applying this method, I suggest people begin by drawing the AB Model diagram on a piece of paper and apply it to their own situation. Choose a simple and current challenge and begin to discipline your thinking so some things you know are "A" and some things are "B." In the center, I've created a little strategy "parking lot" as a placeholder for strategic problem-solving ideas. A word of caution: as you begin to name "A," you are likely to start naming those things with language that describes the "absence of" or names of those things that are missing versus what is actually happening.

For example, you might reference a lack of communication or a lack in teamwork, when really those things are suggested solutions for the issues at hand. In the case of communication issues, you might actually have confusion, frustration, and duplicated effort. In the case of teamwork issues, you might actually have competition for resources, isolated workers, or one person carrying the bulk of the workload. Do this wordsmith exercise using language to describe where you are and then name where you want to be. Do you want to be in a place where work is effortless, efficient, and highly productive? Do you want employees who are passionate, collaborative, and inventive? Perhaps "B" is a place where customer happiness is evident in unsolicited referrals of new customers, momentum in brand strength, or customer service reps asking for extra projects because the warranty call center is slow with work to do?

You want to be able to thoroughly understand your situation. Discipline your thinking so that in meetings you can clearly identify when people are talking about strategy and be reminded to let go and be flexible on strategy but fixed on the most important part of the situation—the pain point of "A" and the place of success at "B." Creating success with this visualization technique first starts with honing your ability to discipline your thinking according to the AB Model and then play with it.

WRIGHT

Let's assume Larry is the owner of a company. Larry has been really good at what he has done for years and he has opened up his own company. The company begins growing and Larry sees very quickly that he is going to have to start hiring more people. Business is good but Larry is not very inspirational—he's not the kind of person who can hold pep rallies or inspire people. What does Larry do?

DALLAS

A lot of owners do feel that way—not many people like to stand on that stage. The same principles apply because you're going to be able to get a bigger bang for your buck when you can anchor what is happening in your organization in these two places: "A" and "B." This is a tool for getting back on track and getting reconnected with why owners got into the business in the first place and worked so hard to grow to this point of opportunity.

In many ways, people don't create these big things for no reason. They create things because it helps them connect with what's most meaningful and there they will find their inspiration. This is the tool that can be used to communicate to people who deliver those speeches, for people who grab others in the hallway and connect with them personally. This is a tool where one of the million different ways you might speak to people is through the other people in your organization!

WRIGHT

Very interesting. Well, what a great conversation. I've really enjoyed talking with you. I've learned a lot here today and I'm sure that our readers will. I really appreciate the time you have given me in answering all these questions. I think this is going to be a good chapter for our book.

DALLAS

Good it's been my pleasure and I'm looking forward to seeing the book in print.

WRIGHT

Today I have been talking with Liz Dallas, executive coach, speaker, inventor, and founder and co-owner of The Coaching Center of Vermont Inc. A professionally trained coach drawing on twenty years of international business management experience, she has coached hundreds of leaders to create success.

Liz, thank you so much for being with us today on *ROADMAP to Success*.

DALLAS

It's been my pleasure, David.

About the Author

Liz Dallas is an innovator who shares her gift through her role as an executive coach, speaker, inventor, and founder/co-owner of the Coaching Center of Vermont, Inc., which is built on a unique business model that supports constant innovation. A professionally trained coach drawing on twenty years of international business management experience in product development and sourcing manufacturing, she has coached hundreds of leaders to create success.

Liz and her family are blessed to live in Vermont where they enjoy village living and efforts to create sustainable life for the sake of the planet and the evolution of humanity.

Liz Dallas

Coaching Center of Vermont, Inc.
Champlain Mill, 20 Winooski Falls Way
Winooski, VT 05404
802-654-8787
lizd@coachingcenterofvt.com
www.coachingcenterofvt.com

Chapter Fifteen

SELF-ACTIVATE AND CREATE TRANSFORMATION

JENNIFER KERN COLLINS

DAVID WRIGHT (WRIGHT)

Today I'm talking with Jennifer Kern Collins. Jennifer has a Master of Science in Psychology and is a Certified Professional Co-active Coach, trained by CTI, the premiere coaching institute in the world. Her coaching addresses all facets of life including success in career, relationships, and personal development, while enhancing clarity on direction, goals, and life purpose. She partners with her clients on their individual journeys and urges them to live their fullest, richest lives. She has experience in tobacco cessation at the Mayo Clinic Nicotine Dependence Center and she currently coaches for Health and Wellness at the Hennepin County Government Center in Minneapolis, Minnesota. Jennifer is a member of the Minnesota Coach's Association and a Professional Certified Coach with the International Coach Federation. Furthermore, she owns a private coaching business called Intrinsic SOULutions.

Jennifer, welcome to *ROADMAP to Success*.

JENNIFER KERN COLLINS (COLLINS)

Thank you, David.

WRIGHT

So what is your definition of success?

COLLINS

My definition of success is actually characterized by several different elements. First and foremost is living in alignment with one's spirit, which for me has to do with living a life of purpose, continuously seeking self-improvement, and being responsive to the present moment. Success is living with an absence of fear and doubt, so we're able to live by choice instead of being driven by worries. For me, an essential part of my spirit flourishing is living in a healthy body that lets me engage fully in life. I think it's also important to live with an outward authenticity and transparency in order to create fulfilling, honest relationships. Having been raised as a first-class appeaser and wild perfectionist, this is a tricky one for me. I am constantly stretching myself to go new places in all areas of my life. Anything I offer my clients, I am practicing myself in one form or another.

WRIGHT

So how have you created success in your own life?

COLLINS

Well, since I started waking up to myself and to my life, somewhere in 2007, I've become very deliberate about applying to my own life techniques that are universal and can be used by anyone. Becoming conscious about how I feed my mind was a big first step. I used to watch television every night, starting with the early evening sitcoms, moving into the dramas, ending with the late-late shows, and somewhere in there was the news.

I realized at one point how emotionally wrapped up I became in the fiction before me. It evoked an emotional rollercoaster on a daily basis, complete with waves of laughing and crying, based on the show I was watching. In the meantime, I was largely disconnected from myself and when I *was* with me, I was creating my own inner dramas.

With new learning about how our thoughts and emotions create our world, I purposefully cut out all forms of media that were not an expression of what I would want to create in my own life (I actually did a full television purge for about a year.) Now, when I select the music I listen to I make sure it has "healthy" lyrics. I listen to a lot of inspirational lectures, and I almost always begin my days in silence. What I've learned is that in the absence of the electronic barrage, there is a peacefulness that is much more enriching. It fuels my day in a way that has me more present to myself and to others.

Another process I've engaged to create success in my life is getting clear on what I want, creating the images in my mind and the feelings in my heart, and then somehow externalizing them.

In 2009, I was in a rollercoaster relationship, stuck in a job I hated, sure that I had no skills and nothing to offer the world, and convinced that I needed a(nother) man to rescue me. This was a chronic condition that was sucking the life out of me. One winter night I finally decided, *"enough!"* I walked into the dinky little bathroom of my crummy apartment, looked myself in the eye, and declared to myself aloud, "Jennifer, I love you, I accept you, and I will *always* take care of you." I was trembling and crying and fell to my knees, overwhelmed by that profound acknowledgment. Little did I know, from that moment my life would be different. Something in that willingness to inhabit a conscious love of and devotion to myself lit a fire inside me.

I immediately sat down and got very clear and specific about what I wanted in a new job. I wrote it out in detail, including everything from the kind of boss and coworkers I wanted, to the actual work, salary, and environment. (I even requested an office with windows, which would be an upgrade from the Cubeville I was languishing in.) I shared my intention with a close friend who responded, "You think you can really get all that?" I shrugged my not-knowing, and internally stayed with the hope.

Within two weeks I found a job posting that fit my skill set, and I applied immediately. To cut to the chase, I got an interview within a week and an offer twenty-four hours after that. It took another two weeks to negotiate a salary I was satisfied with, to which people exclaimed, "In *this* economy!" And within a few months of starting, I even got my corner office with floor-to-ceiling windows.

I eventually ended the rollercoaster relationship to make space for what I really wanted to have in my romantic life. The same process applied. I visualized the kind of man I wanted to be with, and how our relationship would feel. I wrote out all the qualities that were important to me, and I created a vision board to support my internal creation. Again, within a matter of weeks, I met the man who is now my husband. And he's even better than my dream!

All this, David, is to illustrate the power of intention, willingness to act and take risks, and the transformational force of self-love.

Other methods I use to create success in my own life include continued education through reading, lectures, and attending workshops and retreats. I also work with a coach myself and set goals to continue forward action in my business, my relationships, my physicality, and my self-connection.

If we want to move forward in life, we have to take the opportunities that present themselves to us. We have to be willing to take responsibility for what we want to be different in our lives and not just give in to the circumstances. We have to be willing to boldly follow the guidance we are given and trust that we will be safe, even when we stumble. And sometimes we need a partner in that journey. That's what coaching is about.

WRIGHT

Your company is Intrinsic SOULutions, spelled SOUL, what is that about?

COLLINS

At Intrinsic SOULutions, the core belief is that each individual holds his or her own answers within. Most people try to solve their internal problems by seeking external changes. They're looking for ways to make their circumstances different to make them feel happy or more fulfilled, such as losing weight, changing jobs, getting married, getting divorced, having children, and so on. It's not to say these conditions should or should not change, but we need to be clear that an external change alone will not bring us the balanced life we seek. Since our outer experiences are a reflection of our inner world, changing our circumstances without self-awareness or personal exploration will only lead us to recreate the same problems and conditions we just left.

In actuality, happiness can only emerge from within, and true fulfillment can only occur when we are in touch with our soul and acting on the purpose it wants to live out. I like the analogy that if you lose something inside a dark house where the power is out, it doesn't make any sense to go outside the house to look for it just because the street lamp is on.

Intrinsic SOULutions is really about finding, or maybe better put, turning on that inner light in order to get more deeply in touch with your soul, your true essence, and start creating greater fulfillment and personal happiness in relationships, career, health, and any other area of life. In a sense, it's making your own inner wisdom conscious and user-friendly.

WRIGHT

You have extensive experience with coaching for health and wellness, as well as tobacco addiction. How do you motivate people to change?

COLLINS

Well, motivation to me is an interesting concept. What I have found in working with people is that the term "motivation" is used very negatively. I frequently hear people say, "I want to get motivated. I have to get motivated!" When I ask what motivates them, it usually has to do with pushing away from something—"I don't want to get diabetes," "I don't want to lose my relationships," "I don't want to gain weight," "I don't want lung cancer," "I don't want—" whatever it is. Those certainly are very valid issues that can create importance for making changes, but what I find is that people actually get into action more easily through *inspiration* as compared to motivation. So when I work with clients, my target is not motivating them to change, but having them get inspired to create new results in their life.

Part of that comes through developing a vision and knowing how you are linked to that vision. What is it that you really want? What makes it important? And if you got it, what would you have? What would life really be like? Painting that picture and getting inspired to move into that vision are more powerful than simply "getting motivated." It's a positive pull toward something better rather than negatively pushing away from something undesirable.

WRIGHT

So what do you find gets in the way of making progress toward desired change?

COLLINS

Well, there are a number things. For one, I find that some of the inertia around change is simply rooted in conditioning. We are used to our habits and the way we've always done things. We don't want to make the effort to find something new when nothing's broken. Or sometimes we know we *want* to do something differently, but we don't know where to start. We may not know what the possibilities are for altering our daily choices in order to get new results. I think that the lack of a clear vision can interfere with making progress. How do you know what you're working toward if you don't know where you want to go? Without a vision, we cannot know what daily thought and behavior changes we need to implement to get where we really want to be.

Another thing that interferes with progress is fighting internal signals. Many people get into the habit of overriding their biofeedback. What I mean by that is when the body gets a signal that it needs something, people ignore it and continue a behavior that is not getting that need met. An example would be eating behaviors that do not honor hunger levels. People ignore biofeedback, eating past full, simply because there is still food on their plate. They eat out of boredom or the desire for distraction; they eat out of loneliness or the need for self-soothing, regardless of whether the body actually needs fuel. People also ignore their tired meter, staying awake too late watching television, or surfing the Internet. They're not listening to their body's signal of the need for sleep.

Ignoring biofeedback and not honoring the body is something that can interfere with progress in any area of life that you want to have changes, particularly physically, but also including changes in creativity, work performance, or depth of connection in relationships.

How we take care of our physical body is a reflection of how we value ourselves. Our self-honoring on this plane will affect every area of our lives. In fact, I often find that the inspiration for people to make changes in their nutrition, exercise, and sleep habits comes from a desire to improve self-confidence or self-esteem rather than the compulsion to lose weight.

A lack of insight into what drives current behavior also gets in the way of making progress toward change. It's not uncommon for people to just act without understanding what their actual need is. I'll give an example: I was working with a client who was taking action steps for weight loss and she was doing very well. Following a death in the family, she explained to me that that the grief caused her to indulge in donuts. What I highlighted for her is that the donuts weren't actually the indulgence—the indulgence was in avoidance and instant gratification. It was a means of self-soothing. The donuts were simply the vehicle for instant pleasure and creating distraction from the pain.

When we can identify what our needs are (such as soothing pain), we can consciously choose how to meet them without defaulting into unhealthy eating behavior, distraction as avoidance, seeking instant gratification (smoking will do this), and so on.

In our society, we are seduced by distraction, which actually becomes the modus operandi for a lot of people. We make ourselves very busy being focused on following diet plans, checking our Facebook accounts, getting a new date, having a snack, searching for a different job, Googling the latest book to solve the problem, or finding a new whatever-else-might-be-the-answer. We're continuously seeking a different condition or more information, but it actually keeps us distracted from developing ourselves in areas that would really produce change. If we were to go within ourselves and practice what I call "self-activation," we could break through barriers and make progress like nobody's business.

Finally, limiting beliefs are actually one of the top things that interfere with making positive changes.

WRIGHT

So what exactly are limiting beliefs?

COLLINS

Beliefs in general are thoughts you think repeatedly that you hold to be of truth. A belief is a deep-seated opinion that informs your emotional responses, your actions, your choices. It's almost like an internal declaration that shapes your life. So a *limiting* belief, then, is a belief that keeps you from achieving your goals or creating the results you want.

WRIGHT

How can our readers start to change what they believe in order to support getting what they want in life, especially when the world around them is the same way it's always been?

COLLINS

That's a really great question, David. What you are highlighting here is that in order to get new results, you have to create new beliefs. We actually can't wait for our circumstances to change. We need to take charge. A different experience of life emerges from *internal* change, since we'll always act in a way that is consistent with our self-image and our world-view.

The process for creating new beliefs has several key elements. The first thing is finding the limiting belief—what is getting in the way of the actions that will get you what you want? One way to identify your limiting beliefs is to look for where you tell yourself you *can't* and where you tell yourself you *should*. The *can't's* and the *should's* point you to a belief you hold that something is not possible or that you are bad or wrong for being a certain way. Neither of these attitudes will lead to new opportunities or experiences.

Another place to look for limiting beliefs is in thought distortion such as negative self-talk, judgment and criticism, catastrophizing, global negativity, etc. Those are things that would shine a light on a limiting belief about yourself or how you see yourself as a victim of your circumstances. Some of the most commonly held limiting beliefs come from a condition I call "not-enoughism." We think to ourselves, "I'm not good enough, smart enough, thin enough, big enough, young enough, old enough, rich enough, disciplined enough, educated enough," and so on. These are simply thoughts we *choose* to believe. Gaining awareness of them is step one.

The next thing to look for is the evidence of that belief being bullshit because every limiting belief is a *lie*. One place to look for evidence is in past exceptions, meaning a time in your life when this belief was not acted upon and the opposite was true instead. For example, a belief of "I can't lose weight" or "I can't quit smoking" is proven wrong when I reflect on a time when I did lose ten pounds or I was smoke-free. So I now know that belief is false. It may be relevant to explore what was happening during the time when it wasn't true and how my choices or routines differed from what they are now. Or, since life never goes backward, the more potent thing could be to simply acknowledge the lie in the limiting belief and look forward to what's possible when you come from a place of believing "I can."

In order to start consciously creating new beliefs, consider your desired results. What would you have to believe in order to get them? This is the place where you clarify your vision and deliberately write the internal dialogue you need to achieve it. This new script may take on the form of affirmations to reprogram the mind. However, there is another step that is essential to this process and that is granting permission while engaging self-love. We are so conditioned to keep ourselves small (usually to manage other people's egos and insecurities) that we actually need to grant ourselves *permission* to be that person who lives into our greater vision. We need to make it acceptable for ourselves to be physically fit and attractive or to be financially successful or to be happy in a relationship.

Engaging self-love is a way of getting in touch with your inner worthiness to allow the new empowering beliefs to take root in the subconscious. Life is going to look different as a result of your new beliefs. In order to really solidify them, the last piece is creating action steps by setting specific, measurable, and exciting goals along with implementing a means of accountability. (Working with a coach is great for this!)

WRIGHT

What is your view on life changes in general? Where do people get hung up?

COLLINS

I think life change is something that's really personal. The more I work with clients, the more I believe they know what's best for themselves. The process of coaching helps excavate those solutions, create clear actions, have a deeper, more accessible understanding of values and vision, and then lock in the learning that will solidify the changes. I use the word "change" since it is familiar, but I find it is a loaded term. I sometimes reframe for clients that change is simply a redirection of energy and resources.

That being said, effective change comes down to knowing what's most important to you, committing to it, and then adopting habits to support how you really want to live. New habits or routines are essential to long-term success. For example, we all know that "diets" are temporary—after you're done you can go back to the old ways, right? Well, sure, if you want to get the same old results. So creating new habits is the key to lifestyle change.

What people get hung up on are these myths—the Myth of the Wagon and the Myth of Willpower. I hear it all the time, "I'm on the wagon. I'm off the wagon." Sorry, folks, there is *no* wagon. The wagon implies that a change is temporary. When you are committed to a lifestyle that gives you the result you want, there is never an off or on; there is simply a way of living.

I have a girlfriend and colleague who is very fit. She is a runner and she eats healthy foods in comfortable portion sizes. One day, while she was eating a big chocolate bar, I asked her if that indulgence made her think she was "off the wagon." Her response was no, and that's because she didn't consider her overall healthy habits to be temporary. Chocolate is something she enjoys in moderation and it does not overrun or interfere with the general lifestyle that keeps her healthy in the long run.

Thinking or speaking of lifestyle choices in terms of being on or off the wagon is a surefire sign that there isn't actually a commitment to, or embodiment of, the lifestyle you're saying you really want that will get the physical, mental, emotional, or spiritual results you truly desire.

There is something else that I call the Myth of Willpower. David, do you brush your teeth every day?

WRIGHT

Every day, yes, of course.

COLLINS

And does it take a huge act of willpower to brush your teeth?

WRIGHT

Not really.

COLLINS

Not really, because it's a habit—it's something you do every day. You don't have to think about it, so it's not a struggle. It's automatic. This is the kind of relationship you want to create with whatever behavior corresponds with your desired outcomes, be it fitness level, financial saving or spending, improving relationships, being on time, etc.

When you know what's most important to you, when new choices honor your deepest values, and when you're committed to a vision, the action steps flow more naturally. It's not a struggle.

I had a forty-something client come into my office with concerns about her stress level. She described herself as being "type-A" and obsessive about getting her work done before play. With the best of intentions, she would get home from her job and brush past her family to "get her chores done so she would have time with her children and husband." This habit created stress for her and sent her family the message that "getting stuff done" was more important to her then they were.

In realizing that her routine was not honoring what was *most* important to her, my client changed her habit to spending time with her children *first* when arriving home, before anything else. She commented to me in a subsequent session that she had been concerned about her eight-year-old growing into a depressed adult. Since she changed her routine to make time with her children more important that her checklist, she's noticed a turnaround in her eight-year-old's behavior, so much so that she no longer has this worry.

This new routine was difficult for my client initially, but using an affirmation and focusing on her values have yielded results that reinforce her new habit, so it's no longer a struggle for her.

When you start to establish new habits and routines, instead of "summoning willpower," rely on being connected with your values and from there be deliberate about your choices and intentional in your actions. Willpower is not essential, but consciousness is. Be awake to your every-moment decision, and let your new choices evolve into habits.

Finally, I have to mention that failure is also a myth. It's another thing that people get hung up on. Failure is simply the lack of reaching a desired result. Nothing more. But we make such drama over it. In the avoidance or fear of failure, people miss out on a rich place of learning. If something doesn't work, you then know what *not* to do next time. You can look at what you've done and see what has to be different. Then you start asking the questions: What else do I need for support? What other resources do I need? What's another approach I could try? What's working and what's not? So if you miss the mark, don't make yourself "bad" over it. Reframe "failure" to be a new opportunity and a process of honing in that will lead you to your greatest success.

WRIGHT

So how does health and wellness relate to success in business?

COLLINS

What's most obvious is that we rely on our bodies for our ability to focus, to be productive, to engage with others, and more. So it's really important to have the mental, emotional, and physical energy that is necessary to do that.

We know a lot of people who have been seduced into the culture of having to function continuously at full throttle and produce at high levels. That can only last so long, however. We need time to replenish that energy intermittently in order to function at highest capacity.

That means knowing what foods you need to eat, at what time of day, and in what quantity, and knowing when you need to exercise or take rest. You might be a person who is not hungry until lunchtime and can work through those hours with no problem. Others might need a mid-morning break or snack to keep their energy level high and be most efficient.

I personally tend to eat frequently throughout the day, about every three to four hours, with each "meal" being about three to five hundred calories. That is the amount that's most comfortable in my body that my system can use efficiently. When I'm in the office, I use my lunch break to exercise; I either run, walk, or go to the gym. Exercise is another way to re-energize. Every once in a while, however, if I recognize that I'm particularly tired I use my lunchtime to either nap or just lay quietly. It's another way I honor my body that makes me more effective in my work.

Pay attention to when are you most productive—is it early in the morning or is it late at night? Whenever possible, structure your work around those times. For people who deal with chronic conditions, such as a bad back, neck pain, or any other number of conditions, physically moving the body at regular intervals is essential. As a girlfriend of mine taught me, "motion is lotion." Connect with yourself and start creating more habits to meet your needs on that physical level in order to respond to the external demands. As a business owner or manager, give your employees the flexibility to take care of their needs based on *them*, not based on you or the company culture or "how we've always done it." I would bet their level of productivity will go up and they will be more satisfied in their work. A great resource for more on this is Tony Schwartz's Energy Project, which you can find online.

Another way using the body can enhance business success is by building self-efficacy and self-trust. The body is one of the only areas in life where we have almost complete dominion. We are fully at choice with how we feed, exercise, clothe, and rest the body; we choose how to direct our physical energy. So with this we can deliberately set physical goals that, once achieved, increase our self-reliance and confidence.

That leads to what I call the Confidence Overflow Effect. This is when success in one area of life enhances confidence in another area.

I had lower back surgery in 2003, after which I told myself I would never run, rollerblade, ice skate, or learn to ski. In 2009, I began working with a new company that promoted departments forming teams to take part of a series of Twin Cities races. I decided to sign up to get to know my coworkers better, with the intention of walking the 5K course. The race day came and I was the only one there from my department. Surrounded by strangers at the start line, when the signal went off and they started running, I began a light jog, thinking there would be other walkers in the crowd whom I could join. The funny thing was that no one else slowed to a walk! Not wanting to be the only one, I kept jogging, which gradually built up to a decent pace. I remember thinking, "This isn't bad. It actually feels good. I think I can keep going." I ended up running the entire race. I was not only proud of myself, I was surprised and left inspired to see what else I was capable of that I was "sure" I couldn't do.

That event helped me break through the limiting belief of "I'll never run," and spurred me on to try new things. The following summer, I learned to water ski for the first time, which continued to break through my self-imposed limitations. This story is an illustration of how to use the body to build your confidence and thereby expand your realm of possibilities. Now, I can never go back to those old beliefs because I've proven them wrong. What's more, I have to continuously challenge my current limiting beliefs (yes, I still have many) because I know there's a good possibility that they're total bullshit.

Building on this concept, the body can also be used to build self-trust by way of honoring physical commitments. When we make self-promises such as, "I will exercise for forty-five minutes, five days a week," and then we *don't* follow through, we actually chip away at our relationship with our Self. There is an erosion in our self-trust that occurs when we repeatedly lie to ourselves by making promises we don't keep. The good news is the opposite is also true. Self-trust is fortified by honoring personal commitments. We can use physical goals to deliberately deepen our confidence and trust in both our abilities and our reliability. I used to be one of those people who would blow off exercise for something else that was more fun, convenient, or important, thinking it wasn't that big a deal. I would tell myself it didn't matter, which in effect was saying that "*I don't matter.*" Now, when I am tempted to skip out on my planned workout my response to myself is, "No. I said I would do it, and I'm going to do it!" I make honoring my self-commitments more important than giving into a momentary mood or desire. Similarly, I've worked with clients who have had great results with increase in overall self-esteem and improved follow-through at work and other areas of life by developing a practice of keeping self-promises, beginning on the physical level.

So engaging the body is a great access point for learning and building skills to help you be more present in relationships with others and to show up more fully in the business world. Taking care of your body will naturally enhance your mental, emotional, and spiritual capacities as well, improving all areas of your life.

WRIGHT

So what are the steps to start getting results?

COLLINS

First we go back to having a vision. You really have to know where you're going in order to create the road map to get there. Decide what success is to you. Create that picture of your ideal physical body, business or career life, and relationships. What about each of the components of your overall life vision is important to you? Also ask yourself, "Am I willing to live with the short- and long-term effect of that vision?" Changing anything in your life will have a ripple effect of some sort on some level. You may not know what that will be, but in order to have the success you envision, you have to be willing to step into something new and be with the outcomes that show up.

Once your vision is clear, take a closer look at your current behaviors. Chances are, some of your current habits are perfectly in alignment with your goals. However, since you are not currently living the full vision, *something* needs adjusting. I encourage my clients to look at their current patterns and identify what need is being met by each of those choices. We rarely adopt a behavior, much less make it a habit, unless it is serving some purpose. Understanding the underlying need is essential to creating lasting change. We will always default back to old behaviors until we find a new one that still satisfies our needs, and ideally moves us closer to our goals.

An example is the need for a break from work—a refresher or something to reenergize and refocus. Many people use snacking or smoking or Internet surfing to fill this need, when it would be healthier and more effective to go for a brisk walk, take a short nap, or take ten minutes for something fun like doing a puzzle, calling a friend, or reading a book. These alternatives would get the same need met, while moving closer to the vision of being more physically fit or feeling more fulfilled at work. Take the time to write out your current patterns, the need that is being met by them, and then brainstorm new alternatives you can choose to meet each need in a way that's more in alignment with your vision.

Oh, and make sure that there is some fun in your alternative habits. I think that pleasure, fun, and joy nurture the soul and feed your inspiration, which keeps you gravitating toward the vision, instead of negatively pushing away from undesired results.

Finally, set up an accountability framework and find reminders to help with creating your new lifestyle. Knowing yourself best, determine what is going to help you follow through with the vision-aligned behaviors. Is it scheduling them into your calendar? Is it accessing someone as a support person? Sometimes it can be helpful to use structures you are already familiar with. An example around weight management would be using a familiar "tool" like calorie tracking or Weight Watchers while beginning to learn and listen to your biofeedback as a gauge for indicating when to eat and when to stop. Be sure your environment also supports what you want to accomplish by making certain things either more available or completely unavailable. Also, intentionally structure an environment that inspires your inner processes of creativity, compassion, and perseverance.

WRIGHT

These steps seem like they could be overwhelming. How can people make them doable?

COLLINS

It's important to start small. I notice people getting all excited about making changes so they aim really big. That's great! You want the *vision* to be big, and you want the steps to be small and doable. People want to go from running a 5K to running a marathon in one day, so to speak. You can imagine what the outcome of that leap would be—you'd end up sore and burnt out.

It is essential to start with what you can commit to—physically, time-wise, emotionally—and still make the rest of your life work. One word that flags my awareness that a client is over-committing is "try." Anytime I hear someone say, "I can try," I know they are already letting themselves off the hook, so we need to go deeper into matching a doable action step with the vision. If you can't commit all the way, scale back your short-term goal to something you *know* you can definitely follow through on. Part of what you want to do with that follow-through is continue to build your self-trust and self-efficacy. You want to build your "I-can" thinking. Also, focus on consistency and not perfection. I don't care if it's doing something for ten minutes once a week; just make it *consistent*. You can always build on what you're doing.

WRIGHT

Some people have a fear of success. What are your thoughts on this?

COLLINS

Fear is something that can be very real. Perhaps you know the acronym for FEAR: False Evidence Appearing Real. The fear of success is very intimate and can be consuming. We all have internal "voices," or parts of ourselves, that we respond to and that inform our functioning, our choices, and our self-image. Those fear-based parts of the Self want to keep us safe and protected by avoiding change and rallying to keep us in status quo. Simply understanding that those parts of ourselves exist can help us begin to identify the ways in which we might be frightened of success.

Success is something that can be very threatening, to self-image first and foremost. You may not know how to identify or connect with your successful Self. This happens a lot for people who lose a significant amount of weight, particularly if it's fast. They don't know how to be with themselves when their external body doesn't match their self-image of being a "big person." So they put the weight back on to return to homeostasis, or the comfort zone where their thoughts match their physicality.

In some cases, you may fear how you would keep up with the level of success you desire over the long haul. You may be afraid of managing the publicity or financial gains or the increased level of responsibilities that would accompany it. Success can also be threatening in relationships with friends and family and coworkers. There will always be people who will applaud your success and those who will scorn it. You actually have to become a new level of you in order to, not only let the success in, but also be with it when it shows up.

So the internal change actually has to keep up with the external acts in order to dispel the fear. This is why you need to know what's so important about your vision. Because once you start moving in that direction, all areas of your life will start to change as you do. Your external world will respond to the new you, and you can't predict how that will unfold. You have to decide if living your vision and becoming the person you are capable of being is more important to you than taking care of other people's egos or insecurities. I highly recommend getting solid support throughout this process.

WRIGHT

How does one bypass the fear and commit to the vision?

COLLINS

You grant yourself permission to be successful. You get conscious of your self-talk, of any limiting beliefs that you are holding about yourself, and move forward with adopting the inner dialogue that will get the results you want. Own your successful Self in advance, whether it's being more fit, more free, more creative in your job, more timely, getting more promotions, or feeling happier in your relationships. Grant yourself permission, make the success acceptable (even vital!), and then *act*.

Once you start getting results, celebrate them! Don't let others' reactions—positive or negative—deter you from your success path. Know that the changes you make and the success that you have is actually in service of others. You *have* to keep going! When people see you make changes and be true to your desires, it's a way of leading and encouraging them to be their best selves. This awareness of how you are modeling the possibility for personal success to others can also help quell the fear of success.

Be sure you get the right support for your vision. As the saying goes, "Don't go to the hardware store for milk." Call on the people who are really going to support you. There will be people in our lives who don't want us to change, for whatever reason. They don't want things to be different or they can't tolerate your fabulousness or their insecurities keep them from living into their own vision, and what you represent evokes envy. Lean into the people who are really going to be in your corner and help you get to the place where your light can shine. Change is fragile in the beginning, so as you make progress let yourself gradually settle into the new way of being. Continuously reinforce the transformation and renew your commitment to continued action.

WRIGHT

You stated before that happiness emerges from the inside out, but is there a way to use external change to generate internal happiness?

COLLINS

I would say so. In fact, I think sometimes the external doings are more tangible to begin with. It can help to practice certain actions until you really believe that who you want to become *is* possible. Imagine you are that acclaimed artist or the new CEO or the bodybuilding champ. Think about what you would be doing in your daily life and then start doing those things *now*. It's part of getting into the feeling place of that vision and it is also part of creating new beliefs and habits that are going to lead you toward success.

There is also a way of using external changes to create a daily practice of joy. Find something that is joyful for you or that you are passionate about and work it into your day in small ways. It may be singing, writing, painting, being with animals, walking in nature, or any of a million other creative or connective activities. A joy practice is going to improve your mood and help you feel more inspired about life and about changes, which of course will lead to a greater sense of personal satisfaction and happiness. Just be sure your practices are in alignment with your vision and your true essence. I mean, we're not talking about using food, drugs, sex, gambling, or any other instant gratifier. To be more specific, your daily joy practice should be something you have to actively engage *with* to feel the joy, not just passively experience. We are always both inside and outside of ourselves. We are interacting with what's external from an internal place. So using external practices that consciously and actively connect us with ourselves can be very powerful for creating an authentic inner happiness.

Follow-through is also an essential element of doing things externally to create that inner glow. I've mentioned before that it's a way you can develop your relationship with your Self, by building confidence, self-trust, and self-esteem. Couple that with deliberate self-love and you will take ownership of your life in a powerful new way.

Claiming your own self-authority, courage, and clarity will lead you to create your destiny, your future, and your life, as you want to live it.

WRIGHT

So what else do our readers need to know to create success in their lives?

COLLINS

There may be a deficit in awareness of the basic laws of the universe that actually inform what is going on in our lives. I'm no scientist, but I'll explain them as I understand and find them useful.

The book and movie *The Secret* came out several years ago teaching and illustrating the Law of Attraction. Seeing the movie certainly affected my own life and how I think and act. However, I also think it's incomplete. There are other basic laws that we innately know exist, but haven't made conscious or given a useful name to.

One of them is the Law of Gestation, which highlights that nothing is born into its fully-expressed form, ever. Conscious awareness of this law reminds us of the need for patience. Then we understand that we can't have the vision or idea actualized right *now*, because there is a gestation period that is required for it to come to fruition. Our job, during that gestation period, is to hold the vision, nurture ourselves, take the action steps to make it reality, and trust the process.

Another one that I really think is essential is the Vacuum Law of the Universe. This law highlights that any void created in life will be filled in with *something*. So if there is a habit you want to change, without identifying the need and creating new ways to get it met (filling in the void), this law will kick into effect and pull you back to your default way. I speak about this all the time when I'm working with people on tobacco cessation. You can't just take the cigarette away and not fill that time and space with something *else*. Leaving a void creates a huge vulnerability to relapse because you'll always go back to what is familiar, to what you're used to, if you don't know what to rely on instead.

On the flip side, if you want something new to come into your life, you may need to create space for it *before* it can arrive. Staying in a dead relationship, for example, is filling up the space where a new person might come into your life. When you clarify your vision, firmly grounded in self-love, and you act with courage to make space for something new. Invariably, what then comes into your life is usually *better* than what you just had. Use this awareness of the Vacuum Law to create a space, mentally, emotionally, and/or physically for what you want to allow into your life.

The Law of Polarity is like it sounds. Everything in life has an opposite—dark and light, fast and slow, controlling and compliant, active and passive. We each have a wide range of qualities and attributes within us. What can get in the way of success is when we deny one of those qualities, thinking it is bad or wrong to have it. We need to embrace all of ourselves to be in the flow of life and experience inner peace. A great resource for learning more about this is Debbie Ford's movie *The Shadow Effect*. It speaks to the need for acceptance and integration of all aspects of ourselves in order to experience wholeness.

The last law worth mentioning here is the Law of Rhythm. We all have what we call ups and downs in life. It's normal, but I think what a lot of people experience as a "down" is actually a *plateau*. It's a stagnancy or lack of stimulation. For example, you may start out in a job feeling exhilarated and inspired, but after a while it flat-lines out. It's not as exciting or stimulating as it used to be because you've reached a point where you're not getting any more out of it. You've had the experience, you've learned from it, now you're ready for the next level. But it *feels* like a low point because you are no longer growing in a way that is in alignment with your vision or your purpose. There is more to this law, but for the sake of brevity I just want to highlight that your slump is simply a signal that you are ready for the next "up." So get into your vision, make space for something new, overcome limiting beliefs, create inspiring self-talk, design new habits, and get the support you need to be your most successful Self and live the life you really want!

WRIGHT

Well, this has been interesting, very interesting. Especially the part when you said that for all of my behaviors there is a need being met. I'm going to have to think about that one.

This has been fascinating. I really appreciate your taking all this time with me to answer of these questions. I know our readers are going to get a lot out of this chapter.

COLLINS

Well, I certainly hope so. Thank you for inviting me, David.

WRIGHT

Today I have been talking with Jennifer Kern Collins. Jennifer is a Certified Professional Co-Active Coach. She partners with her clients on their individual journeys and urges them to live their fullest, richest lives.

Jennifer, thank you so much for being with us today on *ROADMAP to Success*.

COLLINS

Thank you, David.

About the Author

Jennifer Collins has a wealth of experience coaching business owners, entrepreneurs, corporate executives, physicians, teachers, artists, social workers, librarians, government department directors, lawyers, and "the average Joe." Her coaching addresses all facets of life, including success in career, relationships, and personal development. She has specialized experience in coaching for Health and Wellness and is a Certified Professional Co-Active Coach. An inspirational speaker, Jennifer offers classes and workshops on a regular basis, tailored upon request. She has presented to such groups as the State of Minnesota, the American Lung Association of Minnesota, and the 2009 Mayo Clinic Nicotine Dependence Center Annual Conference. Jennifer locally represents CTI, the Coaches' Training Institute, as their ambassador to the Twin Cities and surrounding area. Educated in Europe, Jennifer enjoys a variety of cultures and can communicate in the Spanish, French, and Dutch languages. Though Jennifer is a citizen of the world, she calls Minneapolis home, where she resides with her husband, Troy, and dog, Suzie.

Jennifer Collins, MS, CPCC, PCC
Intrinsic SOULutions
P.O. Box 19374
Minneapolis, MN 55419
612-605-6587
www.IntrinsicSOULutions.com

Chapter Sixteen

LET YOUR TRUE SELF SHINE!

CATERINA ALBERTI

DAVID WRIGHT (WRIGHT)

Today I'm talking with Caterina Alberti. Caterina is an Executive Business Coach accredited from Royal Roads University and a director on the leadership team of the Vancouver Island Coaching Association. She brings a unique approach that recognizes the interconnection of our professional and spiritual life, a necessary balance that elevates our attitudes for personal and professional wellbeing. Caterina knows firsthand that people need to believe in themselves and be connected at a spiritual level where they may better understand and fully express their uniqueness to walk their path in life.

Founder of Crossover Coaching, she has a proven track record of business success achieved by developing and implementing creative coaching, visionary leadership, professional development, exceptional service and sales with a keen sense for opportunities. She leads with compassion as an inspirational speaker and creator of the Think Like a Mountain™ Leadership Program.

Caterina, welcome to *ROADMAP to Success*.

CATERINA ALBERTI (ALBERTI)

Thank you; it's a pleasure to be here.

WRIGHT

You have spent your life on the beautiful west coast of British Columbia, Canada, and the most recent years in the coastal mountains of the tourism resort community of Whistler. What can you share about the areas where you have lived and how this has shaped your life?

ALBERTI

Yes, I am truly blessed by my surroundings and the journey of my life experiences have shaped who I am today. My childhood years were spent growing up in a remote logging and mining town in one of the most beautiful seaside communities on the west coast of British Columbia. Our home was a very small, two-bedroom miner's cabin, not much more than five hundred square feet.

We were a large and vibrant Italian family of eight. Since there was little space for playing in our house, my brothers, sisters, and I spent most of our days playing outside regardless of the weather. We had a lot of freedom and we learned so much from the extraordinary environment around us. The forests, ocean, beaches, and rivers were very much our home, too. It was this playful freedom that enabled me to develop the understanding of order, to be resourceful, get creative, and build the strength of spirit within me. We were taught at a very young age to engage our whole being in order to know what we needed to survive in nature.

My mother, being the Italian momma that she is, made our home known in our community for her homemade pasta, breads, pizza, cannoli—I am sure you are getting the picture! It was the after-school stop for many neighborhood kids. She is now eighty-two years old and her home is still filled with the smells of her home cooking and everyone feels the warmth in their own hearts when they enter. When we were growing up, my father made sure we received the good things in life—a lot of sleep, fresh air, activity, laughs, fun, dance, magic tricks, and meals together.

One of the most important and precious moments was to kiss our parents goodnight before bed. This created the message that everything our parents did for us in the day was rooted in unconditional love; the kiss sealed the feeling of respect, appreciation, and peace in our hearts. I grew up with the strength of family and the simple life of a small community as well as a profound connection with the beauty of nature.

Now I live in the coastal mountain resort community of Whistler, where I have worked and raised my own family for the past twenty-two years. Living in a mountain resort town tests one's love, patience, and perseverance. It teaches the acceptance of change and deepens a love of diversity. The beauty in the mountains is unmatched and can be seen in every cottonwood tree seed and each snowflake. There is great learning in the mountains and, as they say, "it builds a different kind of character" because at times there is little room for the soft-hearted.

However, what has happened is that we have been taught that an extreme nature of living has more value than being in spirit with nature. This lifestyle is driving how many of us spend our time in work, play, and our communities today. There is little balance in the world of the driven and in this place, people overlook the time needed to connect. It is similar to the sacrificial ritual of cutting the hearts out in a race for individual power, causing political, economical, and environmental turmoil. This is how I came to create my leadership program called "Think like a Mountain"™ where I assist others with the knowing of a deep connection to the spirit within and around us and the power and intelligence of a loving heart.

Real happiness comes from the knowledge that our true power exists in our positive connections, gentleness, and kindness with all beings and the process and cycles of our own nature. The magic in the nature around me is one of the most precious things that has formed my life, this is where it is possible for all to see the miraculous and beauty within ourselves at any moment.

WRIGHT

With more than twenty years of working for others in the retail, service, and tourism industries, leading and managing small to medium organizations toward success, you made a transition in your own life to become a business and spiritual coach. How did this transition come about?

ALBERTI

Well, David, this was a trying time for me because this particular transition came about from the discomfort of working in many organizations in the past few years. I was working very hard, putting in extra hours providing exciting ideas, opportunities, organizing, strategies, plans, and action to elevate business wellness on many levels at my places of work. I also brought a positive attitude and bright spirit; this energy was integral to the wonderful business relationships and successes we were experiencing.

My environment at work is very important to me. The humanizing elements of kindness and caring that are in our nature need to be in every nook and cranny. These respectful manners assist me to be creative, insightful, inventive, where everyone can enjoy a warm and fun workplace; be engaged, and generate trust and new solutions.

Yet my experiences at my places of work left me feeling completely used, battered, sad, and starving for meaning. There was this terrible letdown and the overwhelming feelings of being taken advantage of that never allows you to know a sense of achievement. It seemed that time after time there was a real drought of key personal and professional nourishment such as basic encouragement, value, respect, teamwork, kindness, and leadership. I discovered that this problem is much deeper with dishonest habits such as justifying and expressing anger in unhealthy ways, unethical choices, undermining others, and projecting a false image. The depriving of accomplishment in some workplaces is entrenched in their culture.

To learn that the culture is quite different than it appears on the surface was a very difficult experience for me because I live in what is supposed to be a world class resort, yet it is not what it seems to be to the world. My children have witnessed what I consider serious acts of abuse toward their mom at work, on personal and professional levels. I know that I am not alone and many other people experience similar situations. It is not only a problem in my community; in fact, it is everywhere and it is based on fear, short-sighted, self-serving environments. Sometimes the team or group you work with may be healthy and wonderful, yet what is hidden is how self-serving the environment is in the bigger picture. When dishonesty occurs and the business is protected by people in various surrounding positions, it is simply not safe. This seriously bothered me and frankly it scared me almost to death!

I felt stuck in this pattern of jobs, as it seemed difficult to find a way out. As a single mom, it felt at times that there was no escape route. Then I began to see how dishonesty is deeply engrained in our public, private, and business connections. Many people have made comprises in their own moral guidance so much so that they have become lost and the choice between right and wrong to them is blurred. It seems that the value of the outcome of the dishonesty has become more valuable than being true to self—our conscience against the golden rules of goodness. "Jiminy Cricket" has been threatened or fired so many times he has lost his nerve and has disappeared on a permanent stress leave.

A business rests in the hearts and souls of its people. If the souls of some are dishonest and cause harm, this affects all good intentions within the business. When this happens, the light of spirit is weakened and the whole is harmed. We can all fall prey to the subtle yet dishonest activities because we do not see or cannot believe it is happening until we are hit by the train of reality. The good thing is we can start to get out from these chaotic situations and begin to do the right things immediately—the right things that get us back on track.

I realized coaching is a great way to shine light on the strengths and dreams of others, providing a sacred space for creative reflection and expression needed for our higher purpose to move into action. I made the transition in my career and it was a blessing and a natural step for me. I have always known that I hold a love for others to succeed. This brings in my spiritual side to my coaching. Not everyone holds this same love for others; quite often it is the opposite. To assist others in these situations, I created a deck of beautiful art cards; they provide a return to light within "A Process for the Whole Person."

Coaching others to experience the achievement of doing what feels right and to embrace their immense value, empowers and opens the door to the joys of the long-term effect.

WRIGHT

Your focus is leadership solutions for women and young adults. Will you share with me what your clients are looking for today? Where do you see your assistance is the most beneficial?

ALBERTI

I believe people need someone they can trust to replenish their soul and mend the divide between their personal and professional lives to achieve a better balance and keep on track. Trust and sincerity in ourselves and relationships elevate the spirit in each of us. Trust provides the necessary balance, movement, and choices for our personal and professional life in every way. Self-worth and confidence is developed in environments that are safe and built in trust. Many who have lost trust within begin to doubt themselves, build walls, or become paralyzed with fear and anxiety. This causes great imbalances and we lose the playfulness of our spirit, our power, and the flow of all things.

My older brother is my mentor. He always leads the way with trust in his heart so that you just know anything is possible. He opens doors and you can walk through with both love and confidence.

Creating trusting relationships is a spiritual leadership skill we must learn and be constantly practicing in the activities and choices of our lives. There is a poverty of spirit in the world when there is a lack of trust. The picture looks bleak when there is no unconditional love and everywhere you turn in life there is always an expectation of an exchange of spirit, love, time, mind, body, resources, and even our souls. These are very high prices to pay! If we get caught up in all the drama, we will not see the truth. Answers are found within ourselves; there is always a way to create faith and hope, move with grace, trust to keep our personal power, and cross the barrier to progress.

I encourage people to expand and deepen a spiritual enthusiasm in their professional life. This will increase the *goia di vivere*—the zest in life—and support their personal evolution as well as those they serve. The benefits of honoring this process opens a royal road map, as it nurtures a way of being and aligns us with a path that is always meaningful.

Unless youth are empowered, they may end up on a path that lowers their spiritual potential. My coaching assists and empowers young adults to align with their inner guidance regarding who and how they want to be, what they know is right for them, and the world they are going to step into. That way they can reach their goals on their own merits, blunders, and all. When we nourish our children's natural qualities, we raise their essential life force. This teaches children to know their truth and to stand with reverence and embrace their inner circle of light. Young adults benefit when they understand better how they want to spend their time, talents, and skills that lights a direction forward, creating a sense of time well spent.

When someone has your back, you gain the sense of team work needed to stay on track, achieve goals, and the kind of support that builds strength and security on your path.

Our learning, creativity, and well-being come directly from being in a special joyful spirit. This experience is a feeling of freedom and to know the magic of a live well lived.

My coaching is based in a practical wisdom to regain trust by assisting others to seek the answer within themselves. If we always seek answers from others, we eventually lose our way; we may feel deceived and lose trust in our own intuition. This can create an inner conflict and an anger that can creep up in our feminine intuitive side and logical masculine spirit within. Shifting attitudes at a deeper level of our nature where there is great honor and value for all that we know is the formation of our integrity. This process begins with taking responsibility for balancing our hearts in the past, present, and future, which is likely the name of my next book.

WRIGHT

Crossover Coaching sounds like you assist others to take that necessary step. Will you tell our readers how you came up with the name and what this can mean for others?

ALBERTI

Yes, "crossover" is a word that has great meaning to me. When I was seventeen, my father passed away from a heart condition. A few days before he passed away, I asked him to teach me how to do a crossover in skipping; it was one of the last expressions of our love. Our relationship was such that I could ask him anything and he would teach me with dignity. One day I was sharing this story with my daughter about her grandfather, when I realized this wonderful gift also represented many beautiful ways to see life. This has become a metaphor for how life is infinite when we cross over with love not fear!

The image of skipping is a lovely, fun activity and we can skip along quite merrily. In order to improve this strength, we may need to do a little cross training. There are times in our lives when we may need to learn how to cross over an obstacle to have a glance at something with another perspective a different way of being or doing that can elevate you in the momentum of the movement. This is the power of love we have in our own hands. Here we can maintain our balance in the journey as we move through the process and embrace the beautiful opportunities that unfold before us.

Many people are often influenced by others and their environment, and they think what they are doing is right for themselves. Unfortunately, quite often it is not the best in reality and if they are afraid of being who they really are and doing what they really want, this meets with the question "what is my purpose?" Crossover assists to provide another view, guidance, and training to seek higher forces and strategies to protect and assert our truth so that the kind and honest heart can flourish in business today. Strenuous, competitive struggling in search of riches and fortune is exhausting and a farce and sends a message to our children that this is the only way to success. What this means for others is they have a clear choice to build the strength within and nurture the integrity of the heart and be connected to source. These are very important foundations that support the steps to reach our goals. Slowing down enough to process our truth where we can engage in the spirit of giving without the expectations of receiving, we will find a pleasant and joyful way to success.

WRIGHT

You have mentioned the need today to blend business and spirit. Let's talk about what you mean by this and how we understand and go about creating this balance.

ALBERTI

I think the best way to explain this and to understand the blending of business and spirit and how important it is, is to share a story with you. Not long ago, one of my clients gave me a business referral and I was to meet my new client at her place of work, a local coffee shop, where we would make arrangements for a coaching appointment. When I arrived, I went to order my usual cup of green tea, when for some reason I had a very strong sense that I needed to have the mint tea instead of the green tea that morning. I placed the order with my new client and she prepared my tea and brought it over to me. She set it down in front of me as we discussed our arrangements for our coaching appointment. She went back to work and I began to read the local paper. When I took a sip of the mint tea, instantly I felt very ill with a spastic urge to vomit. Then, as quickly as this feeling came, it passed. I gathered my thoughts about this very strange occurrence. Hmm, I had felt very healthy when I walked in; my stomach felt fine. I always enjoy the mint tea when I drink it and have never had any adverse effects before. It was only in the moments of the sip, then the feeling passed and otherwise I felt great. I realized this was something outside of me but to be sure, I thought I would just take another sip to confirm the experience. As I took another sip, the very same thing happened. In that moment everything became clear and I made the connection that my new client was not well on an energetic and deeper level; what I was experiencing was a message from spirit.

This is a very rare spiritual gift; not everyone is able to have this deeper spiritual experience happen to them. These are the gifts from my grandmother and my family lineage and the openness in my heart to receive. The mint tea fluid was the source in which I became the conduit or the pure channel in which to receive the message about the potential seriousness of her situation. I was given the gift of this knowledge to assist my client and myself.

When I connected with my new client the next day for our appointment, I shared with her my experience. She was very shocked that I was able to know this and she discussed the symptoms of her problems, such as vomiting and painful stomach upsets. She explained to me that she was drinking lots of this brand of mint tea as it was the only thing that was calming and healing her symptoms.

I want to mention the company that makes the tea I consumed, as this also has great relevance in this story. It is a holistic, organic, local family-run business that does mantras during productions of their teas. Higher business ethics and integrity can assist in raising spiritual vibrations. My ability to be a clear spirit channel enabled me to receive the message. There is great courage and trust that comes with the ability to receive such spiritual gifts. It takes an open heart filled with the wisdom to understand the situation, make the connections, recognize the call for aid, and guide the appropriate and timely action.

We will find not only is the quality of the product important, we will also have to take into consideration how healthy is the spirit of the people in which the processes and production are being handled in business. When the spirit is suffering, this lowers the vibrancy of the entire being and the entire product and the entire organization we work in. You can see how it is very critical to recognize the signs and how it needs to be attended to quickly. By the way, my client made some important changes on her path and is now experiencing a healthier and more balanced life.

Organizations and leaders must take responsibility for compassionate awareness and health of their employee's energy. It is similar to being in the same room with a smoker; it is potentially damaging to everyone. Often, I hear others say that if you blend business and spirit, people won't take you seriously. I want everyone to know that being in spirit is seriously the best preparation for business. A clear spirit channel is very important for success; it opens doorways, dissolves patterns, releases blockages, and streams in pure love. Your intuition becomes stronger, clearer, and the messages arrive to assist and guide you. What I have noticed in my coaching is that sometimes we just need one small adjustment to release the blockages that cause our spirits to suffer and hold us back from feeling joy, freedom, love, fun, and our deep light.

WRIGHT

That's quite something. I think our readers will also want to hear about your leadership program, "Think like a Mountain," and how we can get involved.

ALBERTI

Yes, the program is so much fun and gets the senses going. Of course, people can contact me if they want to experience a workshop and inspiring presentations. There are various workshops that unleash the leader within. It's a very creative business and a spiritual adventure. It follows a process of vision and imagination, understanding of our connections spiritually, to evolve, lift, and improve our attitudes. Think Like a Mountain is all about improving our attitudes and gaining a deeper and wider vision, like the eagle that sees both the large picture (the whole) from high above and with an eagle eye can focus on the important parts so we may attend to what is most needed.

We build abundance with our truth, talents, and our resources at hand. Learning to utilize our skills for balancing, creativity, imagery, we can discover the magician in each of us. I love to encourage this insight and awaken our personal power. One of the most important steps we can do for ourselves is to create the feeling of being connected to our inner source and opening a channel for higher wisdom, trust, guidance, and standing in our resolve. I facilitate activities that encourage a visual map for our own rhythm, voice, breath, and value to reconnect with our own nature.

Teaching ourselves how to raise our spirits, we learn to accept the love within our own hearts first. What we offer is certainly not business as usual, thank goodness. I think what we have been handed over the years lacks luster. It's time to have a fresh approach to restore our trust, dreams, creativity, and inspiration so we can truly enjoy our contribution to the world.

The program is based in the understanding that all things are intricately connected and we assist to restore this feeling. What we hold most sacred is the right to know the light of our paths, our connection to all things, and respect our own spiritual source.

WRIGHT

You've created some of the first of many successful community celebrations. Tell us about these and what moved you in this direction on your path.

ALBERTI

Thank you for mentioning this. Bringing people together in community and celebrating is such a joy and is a healing direction to take. It is the right thing to do.

I created the first indoor Winter Farmer's Market in my area in collaboration with the Squamish Lil'wat Cultural Centre in Whistler. This is all about love and the initiation of an opportunity that brings fresh farm products, local artisans, and First Nations artists together. It provides a venue in the fall and winter months to bring local products to market and increase cultural awareness.

As a spiritual coach, I realized that a profound way to accept spirituality in business would be to bring alternative healing practitioners together. The Metaphysical Market was born and so far, this event occurs twice a year on the spring and fall equinox. When we give and receive healing in community gatherings, we humanize the need and gift of natural healing beyond the physical.

In 2010, I initiated the first celebration of peace in my community on September 21, during the International Day of Peace, as a way to encourage people to cultivate inner peace. In 2011 we expanded the event and opened the peace celebrations with the lighting of the Peace Flame and a candlelight circle. It included the Whistler Children's chorus and a prayer/meditation in our Olympic Plaza. We hope you will join us here next year for this amazing, purposeful, and spiritually engaging celebration.

An amazing Multicultural Celebration was also achieved in 2011 with the leadership of many. It is such a joy to be in the midst of all the healing that celebrations like these bring. These celebrations are grassroots initiatives that empower others to share their true, authentic selves bringing love, light, food, economy, purpose, and peace. When we bring community together to celebrate, we learn the art of being together and we find a path glowing with warmth, caring, and the potential for a movement within that represents a deep joy of our true source. Teaching all the beautiful differences of our diversities and how we are alike joins us in the stories we weave together as one.

WRIGHT

What might be some key ingredients you can share with others in taking the first step in the right direction?

ALBERTI

When I make a beautiful pot of homemade tomato sauce, I must have all the ingredients—lovely, fresh garden tomatoes, onions, and basil are a must and so are the tools like my wooden spoon and, of course, the time needed to prepare the meal. The secret ingredient is the love and enjoyment in every step of cooking and serving of the dish.

If we are not sure where the love and enjoyment has gone, then imagine you have a wooden spoon in your hand. Now begin to stir it in the air all around you. As you do this, imagine gathering up all the anxious energy spent on any misused value of time. Now gather the kind, caring and loving energies to ease a worried heart and mind. Once that is accomplished, you will be able to fall into a deep and nourishing sleep so that you may awaken to the fondness within.

Remember "home is where the heart is." Never leave home without your heart. The ingredients in our relationships and the friendship we have with ourselves will lend a hand in the alignment and courage in taking the first step in the right direction.

WRIGHT

Will you share with our readers your spiritual side and what influences you in this area?

ALBERTI

Yes, I would be happy to share because I believe sharing these things assists others to understand their spiritual side and what influences them. For me, it really begins with my mother. My mother is the strong, spiritual influence in my life. My mother is very spiritual and has a deep understanding of our connection to our higher source and the importance of our generations. Ever since I was a little girl, my mother has always shared her dreams with me—what the dreams meant, the messages, and the guidance from these dreams. She has received and shared many spiritual messages and is extremely intuitive, as is my older sister. I believe our ancestors have walked a path that has blessed ours.

One time I was feeling a little stressed out. I told my older sister that I was getting many spiritual messages. At first, I was a little frightened. She said, "Don't be frightened. This is a good thing. I would be frightened if you were *not* receiving these messages," she said. I completely understood.

I am first-born Canadian and my heritage is Italian; both of my parents are immigrants from Italy. My mother is Sicilian. Immigrants leave behind their family and their ancestors. I never had the privilege of knowing my grandparents or experiencing the gifts that they would have wanted to pass on to me. However, I have a special spiritual inheritance—the path my ancestors walked has left behind some beautiful gifts in my generation. I feel a great influence from my grandmother on my mother's side. I am named after her and even though I never got the chance to meet or know her, I feel her spirit with me. I have a beautiful picture of her and she has the most amazing smile. Her spirit is warm, loving, gentle, kind, and carries a beauty and inner peace where I am able to see myself through her eyes. The most beautiful, unconditional loving and powerful feminine spirit are what she has left behind for me and the next generations in my lifetime.

WRIGHT

So how does one begin to connect to these deeper levels of ourselves and discover our spiritual strength?

ALBERTI

First of all, this is something that is very personal, and belongs to each one of us uniquely. There are many activities that can be put into our daily lives to help us center and connect us with spirit. We are learning to bring more of these things into our lives with meditation, rituals, and creating disciplines in our lives that bring us closer to our core. For me personally, it is being in nature, prayer, the wisdom of the candlelight, writing, and staying true to me. These are simple ways of connecting to my spiritual side. My parents, grandparents, and ancestors have graced me with a deep connection to spirit; therefore, for me, I follow this light and this is in my core.

Being in nature is a great way to connect with the disconnected parts of our self. Nature always speaks the truth so here we can be ourselves. To get to a deeper level we must slow down, take the time to bless others, and find quiet places and reach for higher ground to empower our spirituality. We can simply ask ourselves the questions we want to know, listen to the guidance, and slowly we find a path filled with peace and harmony that seeps into our bones. How we communicate to ourselves and others and our thoughts, words, and actions will create the energy we carry and can assist us in staying positive. We can use our imagination and creativity in our own unique ways to connect us to our source. As a coach, I bring my gifts that elevate the energy that motivates and assists in being true to ourselves and the discovery of our spiritual strength and inner peace. When we use this power in action, we connect vision and spirit to develop the determination and positive attitude needed to realize our ideas and plans from start to finish.

WRIGHT

Leadership is critical today and maybe more so than ever. Will you tell me about where and how you see leaders achieving the necessary changes?

ALBERTI

I feel that this is a very difficult situation today and one of the main concerns is the use of power in one's position of leadership. There is a responsibility within leadership today to recognize the gifts of others and elevate each person within his or her organization. The economy is shadowed by fear and the abuse of power and at the same time, there is a leadership crisis in business today. It is so severe that people have become indifferent, completely worn out, and have spiritually left the building. We now have a serious deficit in connecting with spirit and honesty in both our business and personal lives. Those who are based in love and in wholeness are seen as a threat in today's business world. They therefore feel quite vulnerable and voiceless. If you are to be true, you may need to question the dishonest decisions and behaviors of others in business. When you challenge the morals of how decisions are being made, you become a threat to the inauthentic value of the dishonesty. The threat becomes very real and damaging because underling the dishonesty is great insecurities, fear, jealousy, and a flaw in human nature's ability to live within the natural law.

Many relationships with those in positions of power seem to be based in the corrupt practices that use money and fear to influence others.

This leadership style is separated from the whole and everyone loses. It does not take into consideration the individual as a whole, the organization as a whole, and the community as a whole. New methods for leadership need to incorporate a universal love to build self-assurance, creative thinking, decision-making, and the kind of physical, emotional, and spiritual intelligence that nurtures the whole individual and the common good for all.

To achieve the necessary changes, we must bring a balance into our everyday lives and understand our deeper connections with each other and nature beyond the obvious. We need to remember we are also leaders in our homes and communities, too.

There is a process to return to wholeness and a great need for balanced leaders in this world who are connected spiritually.

The challenge for leaders today is to have the courage to know and be in a relationship with the spiritual force.

WRIGHT

Success can be measured in many ways. How do you evaluate the road map to success?

ALBERTI

When I first think about this question I want to say feedback, feedback, and more feedback. Be sure to talk with people and hear what they want to share. Also reflection upon what we have done well and what we have learned along the way is extremely important because it brings value, recognition, and it reminds us to see other perspectives. It demonstrates we are interested and we care about the thoughts of others, which deepens our relationships. We need to celebrate together our accomplishments and milestones along the road. When we bring people together to collaborate and celebrate, we are giving an opportunity to value each of us for what we bring to our community.

Measuring along the way is also about asking ourselves questions such as:

- Am I content with where I am going?
- Am I sleeping well at night?
- What needs to change so that I can enjoy who I really am?
- How can I improve the long-term vitality of my spirit?

Taking the time to see how amazing you are in the present moment, you realize that the real you is a very important part of the whole. These things will assist us to know ourselves better and strengthen our positions to place us in the driver's seat.

When the road map is paved with the light of spirit within us, we will touch the spirit within everyone on our journey. There is no better way to measure true success.

WRIGHT

So if you were to share some golden nuggets of wisdom on the road to success, what are some that the readers can cherish?

ALBERTI

There are so many beautiful words of wisdom out there and I feel very honored to be in the presence of Deepak Chopra and Ken Blanchard in this amazing book, alongside many other talented authors. I have my own little personal nuggets and I hope that these will benefit others.

Sometimes the path has corners, hills, and even the occasional pothole along the way. To unearth a delightful way to look at the turns and the hills on the path, we bring joy and a positive attitude. This way we keep our options open and interesting. We have to ask ourselves to see the beauty in all things, to listen, and to speak from our heart. Spirit is everywhere; if you look deeply, you can see it through the window of nature where it is acknowledged within you. Fill your soul with good deeds, reach for the stars, and believe you will find them twinkling in your own hands. And, remember the gift of faith in your heart, that no matter what happens, something beautiful will come of it! Reclaim your truth and your freedom awaits!

I leave you with these questions to ask yourself:

1. Have I opened myself to the light inside?
2. Is it beautiful and joyful beyond anything imagined?
3. How do I love and believe in this light?
4. How am I letting my true self shine?

WRIGHT

What a great conversation. I appreciate all the time you've taken with me to answer these questions. This has been very enlightening for me and I know it will be a great chapter in our book.

ALBERTI

Thank you very much David. It is an honor and so much fun to be here.

WRIGHT

Today I have been talking with Caterina Alberti. Caterina is an Exectutive Business Coach accredited from Royal Roads University and a member of the International Coaching Federation. She is the founder of Crossover Coaching and Think Like a Mountain Leadership. She has a proven track record of business achievements by developing and implementing effective coaching, leadership, exceptional service, with a keen sense for opportunities.

Caterina, thank you so much for being with us today on *ROADMAP to Success*.

ALBERTI

Thank you David. I'm very excited and look forward to the road ahead.

About the Author

Caterina Alberti is an inspiring coach and speaker who transmits an energy within that touches her clients and audiences in a way that changes and evolves attitudes to a whole new level.

She loves to share, co-create, and build trusting relationships. Join her in conversation over a lovely cup of tea and enjoy your personal and professional success. Caterina is also an artist, poet, and kind-hearted soul who has been described as a gift to her community. Her human approach is known to achieve results and leave a positive and lasting impact. She leads a workable union of business and spirit by assisting others to incorporate higher forces in their lives to free their dreams and reach their goals.

Caterina Alberti, CEC
Crossover Coaching
www.crossovercoaching.ca

CROSSOVER COACHING